MNEMAI

Scholars Press
Homage Series

MNEMAI

Classical Studies in Memory of Karl K. Hulley

edited by

Harold D. Evjen

Scholars Press
Chico, California

MNEMAI

Classical Studies in Memory of Karl K. Hulley

edited by

Harold D. Evjen

©1984
Scholars Press

Library of Congress Cataloging in Publication Data
Main entry under title:

Mnemai, classical studies in memory of Karl K. Hulley

(Homage series)
Bibliography: p.
Contents: The Classics Department and Karl Hulley /
by Edward F. D'Arms—The epic of Gilgamesh, the Bible,
and Homer / by Charles Rowan Beye—Works and days
1–285 / by Peter Green—[etc.]
1. Classical literature—History and criticism—Addresses,
essays, lectures. 2. Hulley, Karl K., d. 1983. I. Hulley,
Karl K., d. 1983. II. Evjen, Hal. III. Series.
PA26.H8M59 1984   880'.09   84-5362
ISBN 0–89130–743–5

Printed in the United States of America
On acid-free paper

CONTENTS

KARL KELCHNER HULLEY
1898–1983

INTRODUCTION

HAROLD D. EVJEN

This volume was to have been an expression of affection for Karl K. Hulley and a celebration of his eighty-fifth birthday. Fate has ordained otherwise and the hope of presenting this volume to Karl has been frustrated by his death on January 24, 1983. The contributors have all participated in the Hulley Lecture Series sponsored by the Department of Classics at the University of Colorado at Boulder. The genesis of this homage was the Departmental Lecture Series inaugurated by John N. Hough on December 8, 1965. When Karl's retirement approached, his colleagues voted to recognise his long service to the department and the university by renaming retroactively the recently established lecture series in his honor. Fittingly the change was announced by the then chair, Hazel E. Barnes, on the occasion of Karl's contribution to this nascent series. He thus appears as the third Hulley lecturer.

Karl's forty-year tenure at the University of Colorado (1927–1966), although not quite reaching back to the period when a wolf pack roamed the campus, did witness much of the formative period of George Norlin's presidency (1919–1939) and the entire period of dramatic post-war growth of the university in size and quality which brought membership in the AAU. Karl participated actively throughout both as a demanding and much respected teacher and in a number of administrative posts, serving as acting head of the department, several times as chairman, and as editor and chairman of the Editorial Board of the University of Colorado Press during its very active phase (1947–1964). His teaching was in many ways the mainstay of the department's offerings in Greek and Latin at the upper division and graduate levels. The time-consuming assignment with the Press was undertaken with little or no relief from other duties. In addition Karl was the primary liaison with the state's high school faculty. He was also active in professional societies locally and regionally, serving 25 years as the State Vice-President of the Classical Association of the Middle West and South and chairing sessions at its annual meetings. He was a contributor to the *Classical Journal*. His co-authored article, "The Oresteia Story in the Odyssey," *TAPA* (1946), 207–15, has been frequently cited and also reprinted. He was a Trustee of the Vergilian Society and participated in several of its sessions in Italy.

Harold D. Evjen

Karl's undergraduate education was at Bucknell University, which granted him an honorary doctorate in 1957, and he earned the M.A. and Ph.D. degrees from Harvard University. His mastery of Latin and Greek languages and literatures was impressive and I turned to him for identification of sources of quotations. As editor of the *Classical Journal* I frequently imposed upon him after his retirement for evaluation of manuscripts, especially when they involved Aristophanes and Horace. His editorial expertise complemented his scholarship and any manuscript which survived his scrutiny was much improved. He continued throughout his long and productive retirement to keep abreast of his field, to read faithfully a number of journals, and to purchase scholarly books and subject them to critical commentary. He was co-editor of Sandys's translation of Ovid's *Metamorphoses* published by the University of Nebraska Press and continued to work until a few days before his death as a volunteer cataloguer for the Special Collections Division of Norlin Library. During his retirement years he received one further recognition, an honorary doctorate from Alderson-Broaddus College where he began his teaching career.

I became acquainted with Karl in 1962 and therefore missed observing one of his passions—tennis. Reports of his prowess in this sport, however, were readily available from many people. I did enjoy many a pleasant game of snooker with him and had the pleasure of sharing with him and his wife, Helen, a number of trips to Greece, Turkey, and Alaska. His July ascent of the Akrokorinthos, impeccably attired as usual in a wool suit and bow tie, is still a vivid memory, as were his general good humor, constant curiosity, and indefatigable spirit, all necessary attributes of a congenial travel companion.

Karl K. Hulley was the link with the department's past. His tenure overlapped that of Fred Hellems, Professor of Latin and Dean of the College of Arts and Sciences from 1900, and George Norlin, Professor of Greek and President of the University. The department in this respect has been greatly diminished by his loss. However, personal affection and admiration for a close friend and wise mentor are the primary reasons his colleagues have chosen to publish a memorial volume and we all thank those scholars from other universities who have contributed their time and scholarly talents. I wish especially to thank Edward D'Arms who was head of the Department during the late 1930s and the middle 1940s for his reminiscences of the university and of Karl. Thanks are also due to the Committee on University Scholarly Publications of the University of Colorado for granting a subvention for this volume.

THE CLASSICS DEPARTMENT AND KARL K. HULLEY: 1937–1946

EDWARD F. D'ARMS

I was greatly surprised and flattered when Professor Evjen asked me to make a written contribution to the memorial volume in honor of Karl Hulley. After the customary disclaimer and a renewal of the invitation, I consented to try my hand at something. Unfortunately, I have no written records of what happened in detail during the years 1937–46. Nor do I have access, at this distance, to materials which must certainly exist in the archives of the university.

Nevertheless, I shall do what I can to recapture some of the major events of those years, along with some minor ones, and the inevitable addition of trivia. So, I ask tolerance for errors of omission and commission in what is certainly far from an official history of the period, or indeed a full biography of Karl during the time of our closest association.

When I arrived at the University of Colorado at the beginning of the fall term in 1937, the resident members of the Department of Classics were Associate Professor Maud Whiting, Assistant Professor Karl K. Hulley, and Assistant Professor William Wallace. Student enrollment was good, with approximately one hundred fifty lower division undergraduates taking courses in the Latin language and about twenty-five in beginning Greek. Upperclass courses were sparsely attended, majors were few, graduate students non-existent during the three quarters from September to June.

During the two six-week summer sessions, the situation was quite different. Undergraduate courses were few, if any. Graduate students, the great majority of them teachers of Latin, were comparatively numerous. They came from a surprisingly wide range across the United States. Some of them were working for an M.A. degree; others for promotion or for merit credits; others because they liked the Classics, the country and the climate. And during the summer we had as visiting professors Marbury Ogle of the University of Minnesota in 1938; Francis Godolphin of Princeton in 1939; and Gilbert Highet of Columbia in 1940.

In order to become acquainted with the curriculum and students, I arranged my first year to teach two sections of the large Latin course (for those who entered with credit for two years of Latin) and the beginning Greek course. Each of these classes met five times a week. In addition, I had a few students in an upperclass Latin course, as I recall. I was surprised to discover that the Latin sections had few good students and fewer who were really interested. Those in the Greek class were, if anything, less bright and less interested than the Latin students. (There were, I was pleased to find, a few outstanding exceptions to these generalizations.)

I soon discovered the reason for this situation. There was a regulation that required each student in his freshman or sophomore year to take a full year's work in two of three fields: mathematics, science and classical languages. Those who were not keen on a dose of both mathematics and science enrolled in Latin or Greek. The largest number by far signed up for Latin, on the basis of the two years of the language they had had in high school. Those who had not taken Latin in high school, or had done badly in it, enrolled in beginning Greek.

During the year, there was a proposal before the faculty to revise this requirement. I do not recall just how things were to be changed, but the new version would take away the exclusive status of Latin and Greek and probably substitute a general foreign language requirement. When the proposal neared a faculty vote in the spring of 1938, I, having experienced the difficulties of trying to teach seventy-five reluctant students, spoke in favor of the change. I was immediately rebuked by the presiding officer, President George Norlin, himself a Classicist and former member of the department, on the ground that the change would be harmful to the Classics Department; he further pointed out to the faculty that this was my first year at the university and that I probably did not appreciate the effects the new requirement would have on the department. Nevertheless, I persisted. The proposal was passed, as it probably would have been without my support. Dr. Norlin proved to be correct, in that enrollment in lower division courses in Latin and Greek declined, although not so much as might have been expected. To compensate, the students who did elect Latin and Greek seemed to be brighter and better motivated. In later years I often wondered if I had made the right decision. Perhaps better teaching than I had provided might have struck sparks from some of the less diligent students and classics enrollment would not have suffered. Furthermore, as any Classicist knows, Latin or Greek would have been Good For Them.

In addition to courses in the Latin and Greek languages, the department also offered courses in translation. One year in the fall term I had a student who was one of the outstanding linemen on the football team. At some point during the season the team traveled to Utah to play one of its interconference rivals from that state. A story in *The Boulder Camera* described the team on tour. Among other items mentioned was the fact that our burly tackle had with him "a book called Homer's *Iliad*."

Arrangements had also been made with other departments for Classics personnel to teach some courses which were part of their regular curriculum. The English Department, for example, had a series of two-hour courses, which I believe were required of all English majors. In the fall term the subject was Biblical Backgrounds of English Literature; in the winter term, Classical Backgrounds of English Literature; and in the spring, English Backgrounds of English Literature. The Classical Backgrounds course was taught by someone from the Classics Department, at first Professor Whiting. After her departure, I inherited the course. It was a real challenge to squeeze into barely twenty class sessions the outlines of Greek mythology, literature, philosophy and history, with a final dash at the Roman scene as well. I still remember with horror the day I discovered that Plato had never been mentioned. I had exactly two minutes left before the bell rang to convey something of his life, writings and significance. Somehow or other, I managed to present a brief sketch within the alloted time, but I have always felt very apologetic to the students—and particularly to Plato—for such short shrift.

Later, after the war in fact, the English Department inaugurated a year-long course in Great Books, one term of which was devoted to Greek (and Roman?) examples. I recall that with the influx of students under the G. I. Bill, Donald Sutherland and I were asked to teach one section each to help out the overcrowded English Department. One day Sutherland came to me in as close to academic anger as I ever saw him. He had just learned that a senior member of the English Department was teaching the *Odyssey* as the story of the returned veteran of foreign wars. Donald himself had just returned from almost three years in the army, a good part of it spent in heavy combat and with a Purple Heart to show for it. But he resented this demeaning of a work of literary stature by equating it with the veterans' experience.

The survey course in Ancient History was also taught by a member of the Classics Department. This arrangement seems to have coincided with the arrival of William Wallace, who taught the course; at times there were hints that the History Department was not altogether happy with the situation. This was not because of William's performance, which was excellent, but for other reasons at which we could only guess. But as time went on, relations became smoother and a few advanced courses, also taught by Classics personnel, were added.

William's particular interest was in Greek history and related fields, such as archaeology, epigraphy and numismatics. When he discovered that I was especially interested in Roman history, he suggested that I take over the spring quarter of the survey course, while he devoted himself to some of the more erudite areas of ancient history. One of these projects was the preparation and publication of the Greek and Roman coins possessed by the University of Colorado, done with great care and skill by William and his wife, Barton Wallace; she, incidentally, was a Ph.D. in Classics from Yale. William's doctorate was from Johns Hopkins.

I mentioned above that Professors Whiting, Hulley, and Wallace constituted the department in 1937. Many changes soon took place. Mrs. Whiting left permanently in 1939. Donald Sutherland arrived in 1940. William Wallace left for the Canadian Navy in 1941. Sutherland left for the U.S. Army in 1942; I, also for the Army, in 1943. Donald Swanson came, I believe, in 1942 and in 1943 went into the Japanese Language School of the Navy, located on the Boulder campus. Wallace, Sutherland, and I returned in late 1945 or early 1946. Wallace and I left permanently in 1946.

The one constant factor throughout this time was the presence of Karl Hulley. He had arrived as a member of the Classics Department in 1927, and served it well—and on the job—until his retirement in 1966. The completion of his Ph.D. was delayed by the shock over the death of his infant son; and by the emotional and financial strain of looking after his aging parents, who lived with Karl and his wife Helen. But with the award of his doctorate by Harvard in 1941, his progress was rapid. He was promoted to Associate Professor in 1942, became acting head of the department 1943–45 and again 1946–47, chairman of the department in 1947–49, full professor in 1948, and editor of the newly created University of Colorado Press from 1947 until his retirement. But these last developments were after my time in Boulder.

(For those rare few who may have noticed and been made curious by the difference in nomenclature, I might say that faculty members appointed as "heads" of given departments retained this designation until their retirement or departure. But about 1940 the introduction of "chairmanships" was instituted. Henceforth, whenever a "head" left or retired, his department changed to "chairmanships," on a rotating and elective basis.)

Karl's teaching, in my time at least, was almost entirely in Latin courses. He was a fine Latinist and a helpful, patient instructor. Quite a few of the students who had him as a teacher in the general Latin course went on to take further work in Latin, under his tutelage if possible. He was also a favorite adviser to graduate students during the summer session, which he taught regularly. In fact, here, as in the regular year, Karl was a constant factor. As I recall, Wallace and Sutherland rarely, if ever, taught during the summer sessions, and I only during the first six-week term. Karl was the one member of the department to whom graduate students returning over a period of years could look for guidance and assistance.

It was not only students who turned to Karl for assistance. In the spring of 1946 I read a paper on the *Odyssey* at a meeting of Colorado–Wyoming college and university humanists held at Colorado College.

The paper was full of broad generalizations and unfinished suggestions. Since I was soon to leave for Washington, I knew I would not have time to revise it and I suggested to Karl that he might be willing to see if he could make anything of it. He loyally agreed to try his hand. The result was published in TAPA, LXXVII (1946), pp. 207–15 under the title, "The Oresteia Story in the *Odyssey*."[1] Karl had limited and sharpened the focus of my paper, rewritten it completely and improved it enormously. As published, the paper owed 80 percent of its virtues to Karl. It should have been published under his name, as I tried unsuccessfully to convince him.

But Karl did not spend all of his time in the classroom or over books. He was by far the best tennis player on the faculty, and he was kind enough to let me play with him quite often—both with and against, I should say. As a doubles team we fared well. In mixed doubles we were frequent opponents, where our partners were often Amy Stearns, the wife of the president, and Phyllis Lockwood, a quondam Colorado champion. During the summer of 1940, Karl and I played frequently with Amy Stearns and Helen Highet, wife of the visiting professor. It often happened, when we stopped to pick up Helen on our way to the courts, that we had to wait a few minutes before she came out to join us. She apologized for being late but said she had been scribbling away at something and had forgotten the time. A year later we discovered that what she had been "scribbling away at" was the manuscript of *Above Suspicion*, the first of the thrillers by Helen MacInnes (Highet), since followed by many, many more, which have brought her fame and fortune.

During the years 1937–39, the major concern in the university community was the retirement of President Norlin and the choice of his successor, Robert L. Stearns, Dean of the Law School. The situation was enlivened, if not edified, by the activities of an anonymous character who appeared to have had access to all of the university's workings, including those of the Board of Trustees. He deluged the faculty with a series of communications containing information of various kinds. The most startling of these was a full listing of faculty salaries. The campus buzzed. Those who appeared at the top of the list, financially, pretended to be embarrassed, but bore their embarassment easily. Those at the bottom were truly embarrassed. When I was appointed full professor and head of the Classics Department in 1937, my salary was $3500. This turned out to be quite respectable, but not outstanding in comparison with similar appointments in other departments. There were many instances of associate professors in one department receiving higher salaries than full professors in other departments; and so on, with other

---

[1] It was later republished under the title, "Guilt and Free Will" in *Homer's Odyssey: A Critical Handbook* (1969) pp. 121–27, edited by Conny Nelson.

ranks. One department head was revealed as receiving only $2800, a source of gossip on many fronts. One associate professor and acting head of a department was listed as receiving $2500, as I recall. His wife, in a group of other faculty wives, made it clear that she and her husband could not live as they did without private income. To this another faculty wife replied, "Oh, do you live nicely?"

While on this subject, I might add that our department paid its visiting professors $300 for a six-week session of summer school. All these figures must be put in context, however. A three-course steak dinner at Howard's, the best restaurant in town, for example, cost sixty-five cents; and a generous hand-packed quart of ice cream from the Alba Dairy was thirty-three cents.

The years 1939 to 1941 were relatively calm and pleasant. Then came World War II. The numbers of male students fell off as military needs were established. The Navy set up its Japanese Language School on the campus; plans were made for receiving, housing, instructing and training increasingly large Navy contingents. By the spring of 1943 the situation at the university was chaotic, but beginning to settle down. The Navy V-12 program began during the summer and preparations for the arrival of large numbers kept everyone very busy. The Navy added its Russian Language School to Japanese. The university was in process of changing from the quarter to the semester system. As Acting Dean of the Summer School, I was very busy indeed. Most of the work of the Classics Department fell upon Karl Hulley, who performed a multitude of tasks and adjustments with his customary efficiency and cheerfulness. I have no idea how Karl survived the next two years, with all the changes and uncertainties, but everything was proceeding smoothly when those of us who had been away returned in late 1945 or 1946.

Karl and I became friends in 1937 and we continued our friendship through occasional meetings in Boulder and Princeton, but particularly through long, chatty communications at Christmas time. In the last one, written in December 1982, Karl told me of his continuing work on Jean Stafford's papers; he also said his doctor had advised him to resume and extend daily walks. As always, he sounded in good spirits and had a constructive attitude toward the future. He was a good friend, a fine person, and a true credit to the Classical profession.

THE EPIC OF GILGAMESH, THE BIBLE, AND HOMER: SOME NARRATIVE PARALLELS*

CHARLES ROWAN BEYE

In the last century increasing attention has been paid to the similarities which are to be found in the literatures of the archaic age Greeks, the Hebrews and the early peoples of the Near East. The fact of the Mediterranean itself makes this a natural kind of study; the easy communication over water meant that each port city developed a kind of international style side by side with the indigenous culture evolving in the land mass around it. Archaeological evidence bears witness to the cross culturization in the Mediterranean in trade and art. George Smith's discovery in 1872 of Utnapishtim's account of a flood, a Babylonian parallel to the *Genesis* flood story,[1] has encouraged the search for more literary parallels. Similarities between the hero, Gilgamesh, Moses of *Exodus* and the Gospel Jesus have been suggested.[2] The other side of the triangle has been filled in by noting parallels between the Gilgamesh epic and the Homeric poems.[3] There is an unusual and hence provocative parallel between similes and their contexts in the *Iliad* (18.318ff.) and in the Assyrian recension of the Gilgamesh story (tablet 8, column 2). Moreover, the Enkidu–Gilgamesh relationship bears striking similarity to the Patroklos–Achilles friendship. A great number of parallel details in a variety of Greek, Near Eastern and Biblical narratives has

---

*This paper began life as a lecture in the Hulley Lecture Series at the University of Colorado, Boulder in November of 1976. I should like to thank the several members of the audience whose observations after the talk gave me a number of ideas for its improvement. I should like also to thank my colleagues, Howard Kee and Herbert Mason, for their kindness in reading a draft of this paper and bringing their knowledge of things Biblical and Near Eastern to bear upon the imperfect ideas of a classicist.

[1] G. Smith, *Chaldean Account of the Deluge* (London 1976³).

[2] Cf. P. Jensen, *Das Gilgamesch Epos in der Welt Literatur I: Die Ursprung der altestamentlichen Patriarchen, Propheten und Befreier-Sage und der neutestamentlischen Jesus-Sage* (Strasbourg 1906); see also A. Heidel, *The Gilgamesh Epic and Old Testament Parallels* (Chicago 1949²).

[3] Cf. e.g., C. H. Gordon, *The Common Background of Greek and Hebrew Civilizations* (New York 1965) 61–85, 218–77; T. B. L. Webster, *From Mycenae To Homer* (London 1958) 79–84.

been noted.[4] This essay is an attempt to suggest further parallels in these narratives, specifically in the principal story lines of the Gilgamesh epic,[5] the *Genesis-Exodus* narrative, the Gospel story and the Homeric epics. It is to try to discover a common shape of narrative to which early story-tellers instinctively molded their materials.

Some argue[6] that common elements in these narratives derive from borrowing, or, at least, the influence of a tradition. In this view the Gilgamesh story becomes the exemplar or matrix. Others would argue that there is an archetypal story pattern underlying these narratives, that Batman must always have his Robin, the Lone Ranger his Tonto.[7] Variants on some of the story elements surface in very different times and places: consider, for instance, the late medieval story of Valentine and Orson[8] or Huckleberry Finn and Nigger Jim or Jacob and Esau. Some would insist that this phenomenon is no more than coincidence. But coincidental parallels in narratives betoken habits of mind which coincide.

What these narratives share *au fond* is the portrayal of a male's experience of growing to manhood, becoming in the process conscious of himself and of the female sex which both attracts and repels him. This claim may seem to some to be reading a good deal into these narratives. Interpretation is hazardous since often some of the motifs which in my view were originally meant to establish this portrayal have been rearranged for other narrative goals. We are not talking about mechanical narrative gimmicks, but about motifs, traditional associations which made certain narrative events or details of these events occur subconsciously to an author; they seem right or natural.

As an example of this we may take for comparison the passage in the

---

[4] Gordon, op. cit. (note 3); also his "Homer and Bible," *Hebrew Union College Annual* 26 (1955).

[5] Although the Gilgamesh narrative has not been discovered anywhere transcribed as one continuum, its essential unity cannot be denied. It has been well said by Kupper: ". . . mais, en définitive, pour une oeuvre qui a connu une vogue aussi persistante, qui s'est maintenue aussi vivante à travers les siècles, ces divergences ne représentent-elles pas peu de choses? Si nous quittons un moment l'optique de la pure critique littéraire pour nous attacher seulement aux traits essentiels du mythe de Gilgameš, à cet ensemble de légendes qui se sont cristallisées autour du nom du héros, nous pouvons affirmer que l'épopée de Gilgameš etait déjà formée tout entière a l'époque de la 1ere dynastie de Babylon." J. R. Kupper, "Les differents versions de l'épopée de Gilgameš," in *Gilgameš et sa légende, études recueillés* par P. Garelli (Paris 1960) 102.

[6] Cf. G. Germain, *Genèse de l'Odyssée* (Paris 1954) or L. A. Stella, *Il poema di Ulisse* (Firenze 1955). A. Huebsch, "Betrachtungen zur Genesis des homerischen Epos" in *Gilgameš et sa légende*, op. cit. (note 5) 185ff., theorizes that the "vor homerische" singer had Märchen material which was "heroisiert" by the *Iliad* and *Odyssey* poets.

[7] For a wide variety of examples see C. A. Williams, "Oriental Affinities of the Legend of the Hairy Anchorite: Part I Pre-Christian," *University of Illinois Studies in Language and Literature* 10 (1925) 5–138; ibidem "Part II Christian" 11 (1926) 429–510.

[8] A. Dickson, *Valentine and Orson* (New York 1929).

Gilgamesh story when the goddess Ishtar invites the hero to have sexual intercourse with her and he declines, citing the misfortunes which befell other mortal men who shared her favors. This idea recurs in the *Odyssey* when Odysseus is warned (10.281–301) about the dangers in sleeping with Circe who turns men into swine afterward. Because he is forewarned and forearmed with the mysterious *moly* he makes love unscathed. At first glance the malevolent, sexually inviting partner, Circe, may seem to be the obvious analogue to Ishtar but in fact elements of the Calypso scene more exactly repeat the Ishtar-Gilgamesh language. On the surface of the narrative, of course, there are real differences: Odysseus declines Calypso's offer of eternal connubial bliss on Ogygia, not because he fears her but because he pines to return to Penelope and Ithaka. We may note, however, that prior to this rejection of her offer, when Calypso complains to Hermes that female deities do not have the luck in consorts which their masculine counterparts enjoy, the poet puts into her mouth a list (5.121–28) of mortal males upon whom dire misfortunes fell once they had entered into sexual liaison with a deity. Here we have the same constellation which was present in the Gilgamesh story: a divine female's invitation, a mortal male's rejection, a list of male mortal victims of such a union. This last comes effectively for Homer's purposes in Calypso's complaint, but it surrounds the transaction between Calypso and Odysseus with a certain baleful aura, probably sensed only subliminally, an aura which later becomes altogether more palpable in the stratagems of Circe.

Establishing parallels is, of course, invariably precarious, especially when it involves comparisons between narratives which differ exceedingly in their clarity and precision, as these do. The Homeric poems are notorious for their detail; the poets, or poet, true to the geometric aesthetic, leave nothing out. One thinks of Auerbach's dictum (". . . the Homeric poems conceal nothing, they contain no teaching and no secret meaning. Homer can be analyzed . . . but he cannot be interpreted.")[9] The Gilgamesh narrative, on the other hand, like the Old Testament narrative,[10] is far more sparse, hence more myth-like. Events demand interpretation because the narrator leaves out so much. Ishtar's invitation to Gilgamesh, for instance, is, apart from the immediate and obvious sexual motive, not given context. We are free to, or called upon to, endow the event with symbolic or metaphorical value.

One might say that the narrator insists upon life lived metaphorically in the Gilgamesh story when he introduces so many dreams. The dreams in the Gilgamesh story are quite remarkable, quite unlike those

---

[9] E. Auerbach, *Mimesis*, trans. W. Trask (Princeton 1957) 11.

[10] On the narrative style of the Abraham and Isaac episode see Auerbach, op. cit. (note 9) 3–23; E. A. Speiser, *The Anchor Bible: Genesis* (Garden City 1964) 164–65.

few which are to be found in the Homeric poems, or the many more in the Old Testament narrative. Whereas dreams in these latter narratives generally function mechanically or narrowly as instruction or admonition, they are described in the Gilgamesh narrative as an experience of the character equivalent to action in the wakeful state. Gilgamesh and Enkidu have dreams which are psychic experiences, adventures of the subconscious or soul, in keeping with the importance attached to sleeping throughout the story. Sleeping, waking, voyaging to the Underworld seem to be alternative experiences of equal importance. Whether dying is an equivalent alternative is unclear; despite Utnapishtim's observation that sleep is "like a painted death," Gilgamesh's despair implies that death is not.

The significant events in the Gilgamesh story seem to be:

1. Enkidu's loss of innocence after his sexual encounter with the harlot
2. the friendship between Enkidu and Gilgamesh following their wrestling match
3. the adventuresome journey into the cedar forest culminating in the killing of Humbaba
4. Ishtar's sexual invitation to Gilgamesh and his rejection of her
5. Enkidu's death motivated by the god's anger
6. Gilgamesh wandering and questing
7. Siduri's advice to Gilgamesh
8. the wisdom of Utnapishtim
9. Gilgamesh's attempts to overcome death, and the serpent's theft of the flower of youth
10. Gilgamesh's death and funeral

Enkidu's loss of innocence is one of the more arresting elements in the narrative. This occurs when he comes down from the hills where he has been consorting with animals and has sexual intercourse with the harlot. Afterwards the animals flee him, and the text reads (Sandar translation), "Enkidu was grown weak, for wisdom was in him and the thoughts of man were in his heart." A primary significance of this event is humankind's turn from nature to civilization;[11] Enkidu, deserted by the animals, in turn becomes the hunter of lions and wolves so that herdsmen and shepherds can sleep in peace. He turns from grasses and animal's milk to bread and wine, the one baked, the other fermented, the basic processed foodstuffs of civilization. Otherwise the meaning is less clear. What is the "wisdom," the "thoughts of man" which the Gilgamesh author mentions? I venture that it is the hero's intimation of his own mortality; for, conceivably, the sexual encounter is to be understood

---

[11] The idea is discussed at some length by G. S. Kirk, *Myth, Its Meaning and Function in Ancient and Other Cultures* (Berkeley 1972) 146ff.

as depriving him of his immortality. This seems to be implied when he curses the harlot as well as the trapper as he lies dying. If they had not transformed him, he seems to be saying, then he would not be dying. This interpretation is possibly reinforced in the subsequent remonstrance of Shamash. When he argues that the goods which Enkidu received— bread, wine, the friendship of Gilgamesh, royal splendor—are sufficient recompense for loss of life, he is not disputing the thrust of Enkidu's complaint, only the notion that he has reason to complain.

The matter is ambiguous, but perhaps the *Genesis* narrative clarifies it. When Adam and Eve eat of the fruit of the tree of knowledge of good and evil they become aware, specifically they become sexually aware; this act somehow is related to loss of immortality (*Genesis* 2.17: "for in the day that thou eatest thereof thou shalt surely die.") Although we are accustomed to the traditional "knowledge of good and evil," it has been pointed out that the Hebrew is better translated as "knowledge of pleasure and pain";[12] in this context we may assume sexual pleasure and the deprivation of it as pain. Hence, loss of innocence is sexual awakening, exactly what Enkidu experiences.

Similarly the *Genesis* narrative of Adam and Eve can be interpreted as a movement from nature to civilization. This movement is analogous to Enkidu's switch from a diet of natural foods to processed foods. Toil becomes an ingredient of nutriment; at the same time processed food-stuff is indicative of man's control over nature, and that is what civilization is all about. The consequence of Adam and Eve's sexual wisdom is expulsion from the garden, that earthly paradise, site of spontaneous goodness, very much the adult's nostalgic view of the state of nature. Together with the expulsion comes the obligation to work and the arrival of a family, two commonplace aspects of civilization; the same idea appears in the Greco-Roman tradition, particularly well expressed by Lucretius who introduces work and the family in a pagan version of mankind's fall from grace.[13]

The equation between sexual awareness and the loss of immortality, an idea which appears in both narratives, seems to mirror the biological truth of the male existence. A male's primary role is complete upon orgasm so that the onset of puberty, true sexual awareness, in a boy's life is also his first real intimation of his own mortality, truly, the loss of innocence. While some would insist that the account of the expulsion from the Garden is an imagistic way of describing mankind's uncon-scious recollection of being expelled from the womb, it is probably more likely the imagistic account of the end of childhood, sexual awareness being a child's loss of innocence. Childhood is marked by dependency

---

[12] Speiser, op. cit. (note 10) 25ff.
[13] See my "Lucretius and Progress," *CJ* 58 (1963) 167ff.

upon a parent, and this quality is marvelously captured in the *Genesis*
(3:9) narrative when Jaweh is described out walking in the Garden and
the guilty pair hide from him, but hear his question, "Where are you?",
like that typically parental question, "What are you up to?"

If we may pose Adam and Eve's sojourn in the Garden as mankind's
childhood, then their loss of innocence, expulsion and subsequent punishment, toil, are the emblems of growing up, paralleling Enkidu's conversion to civilized life. Childhood is commonly represented by nostalgic
adults as a period free of responsibility whereas by contrast it is just that
bondage to this struggle for survival which marks adults. Indeed, the
Genesis–Exodus narrative taken as a whole seems to be the figurative
rendering of the course of human life. It is important to notice this
because we can see the same pattern although less clearly defined in
other narratives. In *Genesis* birth and childhood in the garden, sexual
awareness, the discovery of the other, are followed by intense sibling
rivalry in the stories of Cain and Abel, Jacob and Esau and Joseph and
his brothers; and then in *Exodus* we find the fully developed portrait of
the adult man, Moses, who becomes father and patriarch before he dies.
In the later stages of his career, as the father and authority figure, Moses
encounters the wise man who offers him the traditional wisdom, in this
narrative, Jaweh with the Ten Commandments.

The Gilgamesh narrative by contrast has less marked elements which
suggest the human lifetime.[14] Enkidu's loss of innocence and conversion
from the natural state to worker and socialized man stand at the beginning
of the narrative, balanced by Gilgamesh's encounter with Utnapishtim, the
wise man, toward the close. There is nothing more. The Gospels, of course,
give us an account of the lifetime of the Christ whom we can follow from
his birth in Bethlehem until his death at Calvary, a meeting, so to speak,
with his father, akin to meeting the father or authority-figure in these other
narratives.

The notion of a lifetime is particularly well developed in the *Odyssey*. The poem begins with a young man (Telemachus) who is first presented as impotent and irresponsible until goaded into action by the
goddess, Athena. Thereafter, he leaves his childhood home, his mother
and nurse, and in so doing loses the innocence of provincial life, experi-
encing the civilized ways of Nestor and Menelaus, simultaneously learning who and what a man his father is. Thereafter we see the older man
(Odysseus) traveling, having adventures and experimenting sexually

---

[14] A most interesting dissertation has been written demonstrating that the Gilgamesh
narrative inherently depicts the human life cycle at least in its social ramifications. J.
Kakascik in her *The Epic of Gilgamesh and Life Stage Development* (diss. Boston
University 1975) uses Erikson's theory of psycho-social stages of development to establish
the shape of the Gilgamesh story.

(Calypso, Circe, even Nausicaa by innuendo) until he finally secures a homestead and takes a wife. The encounter with the old man of wisdom forms part of Odysseus' travel tale when he describes meeting Teiresias in the Underworld. Just as Utnapishtim talks to Gilgamesh of his mortality, Teiresias tells Odysseus how he will die, obviously a parallel story element. Teiresias' revelation is not motivated in the *Odyssey*, and nothing is made of it, unlike what Utnapishtim says to Gilgamesh, but its presence and place in the story derive from the structure of this kind of narrative rather than the story line. Nonetheless, the *Odyssey* poet needs to have his hero *describe* meeting an authority figure at this point even if he does not need to have his hero meet one.

The *Genesis–Exodus* story establishes Moses as a father figure and an old man when he receives the wisdom of Jaweh. Gilgamesh, on the other hand, is not so identified when he meets the old man of wisdom, Utnapishtim, relict of the antediluvian human race. The connection is made, however, between old age, authority-figure, patriarchy, father and eternal wisdom; this is the lifetime pattern. The meeting between Odysseus and Teiresias seems to be misplaced because it occurs so early in the narrative, except that, as we shall see shortly, it serves other narrative demands. Old age in the *Odyssey* is indeed introduced in its proper place although divorced from any exchange of wisdom. The *Odyssey* poet brings in Odysseus' father, Laertes,[15] toward the close of the poem (24.205–411) to complete his triptych in which Telemachus and Odysseus hold the other panels. It is important to note that Laertes is unnecessary to the action of the story, and the poet only briefly portrays him. His motive in introducing Laertes, however unconscious, must be to show the final stages of man's life which follow upon homesteading and family years, that is, dependent senility. So Odysseus meets his father, and in this sense Laertes is essential to the story form if not to the *Odyssey* plot.

Telemachus, we have suggested, is a conception of early youth and loss of innocence. The poet introduces yet another narrative of the loss of innocence in the fifth book. That he is intentionally repeating himself seems clear from the fact that this doublet version has as its prelude a second council of the gods paralleling the one which had begun the first book. So here it is Odysseus' departure from Calypso's island which constitutes another loss of innocence. We first meet the central figure of the *Odyssey* narrative in the fifth book and he is described in a sexual relationship with Calypso; that is the central fact of the situation on Ogygia. Subsequently he declines her invitation of immortality (he loses his immortality, so to speak) and he sets forth on his adventures. This is analogous to Adam and Eve's fall from grace and to Enkidu's sexual experience.

---

[15] N. Austin, *Archery at the Dark of the Moon* (Berkeley 1975) 102f.

Imposing a lifetime pattern on the events of the *Iliad* is less easy and some will complain much too contrived. The initial quarrel between Achilles and Agamemnon, however, can be called Achilles' loss of innocence. This seems especially true of his angry rejoinders to Agamemnon where he cynically disputes the heroic values, and in so doing destroys the motivational framework of a warrior's existence, and, of course, of his own. Just as Adam and Eve's disobedience can be described as questioning of divine trust, another way of describing loss of innocence, so Achilles' cynical disclaimers betray a loss of faith. The poet dramatizes this idea in Achilles' subsequent withdrawal from the battlefield. While the theme of awakened sexuality is not apparent here (unless it be in Achilles' reaction to the loss of Briseis), the poet notices briefly, very briefly—and probably unconsciously—a conversion from nature to civilization in his description of the speaker's staff (*Il.* 1.234–39) which, as the poet says, was once a flourishing tree, now denuded and carved, that is a product of culture. A similar unconscious gesture to what may be traditional associations occurs at the close of the *Iliad* when Achilles meets the old man and father Priam and is thus reminded of the old man, his father, Peleus, and thereafter speaks a piece of traditional wisdom (the jars of Zeus speech [*Il.* 24.527–33]) which is a summation of the action of the entire *Iliad* narrative. Here the younger Achilles in the company of the old man and father is made to say what in other narratives comes from the mouth of the old man, father-figure or authority-figure.

Another important element of these narratives is the friendship or companionship between the central figure and a slightly subsidiary figure, subsidiary principally because the narrator does not make us care to the same degree about his fortunes. The best realized friendship is that between Enkidu and Gilgamesh to which the relationship between Patroklos and Achilles is immediately analogous. What do these men mean to each other? The Gilgamesh author describes their love as that of a man and wife; Aeschylus wrote a homoerotic love tragedy about the Homeric twosome. I should say that the relationship in neither instance is overtly sexual,[16] although there is sexuality in the wrestling match between Gilgamesh and Enkidu just as there is sexuality in Achilles and Patroklos making love to women in their shared quarters. In societies where women are not highly valued as personalities by the males, masculine friendships inevitably assume primal importance. Consider the nude wrestling between two male heroes in D. H. Lawrence's *Women in Love*, two upper-class English males whose emotional life peaked, no doubt, at their public school when women seemed, as they would always remain, obstacles to be overcome on the road to freedom. The Gilgamesh narrator connects Enkidu specifically

---

[16] For another view on the Homeric pair see W. M. Clarke, "Achilles and Patroklos in Love," *Hermes* 106 (1978) 381–96.

with Gilgamesh's sexuality. The former stops Gilgamesh as he is proceeding upon a mission of lust, stops him with a wrestling match; thereafter Gilgamesh's sexual desires do not appear in the narrative. It seems fair to ascribe undertones of something sexual to this succession of events. Enkidu and Gilgamesh move from hostile encounter to peace to love to symbiosis. A similar progression can be demonstrated in the sibling relationships in the *Genesis–Exodus* narrative, commencing with the violent opposition in the conflict of Cain and Abel evolving into the love and self-abnegation of Judah's wish to substitute himself for Benjamin and concluding with Aaron's becoming, as we nowadays call it, the mouthpiece of Moses.

The epic heroes love each other deeply. The Gilgamesh author wishes to stress their need for each other and uses the marriage relationship as his metaphor. The relationship may also be the poet's way of describing the whole masculine personality. In each instance Enkidu and Patroklos are the alter egos, the shadow figures, an expression of the ambiguity in human personality, our psychological ambivalence. The Enkidu–Gilgamesh relationship has greater psychological intensity than the Achilles–Patroklos relationship because we learn much more about Enkidu than we do about Patroklos. Barely identified or described, Patroklos is little more than an extension of Achilles,[17] so that when Patroklos dies, Achilles hears within himself the bell tolling his own mortality. The externalization of this innermost sensation is true to the psychology of oral literature as it has been described by Russo and Simon.[18] Enkidu, on the other hand, is the externalization of a more complicated set of emotions.

Enkidu meets Gilgamesh as the king is about to act out the arrogance for which his people criticize him. Enkidu stops him forever after from doing so. Enkidu is inhibition incarnate. And thereafter Enkidu shows the appropriate emotions or attitudes: fear, humility, prudence. His death, his dying are important to the narrative. It is the great negation of the life force which so clearly animates Gilgamesh, even to the point of the cruel exercise of power which is the first aspect of the king which the narrator establishes for us. Enkidu's death also furnishes the motive for Gilgamesh's emotions and actions in the latter half of the poem. Gilgamesh's death is by contrast a modest, unimportant, inevitable narrative event which functions more as boundary or frame for the narrative than as action within the narrative. It may be compared to the description of Hector's funeral at the end of the *Iliad* or the description of Achilles' funeral toward the close of the *Odyssey*. These events are not necessary to the story, but they are crucial for the *structure* of the

---

[17] One might say that he is the representation of the Freudian notion of the superego. Cf. Nestor's comments, *Il.* 11.785–88.

[18] J. A. Russo and B. Simon, "Homeric Psychology and the Oral Epic Tradition," *Journal of the History of Ideas* 29 (1968) 483–98.

narrative. They function like the words "The End" which used to appear at the close of films or like the screen credits which begin to unroll in the foreground of a film's final scene.

Fundamentally Enkidu seems to represent the psychic force of inhibition. Consider his hesitation at entering the forest, his tears, his fear of Humbaba; then, finally, when Gilgamesh hesitates to kill Humbaba it is Enkidu who insists. We can read that insistence as his hard-hearted and narrow prudence, inhibiting Gilgamesh's more adventuresome and imaginative reaction to Humbaba at that moment. Notice again at his death how Enkidu curses the trapper, the harlot, curses the things he has done; it is repentance and regret, emotions which are consonant with the personality of dread, prudence and humility. Gilgamesh, by contrast, takes risks. He is ambitious, impetuous, courageous, innocent of suspicion or danger. The narrator arranges a telling juxtaposition: Enkidu's eyes fill with tears at his fear and dread of the thought of meeting Humbaba, while moments later Gilgamesh's eyes fill with tears at the frustration at not yet having established an enduring fame for himself. When Enkidu begs Gilgamesh to give up the enterprise, Gilgamesh characteristically replies that man cannot in any case live forever, therefore, fame is the only bulwark against extinction.

The author of the Gilgamesh story knows the adventuresome personality well. It is a manic-depressive one. Gilgamesh shrinks from killing Humbaba because he knows that the glamour and excitement of an adventurous life will die ("If we touch him the blaze and glory of light will be put out in confusion, the glory and the glamour will vanish"—Sandars translation). Here is the hero's continual problem, that is, confronting what lies beyond the significant act. Consider how indifferent Achilles has become by the end of the *Iliad*, when Thetis asks him to give back Hector's corpse. "So be it," he replies to his mother. "If Zeus wants it in his heart, then Priam may as well bring me the ransom and take the body away" (*Il.* 24.139–40).

The disciples of Jesus function as his Enkidu. Short of faith, timid, they have to be forever exhorted and encouraged. They in turn are reminiscent of the weary, discouraged and complaining Israelites whom Moses must lead in *Exodus*. Like Gilgamesh, the Christ must say to his disciples "he who preserves his life shall lose it" (*Luke* 9.24). This is the answer to Enkidu's timidity and it goes for Odysseus' crew as well, a group of men who demonstrate the same combination of prudence and timidity as Enkidu. They lose their lives ironically when famished, eating the cattle of the Sun God to ward off starvation. They lose their lives violating a taboo, offending the Sun God, just as Enkidu opens the gate instead of smashing it, and just as he offends Ishtar by hurling a bone at her.

Odysseus' crew functions as his companions only during the travel adventures which he himself narrates. Elsewhere Athene is the companion figure, first with Telemachus, then with Odysseus. She is a creation not of the pattern we have observed elsewhere; she seems to represent the strategic thinking of both men, then the more powerful, aggressive aspects of Odysseus' thinking. He does not commune with himself to rehearse doubts, but rather to analyze. Once the poet presents him in the kind of interior monologue we expect in fiction (*Od.* 5.465ff.). Otherwise the poet seems to allow Athene to express the heightened awareness of this exceedingly lucid man.

The crew, as we have noted, appear only in Odysseus' narration of his adventures before the court of King Alkinoos. This narration is remarkable in that it contains several features which are analogous to elements of the Gilgamesh story. Teiresias, as we have remarked, is like Utnapishtim. The journey to the Underworld is comparable to Gilgamesh's journey to find Utnapishtim. Circe is the malign female figure whom Gilgamesh encounters in Ishtar. The Cyclops is the baleful giant which corresponds to Humbaba. The Lotus Eaters offer the temptation to stop adventuring and searching just as Siduri advises Gilgamesh. The episode in which Odysseus narrates his adventures is marked by references to the poetic contrivance.[19] One wonders if the poet of the *Odyssey*, in order to emphasize the art of story-telling which Odysseus so superbly possesses, has carefully constructed his travels on a very traditional and obvious frame, one which the audience of the *Odyssey* would recognize as an artifice independent of Odysseus' experiences.

The poet of the *Odyssey* is fond of creative repetition, whether it is the constant repetition of the theme of arrival or the duplication of Telemachus with Odysseus. Here so much of that travel story reappears in the other narrative. Laertes, as we have suggested, appears as Utnapishtim, the old man at the end of the journey. Calypso, as we have noted, is a kind of Ishtar figure. Nausicaa functions somewhat like Siduri, both the young, nubile maiden herself and the island culture of the Phaecians ("We know how to drink and eat . . ." *Od.* 8.245ff.). As Siduri says to Gilgamesh,

> 'Where are you hurrying to? You will never find that life for which you are looking. When the gods created man they allotted to him death, but life they retained in their own keeping. As for you, Gilgamesh, fill your belly with good things, day and night, night and day, dance and be merry, feast and rejoice. Let your clothes be fresh, bathe yourself in water, cherish the little child that holds your hand, and make your wife happy with your embrace; for this, too, is the lot of man.' (Tablet X, Old Babylonian Version, Column 3)

Siduri tempts Gilgamesh to stop traveling by reminding him of the sensual and earthly delights which traditionally mark human existence.

---

[19] See my *The Iliad, the Odyssey and the Epic Tradition* (Garden City 1966) 184ff.; 203ff.

The travel-torn and weary Odysseus is offered exactly the same seduction at Scheria, a nubile princess, luxury, parties, dancing, a life of ease.

The women of these narratives are another commonplace element. In the Gilgamesh story we see the three aspects of woman as men imagine them: mother (Ninsun); consort, helpmeet or domestic life force (Siduri); and sexual partner (Ishtar). Exactly the same triad appear in the sixth book of the *Iliad* where they seem to be almost allegorical. Hecuba offers her son wine (the nurturent figure); Helen, the adultress, the wife, holding Hector's son, tries to keep her husband from going outside the walls to fight (like Siduri who tries to keep Gilgamesh from going to Utnapishtim). The three women try to prevent Hector from fulfilling himself as a warrior (although, of course, very briefly and superficially set into the scale of the *Iliad*'s plot). Like the Christ who must resist his mother's entreaties with a reminder that mere familial bonds can no longer hold him (Mark 3:31–35; Luke 8:19–21) or tell the Magdalene not to touch him since he has yet to ascend to Heaven (John 20:17), Hector must resist these female restraints upon his action, action which defines him. The same three women of the *Iliad* reappear to lament Hector's death, not unlike the Virgin and the Magdalene in lamentation at the Cross, an idea considerably more developed in Christian art than in the Gospel narratives. The women of the *Odyssey* cannot be so simply categorized because while we may speak of a Siduri figure in Nausicaa, or an Ishtar figure in Circe and Calypso, there are many other women, principally, of course, Penelope who is far more than the wife figure of the Gilgamesh story or of the *Iliad*.[20] She is more the princess, the suitors' prize, like Atalanta or Hippodameia, than she is the wife or consort figure. Indeed, once Odysseus regains her side in bed, she disappears from the narrative.

Most of these narratives have some kind of monster figure who must be overcome, part of the hero's adventure or trial. Humbaba, as we have suggested, may be equated with the Cyclops in the *Odyssey*. In the *Iliad* there is no obvious adventure or giant. Achilles' withdrawal to his tent, his meditation there which produces the stark truths which he conveys to Odysseus and Phoinix in the ninth book, is like the wandering and questing of Gilgamesh. Christ at Gethsemane is like Achilles in his tent. Both passages may be compared to Gilgamesh's journey into the cedar forest and his killing of Humbaba, although a more precise analogue would be Christ's sojourn in the wilderness and his confrontation with Satan.

This story structure can evolve tragically or comically. The Gilgamesh story is tinged with a pessimism and despair which—at least in the

---

[20] See my "Male and Female in the Homeric Poems" *Ramus* 3 (1974) 95ff., now revised in *Ancient Greek Literature and Society* (Garden City 1975) 91ff.

extant texts—is never alleviated. Utnapishtim's devastating, brief and abrupt reply to Gilgamesh's lengthy question when they first meet stands as stark representation of the utter nothingness of man's existence, the finality of his doom. The *Iliad* seems to be equally despairing, except that when Achilles offers Priam food, telling him to eat rather than to grieve, the poet is asking us to believe that Achilles has accepted the essentially comic philosophy of Odysseus (cf. *Il.* 19.155ff.; 216ff.), has accepted life's limitations and impositions; he makes meaning in a meaningless universe. The *Odyssey*, like the *Genesis–Exodus*, has the happy resolution of homecoming. The Gospel story has the Resurrection. Whatever the imperatives of the particular story, one can discern a common complex of elements which betoken the same underlying structure.

WORKS AND DAYS 1–285:
HESIOD'S INVISIBLE AUDIENCE

PETER GREEN

There is a popular delusion that the personal family allusions scattered by Hesiod throughout the *Works and Days*, and at the beginning of the *Theogony*,[1] are straightforward and, for the most part, not in dispute. Careful attention to Hesiod's text should suffice to dispel the first impression, while a survey of modern scholarship in this area will very soon put paid to the second. As J. F. Latimer observed in 1930,[2] "Hesiod's *Works and Days* is a veritable gold mine for those who would not inhibit their hermeneutical aspirations." It is indeed. The operation, however, entails considerable risk. Rival, and mutually contradictory, theories abound. Worse, as Latimer confessed, "often a reexamination of the author or of the passage in question completely upsets one's carefully formulated opinions." Here I myself must plead as guilty as any. In 1960 I published[3] the following statement in the course of a discussion on Hesiod: "It seems clear that Perses not only disputed the terms of his father's will, but bribed local barons to give him the lion's share of the estate at arbitration." There is nothing in that sentence, apart from the first assertion (and I am not too sure about the idea of a will, either) which I would stand by today. Yet no new substantive discoveries have been made; the text, despite all West's efforts, is not all that far from where Rzach left it. True, a great deal of interpretive work has been published, some of it both innovative and methodologically invaluable,[4] but the overall scene remains one of dogmatism and confusion.

---

[1] See *WD* 9–10, 27–39, 190–94, 202–18, 225–27, 248–51, 260–64, 267–81, 298–301, 320–26, 340–41, 363–67, 371, 376–78, 394–404, 631–40, 646–47; *Th.* 22–34, 79–97.

[2] J. F. Latimer, "Perses versus Hesiod" (Latimer), *TAPhA* 61 (1930) 70.

[3] *Essays in Antiquity* (London 1969) 39, in an essay entitled "Hodge on Helicon: a study of Hesiod and his society."

[4] I would particularly single out three articles by Michael Gagarin: "Dikē in the *Works and Days*" (DWD), *CPh* 68 (1973) 81–94; "Hesiod's dispute with Perses" (HDP), *TAPhA* 104 (1974) 103–11; and an as yet unpublished paper entitled "Linguistic and moral ambiguity in the *Works and Days*" (LMA). I am grateful to Professor Gagarin for allowing me to examine this last-named piece in typescript.

Some scholars, from Gilbert Murray onwards,[5] have argued that the entire quarrel between the brothers was a literary fiction, a view very much in accord with contemporary critical trends: Pietro Pucci's discussion, for instance, is conducted at so rarified a level of structural and semantic abstraction that the problem is simply ignored altogether.[6] There was no lawsuit, Krafft argues[7]: "Er ist ein literarisches Motiv." From the time of the early scholiasts there have always been critics eager to theorize Perses himself out of existence, as a mere conventional addressee—in Dornseiff's case, with abundant parallel citations from Eastern wisdom literature.[8] Yet no one supposes that Hesiod invented himself; and since his personal relationships stand at the heart of the *Works and Days*, it is hard to believe, from the circumstantial evidence he offers, that he has saddled himself with a fictitious father and brother for the occasion. (Nor, might I add, do I accept recent attempts to relegate Lycambes, Neobule, and the rest of Archilochus' personal circle to a mere property-closet for the conventions of iambic ψόγος.) As Walcot says, the *Works and Days* is an intensely personal poem: it is shot through with legal preoccupations, and these may reasonably be held to have stemmed from the long-simmering quarrel with Perses.[9] Indeed, many scholars take it for granted that the dispute actually provided the original impulse (*Anstoss*) for the poem, however much Hesiod may afterwards have added to the version that we possess.[10]

Yet even if we grant the historicity of Hesiod's family feud, and the interest it generated in his contemporaries, its details remain highly

---

[5] Cf. *A History of Ancient Greek Literature* (London 1897) 6–7, 53–55.

[6] Pietro Pucci, *Hesiod and the Language of Poetry* (Johns Hopkins UP, 1977) 45ff.

[7] In *Vergleichende Untersuchungen zu Homer und Hesiod* (Göttingen 1963) 90 n. 4, cited by Gagarin, HDP 104 n. 1. Cf. H. Munding, *Hesiods Erga in ihrem Verhältnis zur Ilias* (Frankfurt 1959) 12ff.

[8] See M. L. West, *Hesiod: Works and Days* (West) (Oxford 1978) 33–34.

[9] P. Walcot, *Hesiod and the Near East* (HNE) (Cardiff 1966) 104–6: his arguments are given added strength by Gagarin's contention, DWD 81ff., that the fundamental meaning of δίκη in Hesiod is "'law', in the sense of a process for the peaceful settlement of disputes." For the semantic flexibility of the term depending on context cf. B. A. Van Groningen, "Hésiode et Persès" (HP), *Med.Ned.Akad.Wet.Afd.Let.* 20 (1957) 159 n. 22. Similar arguments in favor of a biographical base for the quarrel are found in T. A. Sinclair, *Hesiod: Works and Days* (Sinclair) (London 1932) xvi, and Mario Puelma, "Sänger und König: zum Verständnis von Hesiods Tierfabel," *Mus. Helv.* 29 (1972) 92 n. 30. Cf. West, 34–35. On Archilochus and iambic ψόγος see now G. Nagy, *The Best of the Achaeans* (Johns Hopkins UP, 1980) 243–49, in contrast to the more judicious warnings of K. J. Dover, *Archiloque, Entretiens de la Fondation Hardt*, 10 (Geneva 1964).

[10] E.g. Rzach in *PWK* vol. 8 col. 1171; K. von Fritz, *Hésiode et son influence, Entretiens de la Fondation Hardt*, 7 (Geneva 1962) 29 ("Die Dichtung selbst sollte ihm die Waffen liefern, den Bruder und die Könige doch noch auf den Weg der Gerechtigkeit zu bringen"); H. T. Wade-Gery, "Hesiod" (Wade-Gery), *Phoenix* 3 (1949) 90; *contra*, e.g., S. Østerud, "The individuality of Hesiod" (Østerud). *Hermes* 104 (1976) 17 n. 13.

debatable. It is widely assumed, for instance, that there had been an earlier lawsuit, or arbitration, between the brothers,[11] even though opinions are divided as to whether Perses won[12] or lost[13] on that occasion. In fact, as we shall see, the very existence of such an event is, to say the least, highly problematical. Similarly, most scholars have, till very recently, taken it for granted that Perses bribed the βασιλῆες who presided over the case.[14] There is no hard evidence to support this allegation in the crude direct sense, and the whole concept of "gift-eating" in Hesiod needs to be modified in the light of modern anthropological parallels, mostly from Greece itself (see below, pp. 28–29). Can we even be sure, as Minna Jensen pertinently enquired,[15] which of the two brothers was the injured party, let alone which of them initiated litigation?[16] Walcot, in *Hesiod and the Near East* (Cardiff 1966), p. 106, argues bleakly that "we do not know as yet, and probably never shall know, whether the pair of brothers quarrelled once or twice, or if their dispute ever reached a court of law." Both Jensen and Walcot seem to me a trifle over-pessimistic. I would like to approach the problem in two stages: first, by scrutinizing Hesiod's text, to determine what he actually does, and does not say—as opposed to the statements more or less loosely attributed to him; and second, to consider the *dramatic setting* of WD 1–285, the context in which we, as readers or listeners, are to think of the poem as being delivered.

At the close of this initial appeal to Zeus (*WD* 1–10), Hesiod, with a

---

[11] E.g. by Paul Mazon, *Hésiode: Les Travaux et les Jours* (Mazon) (Paris 1914) 45; Gagarin, HDP 106–7; Wilamowitz, *Hesiodos Erga* (Wilamowitz), (Berlin 1928) on WD 34 ("Einmal hat das νεῖκος des Perses gegenüber Hesiod Erfolg gehabt"); Van Groningen, HP 155; other instances collected by Latimer 72–73 with n. 10; Latimer himself (76–77) is properly sceptical on the issue.

[12] Mazon and Wilamowitz, *locc. citt.*; R. J. Bonner and G. Smith, *The Administration of Justice from Homer to Aristotle* (Chicago 1939), vol. 1, 46; Sinclair xxxviii–ix (with some characteristic hedging); H. Diller, "Die dicterische Form von Hesiods Erga," *Akad.Wiss.u. Lit.Mainz* 2 (1962) 41–69, repr. *Hesiod* (*Wege der Forschung* vol. xliv, [Darmstadt 1966]) 239–73, see esp. 247 n. 16. Cf. Van Groningen, HP 153 n. 1.

[13] Van Gronigen, HP 164–65 (though earlier, 155, he had written, "Comment le premier procès s'est-il termine? Impossible d'en dire quoi que ce soit avec certitude."); followed by Gagarin, HDP 104, 106 n. 9 (with the same hedging as Van Groningen).

[14] As Gagarin points out, HDP 109–10, with n. 19; he and Van Groningen (HP 157–58) are the only scholars who have seriously challenged the notion that what Hesiod is describing is indictable corruption (rather than a legitimate, if excessive, passion for court-fees). The common view is exemplified by Jula Kerschensteiner, "Zu Aufbau und Gedankenführung von Hesiods Erga," *Hermes* 79 (1944) 156: "Nicht zum *zweitenmal* darf er [Perses] hoffen, die *habgierigen* Könige zu *bestechen*" (italicising mine).

[15] Minna Skafte Jensen, "Tradition and Individuality in Hesiod's Works and Days," *Class et Med.* 27 (1966 [1969]) 10 (hereafter Jensen).

[16] It is most often assumed that Perses originated the suit, but Latimer (77) and P. B. R. Forbes, "Hesiod versus Perses" (Forbes), *CR* 64 (1950) 83, argue for Hesiod, "who corresponds most closely to the modern plaintiff." Cf. also Gagarin, HDP 111.

certain imperative familiarity, delimits their respective spheres of activity. Zeus' job is to keep straight (ἴθυνε) the judgements (θέμιστας) handed down by the βασιλῆες,[17] to ensure that they are consonant with δίκη. The poet's own business is to expound home-truths to Perses (ἐτήτυμα μυθησαίμην). We are, it would seem, in for a λόγος παραινετικός of the kind that Phoenix inflicted on Achilles.[18] Whether we read Πέρσῃ (dat.) or Πέρσῃ (voc.) in line 10—and even that choice is not so clear-cut as, e.g., West (p. 142) would have us believe—Hesiod's addressee is introduced right at the beginning of the poem. On the other hand, he is not formally explained. We can infer (as no doubt the original audience did) that only relatives would quarrel over an inheritance (37ff.); but it remains a fact that not until line 633 are we told, in so many words, that the two men are brothers.[19] The clear implication is that Hesiod's audience was assumed to be familiar with Perses and Hesiod and their differences already. On the other hand, to balance this withholding of background information, we observe that Perses himself, during the course of the poem, hears a good deal about his personal habits and family history with which he must already be only too familiar.[20] Why is this? What assumptions led Hesiod to overdocument his characters at one level, yet at another fail to block in their most fundamental relationships?

We now come to the most crucial passage for any interpretation of the Hesiod–Perses debate: WD 27–39. It is not too much to say that the whole story of the quarrel, with its uncertain outcome and contested number of lawsuits, rests fundamentally on these few lines. Hesiod urges Perses not to abandon work, spurred on by bad Eris, in favor of hanging about the *agora* for the purpose of watching, and listening to, νείκεα, litigation, disputes. A man in Perses' position, that is, a small farmer, would need to have a full year's supply of stores laid by (βίος . . . ἐπηετανός) to cover him through to the next harvest, before he could afford such self-indulgence.[21] It should be stressed that the kind of poverty envisaged throughout the *Works and Days* is always of this seasonal kind, the inability to survive between one harvest and the next: and though, as we know from the Solonian σεισάχθεια, this misfortune could,

[17] Though the βασιλῆες are not mentioned in this context, θέμιστες, like Anglo-Saxon "dooms," were essentially arbitrary, rulings which only they could pronounce: cf. Sinclair, 2–3, West, 141.

[18] Cf. Østerud, 16–17.

[19] Well emphasized by Jensen, 6.

[20] As is correctly pointed out by West, 33.

[21] The situation is at once recognizable as that confronting many of the smallholders in Attica prior to Solon's reforms. See Arist. *Ath.Pol.* 2, 5–6; Plut. *Sol.* 13–14; and the excellent discussion in A. French, *The Growth of the Athenian Economy* (London 1964) ch. ii, "The Breakdown of the Old Order," esp. 12–13.

ultimately, reduce the victim to serfdom, it is still thought of by Hesiod very much as a temporary fluctuating condition. Perses' poverty is never presented as absolute or irretrievable.[22]

"Only when you have your fill of βίος," Hesiod emphasises, "can you promote disputes and conflict over other men's goods (κτήμασ᾽ ἐπ᾽ ἀλλοτρίοις)." The point he is making—no less familiar or applicable today than in antiquity—is that while litigation may be a source of profit to the wealthy, it costs the poor man, win or lose, time and money that he can ill afford.[23] Perses' role, as Hesiod presents it, is seen as more than that of a mere passive spectator: he is involved in the action (ὀφέλλοις), though to what extent is still uncertain. It could mean no more than the shouting of partisan comment or advice (see below, p. 34). There now follows (line 35) a surprising statement: "But you won't get a second chance to act thus" (σοὶ δ᾽ οὐκέτι δεύτερον ἔσται ὧδ᾽ ἔρδειν). To act how? And when are we to place the first action? One point is clear, and should not be fudged: δεύτερον can *only* mean "second," and not, in a loose sense, "further" or "later," a meaning badly needed by those who believe in an earlier trial: if the present altercation is the brothers' second, then Hesiod must be warning Perses that he will not get a *third* chance.[24] But if Hesiod unequivocally says "second," and if ὧδ᾽ ἔρδειν is taken as "bring suit against me," which Perses is in the process of doing, then the conclusion is inescapable: there was no prior litigation. As we shall see, such a hypothesis is perfectly consistent with Hesiod's text.

At first sight, it might be thought that the undesirable activity which Perses is admonished not to repeat is his time-wasting habit of watching, or taking part in, disputes in the *agora*, of encouraging strife over other (unnamed) men's goods. But a moment's thought shows that this is impossible. Such behavior is repetitive and habitual; what Hesiod objects to is something that has happened only once, and which (in his opinion) Perses will not be able to attempt *a second time*. It must, then, have a personal and specific application. In the lines that follow, the on-going dispute between the brothers begins to emerge, and we see it is to this that ὧδ᾽ ἔρδειν must refer.[25] Once again, Hesiod has assumed prior knowledge of the facts in his audience. The meaning is now clear. The present case

---

[22] This at once answers some of the objections raised by West, 35–40.

[23] Gagarin, LMA.

[24] Gagarin, HDP 107 with n. 10, correctly opposing Krafft (above, n. 7) 89 n. 4, who argues for a meaning such as *weiterhin* or *später*. I do not, however, agree with Gagarin's attempt to reconcile this finding with the existence of an earlier trial by treating the present dispute "as part of one long dispute which includes the earlier one." Van Groningen claims (155) that Hesiod is telling Perses that the latter will not be able to bring *this second case*, a desperate resort at odds with all the known facts of the poem.

[25] West (150) duly notes this inconsistency, but without drawing any significant conclusion from it.

coming up for arbitration is a kill-or-cure attempt, on Perses' part, to secure a greater share of his father's legacy. He has not hitherto resorted to the law—that Perses is the plaintiff emerges clearly from this passage: ἔρδειν implies positive action—and he will not, in his brother's opinion, get a second opportunity to do so. Once the case is decided, that is, he will not be able to repeat it. What basis could Hesiod have had for so confident an assertion? Gagarin has argued that the cost of bringing suit would effectively have ruined Perses, and this is possible; but surely a more immediate and obvious cause would have lain in the verdict itself. Since their θέμιστες were binding, any ruling handed down by the βασιλῆες would preclude further appeals on the same issue.[26]

Hesiod now invites Perses to come to a private agreement with him. "Let us settle our dispute for ourselves, here and now, with Zeus' straight judgments, the best." διακρινώμεθα, as Gagarin rightly saw,[27] must be taken in the reflexive sense; it is not a causative middle. This reading is confirmed by the sense of the passage as a whole. Hesiod prefers the sure workings of divine law (a point stressed throughout the *Works and Days*) to the fallible judgments of men.[28] αὖθι, as the majority of scholars are agreed,[29] must mean "here and now." But even if we choose to take it in the (non-epic) sense of "again," that does not imply a previous lawsuit: in fact quite the reverse. The estate, Hesiod reminds his brother, was divided between them the first time (ἤδη μὲν γὰρ κλῆρον ἐδασσάμεθ᾽) without any hint of litigation. Why not repeat so eminently sensible a procedure?

We may assume that the original division was an equal one, at least as regards land, and perhaps carried out by lot: ancient and modern customs in this respect seem to be very similar.[30] Even if Hesiod was the elder son, as has been ingeniously argued,[31] there was no right of primogeniture.

---

[26] Gagarin, HDP 111. On the principle of binding "obligatory arbitration" see Bonner and Smith (above, n. 12) 47–48; cf. West, *Theogony* (1966) 184. On Perses as plaintiff see Jensen 7–8; cf. A. Kirchhoff, *Hesiodos' Mahnlieder an Perses* (Berlin 1889) 40–41.

[27] Ibid. 107.

[28] A point well made by Van Groningen, 156: "A l'appui de son point de vue Hésiode ne fait pas appel à la juridiction toujours faillible, telle qu'elle s'exerce dans les tribunaux, mais à la loi divine que même un auditoire non spécialisé comprend et accepte. Le poème tout entier est un exposé de ses dispositions de Zeus relative à l'existence humaine: il exige avant tout travail assidu et hinnêteté scrupuleuse. Si Persès se soumet à ces règles et à tout ce qui en dérive, l'accord entre les deux frères sera rétabli sans qu'un nouveau procès puisse encore être désiré par l'un des deux."

[29] See, e.g., the conspectus in Latimer, 72 n. 8; Sinclair, 6, and (with some hedging) West, 150. Paley, *The Epics of Hesiod* (London 1883) 11, argued that "it is very doubtful if it can bear this sense."

[30] P. Walcot, *Greek Peasants, Ancient and Modern* (GPAM) (Manchester 1970) 46–50, with further ref. Contra, Gagarin, HDP 107 n. 12. For ancient instances of division by lot see, e.g., Hom. *Od*.14.199ff., *Il*.15.187–89; Dem.48.12–13.

[31] P. Walcot, "A note on the biography of Hesiod," *CPh* 55 (1960) 33–34, equates Hesiod with the "good Eris"; it would be improbable, he argues, "that Hesiod would claim priority

What is more than likely is that the estate at issue was too small to be split in two and for each half still to remain economically viable. Greek farms were, and are, minuscule, so that repeated divisions among heirs has always tended to reduce holdings to a size where they can no longer be worked: the problem confronting Hesiod—and Solon after him—remains endemic, even today. In the famous autobiographical passage describing their father's settling at Ascra (*WD* 631–40), Hesiod shows scant respect, and more than a little resentment, for his patrimony. His recommendation that there should be no more than one heir to a farm (376–78) is surely based on bitter personal experience. To be childless was, and is, an unmitigated disaster in Greece (e.g., Hom. *Il*.9.453–56: *WD* 244, 284, 325:26); to have only one son was, for Homer, a curse rather than a blessing (*Il*.24.538–40). (But then Homer was dealing with warriors, not farmers.) Equally reprehensible, on the other hand, is a failure to provide adequate living standards and material well-being for one's children after one. In straitened circumstances the two principles will come into conflict, and the single male heir Hesiod recommends must be seen as the lesser of two evils for a struggling farmer. "That way wealth *piles up*," he says. "If you leave a second son, you need to die old," i.e., it will take you proportionately longer to build up the capital, acquire tha extra land, and establish the holdings necessary to provide for both of them.[32] It may also help to outlive any other relatives who might enter a claim on all or part of the estate.

It was, then, predictable that the division of their father's patrimony would lead to trouble between Hesiod and Perses. The most likely source of conflict, to judge from parallel cases, would be the house. Hesiod proceeds at once to tell his audience, while ostensibly addressing Perses, the background of their dispute. "For we'd already divided the estate"— no hint of litigation there, merely the implication that that should have settled the matter—"and [yet] many other things you kept trying to carry off by force, while greatly honoring [or perhaps "giving great pleasure with your attentions to": see L-S-J s.v. κυδαίνω II] the gift-eating

---

of birth for the good Eris without being the older brother himself." Cf. Van Groningen 165.

[32] On primogeniture see Latimer 70–71; this is also the clear implication of *WD* 376–78. The largest Attic farm on record, even in the classical period, is that of Alcibiades, about 70 acres (French, *Growth of the Athenian Economy* 181 n. 13), a size which still leaves little scope for further sub-division. On the size of farms in modern Greece, and their sub-division through inheritance, see A. N. Damaskenides, *Balkan Studies* 6 (1965) 25–28, and I. T. Sanders, *Rainbow in the Rock: the People of Rural Greece* (Harvard UP, 1962) 60; cf. Juliet du Boulay, *Portrait of a Greek Mountain Village* (Oxford 1974) 28, and esp. Appendix II, "Land Tenure," pp. 265–73. For other recommendations in favor of leaving single heirs in ancient Greece see West, 251–52. I do not (as should be clear from my translation) subscribe to the theory (supported by West) that what Hesiod means by ἕτερον παῖδα is a grandchild. For the obligation to provide for one's heirs at all costs see, e.g., Plato *Rep*. 2.372b, Du Boulay, 139–40, and E. Friedl, *Vasilika: a Village in Modern Greece* (New York 1967) 18.

barons[33] who are ready to give judgment in this case." ἀλλά τε πολλά
stands in sharp contrast to the κλῆρος: the phrase implies removable
property such as tools, farm equipment, or household furniture.[34]
Though Hesiod and Perses may have argued over the house and
property-boundaries (cf. the simile drawn by Homer, *Il*.12.421–23), we
should note that Hesiod does not say so. Indeed, the word ἐφόρεις is
hardly one to use of such a disagreement. Houses and land stay where
they are; only chattels are transportable. The force of κυδαίνων is temporal rather than causal, while the imperfect ἐφόρεις is surely conative[35]:
Perses' attempts to remove disputed property take place concurrently
with his careful cultivation of the barons, and the most we can infer
about the latter is that it was designed to win their support or approval.
We can only guess at what form it took. Van Groningen (p. 157) argues
that it was by assiduous attendance at meetings of the βασιλῆες, by loud
approbation, by forming part of a voluntary claque. But the βασιλῆες
are described as "gift-eating" (δωροφάγους). This need not *per se* imply
gross corruption, since judges and arbitrators regularly took fees to settle
disputes; nor is κυδαίνω ever found elsewhere in a pejorative context,
meaning to bribe or flatter, but always in the sense of conferring honor
or pleasure on the recipient.[36]

Yet Hesiod is assuredly not being complimentary: the contrast with
Theogony 84–92 alone would suffice to prove that. The βασιλῆες are, if
not corrupt, at the very least rapacious. Even if they perform all the
duties outlined in the *Theogony*, effecting restitution for the injured,
resolving disputes, handing down straight judgments (all of which here is
very much in question), they exact a stiff price for the privilege. We
should also, of course, make allowance for the fact that, at all periods of
Greek history, officials are invariably assumed (whether justifiably or not
is another matter) to be corrupt by definition. The modern Sarakatsani
refer to them as φαγάδες, "eaters," an epithet surprisingly close to
Hesiod's δωροφάγοι, and gifts are regularly offered to them in the (often
illusory) hope of favorable treatment. One gift or service is held to
require another in return, a system that runs flat counter to the non-
tribal concept of public administration. Like Hesiod, who elsewhere
claimed that gifts persuade gods and kings alike (fr. 361 Merkelbach–
West: the implication is that these two categories are harder to move
than ordinary mortals), the modern Greek is convinced that his *douceurs*
work: yet in fact Greek judges are no more bribable than those of other

---

33 Not "kings" in our sense, but local landed aristocrats: "barons" would be a very loose
equivalent. Diodorus (4.9.24) tells us that Thespiae was governed by a group of seven
δημοῦχοι who were, clearly, the later successors of these βασιλῆες.
34 Gagarin, HDP 107 n. 12 with ref.
35 Van Groningen, 156; Gagarin, HDP 107–8.
36 Gagarin, HDP 109–10 with nn. 19 and 20; cf. Van Groningen, 157.

countries. It is the belief that counts.[37] If there is a causal sequence in lines 38–39, it is that the barons' *willingness* to give judgment in the present suit (τήνδε δίκην) may have been increased by Perses' previous cultivation of them. Yet this would scarcely be logical: to judge by *Theog.* 84ff., settling disputes was part of their accepted duty. Perhaps Hesiod is merely hinting, with the epithet δωροφάγους, that their appetite for the task has been whetted by the payment of substantial court fees.

Did Perses have any other kind of influence with the local aristocracy? We cannot be certain, but Hesiod's ironic description of his brother (299) as δῖον γένος, "illustrious-born," in a context which suggests that Perses regarded status as an adequate substitute for hard work, at least gives one pause for thought. From the famous biographical passage concerning their father (631–40) it is clear that Perses' own pedigree was, at best, *déclassé*, and in all likelihood far from illustrious. (βίου κεχρημένος ἐσθλοῦ is a socially ambiguous phrase: "the life of a noble" or "good living"? prestige or wealth? the dream of an ambitious outsider, or the nostalgia of a gentleman who'd been reduced to trade?) Could he have acquired status in his own eyes through marriage? There is something very personal about Hesiod's description of the γυνὴ πυγοστόλος, "prinking her butt," who is only out to get her hands on Perses' granary (373–74). We can trace a clear link between this woman and the *Works and Days* version of Pandora, with her "bitch's mind and thievish nature" (κύνεόν τε νόον καὶ ἐπίκλοπον ἦθος, 78), who is fobbed off, in this version of the story (cf. *Th.* 511–14), on the more foolish of two brothers, Epimetheus (83–89). It is hard not to infer that Hesiod's argument here must have been at least in part *ad hominem*, with himself in the admonitory Promethean role. Was it also *ad feminam*? At line 80 we find Pandora described, very oddly for narrative (so, rightly, West on *WD* 80, p. 164) as τήνδε γυναῖκα. The force is demonstrative; indeed, it is almost as though Hesiod were pointing at someone (I shall return to the significance of this phrase later). It is tempting, if wholly speculative, to argue that Perses had married an aristocratic lady from Thespiae with expensive tastes, a forerunner of Strepsiades' very similar *mèsalliance* in *The Clouds* (41 ff.). If this was how the now-impoverished Perses had wasted his time and substance, much of Hesiod's admonition (e.g., 27ff., 60–89, 94–95, 195–96, 235, 299–300, 356, 373–75, ?586, 695–705) acquires extra point and edge.

A great deal of inconclusive discussion has taken place over the precise meaning of the words οἵ τήνδε δίκην ἐθέλουσι δικάσσαι—mostly in *parti pris* attempts to make them fit a preconceived interpretation of what is going on. We sense, as so often, the ghost of that non-existent

---

[37] For evidence of rapacity cf. West, 151; Jensen, 9. For the widespread and perennial assumption of venality in public officials see Walcot, GPAM 102ff., cf. 80–81. The Sarakatsani on φαγάδες: J. F. Campbell, *Honour, Family and Patronage* (Oxford 1964) 257.

first trial in the fact that so many scholars have, against the evident
natural sense of the phrase in context, wanted τήνδε δίκην to mean "a
suit *of this kind*."[38] Schömann, indeed, not only insisted that τήνδε δίκην
referred to the first trial, but emended ἐθέλουσι δικάσσαι to ἐθέλοντι
δίκασσαν in order to give his perverse reading a more plausible
time-sequence.[39] Another line of approach is the assertion that δίκην
δικάσσαι can *only* mean "to pronounce a verdict," and that the phrase
therefore means "who see fit to make this [but what?] their judgment."
ἐθέλουσι thus has to lose all future sense, and merely emphasize the
"voluntary nature of their actions."[40] The trouble with this is that the
βασιλῆες have not so far, except in the speculative minds of scholars,
delivered a specific judgment of any sort apropos Perses' case: they are
ready to (ἐθέλουσι), but that is all. Those commentators from Proclus to
Wilamowitz (who, nevertheless, believed in a first trial), Mair, Marg,
Jensen, and, now, Gagarin,[41] who take τήνδε δίκην in its natural demonstrative sense, and translate "are ready to give judgment in this [present]
case," have both common sense and syntax on their side. The semantic
flexibility of the word δίκη in Hesiod has been well analyzed by both
Van Groningen and Gagarin,[42] and their findings make the kind of
straitjacketing that West proposes as unnecessary as it is inapposite.

Once we accept the fact that the whole notion of an earlier lawsuit is
a mere scholarly chimaera, and that τήνδε δίκην, not merely in line 39,
but also at 249 and 269, bears a specific reference to the case presented
as pending,[43] two conclusions emerge. The first is that most of the supposed inconsistencies in Perses' actions (well summarized by West,
pp. 33ff.) vanish into that limbo to which they should have been consigned long ago. In particular, we do not have to cope with the problem

---

38 E.g. Paley (above n. 29), 11; Sinclair, 6; Mazon (Budé ed., 1924) translates, "toujours
prêts à juger suivant telle justice," and Evelyn-White (Loeb ed., 1914), "who love to judge
such a cause as this."

39 Well disposed of by Mazon, 47.

40 West, 152.

41 West, *ibid.*; Wilamowitz, 46; Jensen, 7; Gagarin, HDP 107–8.

42 Van Groningen, 159–60 n. 22; Gagarin, DWD *passim*, also in LMA (unpublished)
where he writes that "despite the advantage *dike* has over violence, a poor man may be
harmed by it and should avoid it if possible," and adds that "Hesiod is also aware of a
fundamental ambiguity inherent in the word *dike*, which in a general sense (the peaceful
settlement of disputes, lawfulness, etc.) has a definite positive value, but in more specific
senses (a particular settlement or kind of settlement, a litigant's plea, etc.) has a neutral
value and may be qualified either positively or negatively, primarily by means of the
adjectives 'straight' and 'crooked'."

43 *Contra* Van Groningen, 162, who argues that here "Hésiode parle non pas comme un
homme qui pourrait être engagé, bon gré mal gré, dans un procès privé, mais en
prophète, en moraliste, en défenseur des principes sur lesquels doit se baser la vie commune de la cité." I see no reason why H. should not choose to make his general point
through the specific instance.

of a Perses who, at irregular and illogical intervals during the poem, is alternately rich and poor, but rather one who is poor, and feckless, throughout: what capital he had has already been either wasted, or committed to litigation. Perses never got the lion's share of the estate at arbitration: that myth depends on Guyet's emendation, at line 37, of ἄλλά τε πολλά to ἀλλὰ τὰ πολλά.[44] In fact he never previously went to arbitration at all, and has so far got nothing out of the βασιλῆες: on the contrary, *he* seems to have invested quite a lot in *them*. Even his efforts to carry off bits of moveable property from his brother would seem to have been unsuccessful, or at best inconclusive: the imperfect ἐφόρεις is revealing. We are not even told, in so many words, whether he is disputing the division of the κλῆρος itself. Rather than the successful sharp crook of tradition, he begins to sound both pathetic and ineffectual, perhaps even a man with a genuine grievance.

What we *do* know is that, within the dramatic context of the poem, he is in the process of bringing suit against Hesiod, but that the case—his first and only one—has not yet been determined. Perses' financial status is shown to be precarious. He is certainly in debt (404, 647), and there may even be the possibility of someone buying his κλῆρος (341). He should stop going begging to neighbors—"as so recently you came to me," Hesiod says, adding that Perses can expect no further hand-outs, and should do an honest day's work instead if he wants to avoid starvation.[45] With regard to the suit itself, Perses is pointedly warned against perjury[46]: This must mean that at the hearing he would have an opportunity to testify on oath, presumably regarding his father's alleged (verbal?) disposition of family property, and this solemn oath might well be regarded as conclusive by his judges.[47] Goods, Hesiod reminds his brother, are not to be snatched (ἁρπακτά) or pirated by a clever tongue (ἀπὸ γλώσσης ληίσσεται, 320ff.). Similarly, the βασιλῆες themselves are urged to think over the case carefully (248–49) and avoid "crooked judgments" (250, cf. 225–26, 263–64), since these are not only observed by the gods (249–51, 267ff.), but also liable to possible retribution from the δῆμος (260–62).

The picture is now clear and consistent. Two brothers have, some while ago, divided an inheritance. One of them, Perses, impecunious and improvident (we should always remember, however, that it is Hesiod's account of events that we possess; Perses' side of the story might have been very different), regards this division as in some way unfair. After

---

[44] Among modern editors and translators accepted only, to the best of my knowledge, by Evelyn-White, but still influential (I suspect) at a subliminal level.

[45] *WD* 274–81, 298–301, cf. 397ff., 363–67, 404, 646–47; 394–97.

[46] *WD* 219, 282–84, cf. 190–94, 803–4.

[47] Forbes, 85ff., citing the case of Antilochus (Hom. *Il*.23.573ff.), who refused to take an oath rather than perjure himself in such a case; cf. Jensen, 9–10.

unsuccessful private attempts to alter the balance in his favor, and an
investment of some sort in cultivating the βασιλῆες of Thespiae, who
hold jurisdiction over property disputes, he has taken his case to arbitration. What we have in lines 1–285 of the *Works and Days* is a poetic
evocation by his brother Hesiod of events either at the hearing itself, or
immediately before it, or both: a dramatic reconstruction of a public
difference that had deeply affected them both, and still formed a
talking-point long afterwards. This is the second conclusion that emerges
from, among other things, that tell-tale phrase τήνδε δίκην, and it suggests
that we would do well to scrutinize, not only the dramatic circumstances
that Hesiod presupposes, but also the audience to whom he is addressing
himself. For the purposes of this stage of our enquiry the biographical truth
of the subject-matter becomes irrelevant, and the entire story that Hesiod
tells or implies can be treated as a fictional construct.

On account of the didactic or paraenetic label so regularly attached
to the *Works and Days*,[48] its strikingly immediate *dramatic* qualities
tend to be overlooked. Hesiod himself is too often treated as a mere
quasi-autobiographical literary sage, handing out good advice from
whatever the eighth-century equivalent of a study may have been. Yet a
dramatic *persona* that we can similarly call "Hesiod" is very much present throughout the first 285 lines of the *Works and Days*—and indeed
with certain modifications thereafter. The poem, in short, is not simply a
παραινετικὸς λόγος; it is also a *dramatic monologue*, in the sense that
Browning's "Fra Lippo Lippi" may be so described. Almost no one has
appreciated this crucial point, let alone worked out its full implications.
Wade-Gery took a step in the right direction: he observed, correctly, that
in *WD* 1–285 the crisis, i.e. the lawsuit, is thought of as still being to
come (though Hesiod must have gone on working at the poem long after
the crisis itself had been resolved), and saw the origin of this section of
the *Works and Days* in what he termed "agitation poems," recited while
Hesiod was stumping the countryside to whip up support for his cause.[49]
(It should, of course, be emphasized at this point that we do not know, and
cannot tell, what Hesiod actually said *at the time*: how he went about
defending his position, the actual language he employed before the
βασιλῆες, and so on. All we have is his artistic reworking and dramatization of the event in retrospect, so that questions of literalism—e.g., would
a forensic speech, even ca. 700 B.C., have been couched in dactylic
hexameters?—become irrelevant. A more useful parallel, from a later

---

[48] See, e.g. Østerud (above, n. 10), 16–17; Puelma (above, n. 9), 88; F. Dornseiff,
"Hesiods Werke und Tage und das alte Morgenland," *Philol.* 89 (1934) 397–415 (repr.
Wege der Forschung vol. 44, Darmstadt 1966, 131–50), and, most recently, West, 3ff.,
who—developing Dornseiff's position—sets the poem in the comparative context of Near
Eastern admonitory wisdom literature.
[49] Wade-Gery, 81–93, esp. 88–90.

period, is Thucydides' approach to his speeches: as there, we can only guess at the *degree* of verisimilitude, though it seems a fair assumption that *l'esprit de l'escalier* will have played its part in Hesiod's presentation.)

Only Forbes and Jensen come near the heart of the matter, by identifying both the dramatic nature, and the dramatic setting, of Hesiod's monologue[50]; and even they fail to pursue this striking insight to its logical conclusion, or to analyze Hesiod's text in the light of their findings to an adequate degree. Nor do they appear to have had any effect on subsequent scholarship. West, for example, completely ignores this line of approach, though in fact it could have solved several problems that baffle him in his commentary.[51] "The scene," Forbes states correctly, "is the crowded ἀγορά . . . with the magnates in their places and Hesiod and Perses before them." He also describes WD 1–285 as "a complete rhetorical unit, a forensic speech, representing Hesiod's appeal to the conscience of the people, the princes and Perses." Jensen follows Forbes in detail: for her too the scene is the *agora*, and the opening section of the *Works and Days* forms "the speech for the defence in an action brought against the poet by his brother Perses." She also (pp. 6–7) isolates the force of αὖθι ("here and now") at line 35, and of the -δε demonstrative in such phrases as ὧδ' ἔρδειν (35), τήνδε δίκην (39, 249, 269), or τάδε (268), the "goings-on"—actually in court, there in the speaker's presence—that the eye of Zeus, Διὸς ὀφθαλμός, observes. To these instances we can, of course, add many more. Demonstratives may suggest a dramatic pointing finger: τήνδε γυναῖκα at line 80 is said of the Pandora foisted off on poor gullible Epimetheus, but are we not meant to imagine Hesiod looking hard at Perses' wife? Similarly with the appeal to Zeus at 9–10, the promise to tell Perses some home-truths, the direct apostrophes aimed at his opponent (e.g. 27–29, 213ff.), and, of course, those assumptions of knowledge on the part of his audience that I mentioned earlier—assumptions which have so unnecessarily bothered commentators. In a dramatic monologue, clearly, the audience must be well aware of the relationship between the two protagonists; no need to explain that Hesiod and Perses are brothers. At the same time, since what is being dramatized is a court case, a brief *résumé* of the facts, however familiar these may have been to the principals, becomes essential (37–39). Forbes and Jensen are, I think, over-strict in viewing the

---

[50] Forbes, 83; Jensen, 6–8. The same idea appears to have struck Havelock in passing in *The Greek Concept of Justice* (Harvard UP, 1978) 212, where he writes: "Is this the scenario present before Hesiod's eyes when he asserts that Zeus is actually 'looking down at *these* things' and 'has not failed to notice what kind of justice *this* is, that is being confined within the city'? Are the demonstrative adjectives pointing to the scene?" He does not, however, follow this lead any further.

[51] See, e.g., his notes on WD 35 and 80, and his whole introductory section on Perses, 33ff.

entire 285 lines simply as a forensic speech and nothing else; Hesiod is
more flexible and digressive than that, and the poem as we have it has
clearly been worked on and added to over a long period. But their central point is of fundamental importance.

I would, finally, like to develop further a point that Forbes only
touches on in a phrase, and that is the identity of Hesiod's dramatic
audience. The βασιλῆες and Perses, being apostrophized directly, are
obvious components. But Forbes also mentions, in passing, "the conscience of the people," and here, it seems to me, he isolates a crucial
dramatic element in the poem that has gone virtually unregarded. The
spectators who, like Perses himself, made a habit of sitting in on these
public hearings took a vigorous, and frequently vociferous, part in the
proceedings. We at once recall the scene on the Shield of Achilles
(*Il*.18.487–508), where such a case draws a huge crowd (cf. *Th*. 84–86),
members of which yell advice and encouragement to whichever of the
contestants they favor (ἀμφοτέροισιν ἐπήπυον, ἀμφὶς ἀρωγοί), and actually have to be held back by heralds (503) from physical intervention.
The crowd is a key factor in any Greek lawsuit: its encouragement is
worth getting, its censure is to be feared. When Hesiod dramatized the
litigation in which he had been involved, I cannot believe that he
ignored so integral a part of his experience, even if its remembered
impact emerges only in a tone, an attitude, a series of appeals to shad-
owy and unspecified listeners.

This, then, is Hesiod's silent and invisible audience in the *Works and
Days*: vocal enough in life, very much present at public hearings, a functional element taken for granted by Hesiod and those who listened to his
poem at the time. Whenever Hesiod is not specifically addressing Perses
or the barons it is the crowd, the δῆμος in the *agora*, to whom his arguments are directed, and who—we need not doubt—could make their
views on "crooked justice" uncomfortably clear. Thersites in the *Iliad* has
the ring of contemporary truth about him; whether in Ionia or Boeotia,
he is unlikely to have been an isolated phenomenon. Even passages such
as 27–39 (to Perses) and 248ff. (to the βασιλῆες) are composed, dramatically speaking, with one eye to the effect that they will have on the
bystanders. The repeated attacks on crooked judgments, gift-eating, or
perjury, sometimes aimed directly at those sitting in judgment on the
case (248–51, 262–64, 279–80, cf. 190–94, 225–27), make far more sense
if they are seen as dramatic attempts to win the sympathy of the λάοι
ἀθρῶοι filling the *agora*. νέμεσις, public disapproval, was a force to be
reckoned with in Homeric or Hesiodic society, as indeed in that of modern Greece.[52] If the wise man took care to get the crowd behind him, he

---

[52] Forbes, 84: "We tend to underrate the power of opinion in early society." For νέμεσις
see, e.g., Hom. *Il*.6.351, 13.121f., and E. R. Dodds, *The Greeks and the Irrational* (Berkeley

also, whenever possible, exploited public feeling to discredit his opponents. Hesiod in the *Works and Days* does both. In his dramatization he was drawing upon a universally accepted, and familiar, tradition. This is nowhere more apparent than in his notorious, and puzzling, αἶνος addressed to the βασιλῆες, the fable of the Hawk and the Nightingale (202–12). Forbes's claim (p. 84) that by lines 248–69 Hesiod "evidently feels the support of the crowd behind him" is correct: on the other hand, his assertion that until then Hesiod has handled the princes "rather lightly and circumspectly" cannot be sustained. The αἶνος itself forms its most telling refutation, and, properly interpreted, shows how the crowd's support was won.

Before embarking on his fable, Hesiod has expatiated at some length (174–201) on the almost unrelieved horrors of the present iron age in which men are living: an era of toil and stress, of collapsing social and familial values, of might-is-right ethics, perjury, blackmail, and "crooked accusations" (μύθοισι σκολιοῖς). The most he will concede is that "some good will yet be mixed with these evils" (179). He then narrates his fable, and when it is over, turns to Perses. "Perses," he exhorts him (213f.), "*you* pay attention to δίκη, do not promote ὕβρις." The reason is clear: δίκη wins against ὕβρις in the end (ἐς τέλος ἐξελθοῦσα, 218). Those who act according to the dictates of δίκη lead happy lives (225–27), while divine retribution awaits the perverters of justice (248–51, 260–64, 267–75). Above all, Zeus has made the gift of δίκη that which distinguishes men from the jungle world of bird, beast and fish (276–281): δίκη, in short, must be the good element that is mixed in with the bad for men of the iron age, the principle that can save them. Between these two striking passages—the jeremiad on current ills, and the isolation of δίκη as the one solution to such ills—Hesiod sets his short fable. It could scarcely be more prominent, and we can assume that this was no accident.

> "Now I will tell you a fable for the barons;
>   they understand it.
> This is what the hawk said when he had caught
>   a nightingale
> with spangled neck in his claws and carried her
>   high among the clouds.
> She, spitted on the clawhooks, was wailing pitifully,
> but the hawk, in his masterful manner,
>   gave her an answer:
> 'What is the matter with you? Why scream?
>   Your master has you.
> You shall go wherever I take you,
>   for all your singing.

1951) ch.i ("Agamemnon's Apology"). For the force of public opinion in modern rural Greece see Campbell (above n. 37) 190, 197–98, 201–3, 307–10, 312–15; and Du Boulay (above, n. 32) 73, 81–84, 108–9.

If I like, I can let you go. If I like,
    I can eat you for dinner.
He is a fool who tries to match his strength
    with the stronger.
He will lose the battle, and with the shame
    will be hurt also.'
So spoke the hawk, the bird who flies so fast
    on his long wings." (Trs. Richmond Lattimore)

νῦν δ' αἶνον βασιλεῦσ' ἐρέω, φρονέουσι καὶ αὐτοῖς.
ὧδ' ἴρηξ προσέειπεν ἀηδόνα ποικιλόδειρον,
ὕψι μάλ' ἐν νεφέεσσι φέρων, ὀνύχεσσι μεμαρπώς·
ἡ δ' ἐλεόν, γναμπτοῖσι πεπαρμένη ἀμφ' ὀνύχεσσιν,
μύρετο· τὴν δ' ὅ γ' ἐπικρατέως πρὸς μῦθον ἔειπεν·
"δαιμονίη, τί λέληκας; ἔχει νύ σε πολλὸν ἀρείων·
τῇ δ' εἶς ᾗ σ' ἂν ἐγώ περ ἄγω καὶ ἀοιδὸν ἐοῦσαν·
δεῖπνον δ' αἴ κ' ἐθέλω ποιήσομαι ἠὲ μεθήσω.
ἄφρων δ' ὅς κ' ἐθέλῃ πρὸς κρείσσονας ἀντιφερίζειν·
νίκης τε στέρεται πρός τ' αἴσχεσιν ἄλγεα πάσχει."
ὣς ἔφατ' ὠκυπέτης ἴρηξ, τανυσίπτερος ὄρνις.

                                                        WD 202–12

The immediate message, considered *in vacuo*, is a morally depressing piece of cynical *Machtpolitik* which confirms all the worst of the iron age troubles, particularly those concerning χειροδίκαι, the notion of δίκη subsisting merely ἐν χερσί (190–94). The nightingale, though a singer (καὶ ἀοιδὸν ἐοῦσαν), is no match for the hawk: how, one wonders, could singing ever be presumed to arm one against a predator? (This, as we shall see, is to commit the cardinal error of thinking in hawk-terms.) It is the hawk, in this fable, who bangs the moral home, with a brutal little speech on the realities of power (207–11) that puts one in mind of the Athenians on Melos or of Callicles in Plato's *Gorgias*.[53] This is in sharp contrast with a later fable in the *Aesopica* (Perry §567), where the hawk in turn falls victim to a fowler. As West says (p. 205), "we find here what we miss in Hesiod, the subjection of the bad bird by another, higher power." Why should Hesiod introduce so bleakly pessimistic a motif at this point?

    The situation is further confused by the fact that the nightingale, *qua* ἀοιδός, is naturally identified with Hesiod himself (so almost all commentators), and the hawk with the βασιλῆες.[54] Is Hesiod then

---

[53] See, e.g., Thuc. 5.105.2, ἡγούμεθα γὰρ τό τε θεῖον δόξῃ, τὸ ἀνθρώπειόν τε σαφῶς διὰ παντὸς ὑπὸ φύσεως ἀναγκαίας, οὗ ἂν κρατῇ, ἄρχειν, cf. Plat. *Gorg.* 890a, with Dodds's commentary *ad loc.*; also Thrasymachus in the *Republic*, 338b.

[54] The most useful recent studies are those of L. W. Daly, "Hesiod's Fable," *TAPhA* 92 (1961) 45–51; Puelma (above, n. 9); Østerud (above, n. 10) 21–23; Jensen, 20–22 (though her identification of the hawk with Zeus—a view also advanced independently by C. B. Welles, *GRByS* 8 (1967) 17–19—has, rightly, won few adherents), and Van Groningen, 160–63.

representing himself as a helpless victim of the barons? Surely not[55]: the ἀοιδός of *Th*.79–97 stands equal in inspiration and authority to them, and Hesiod's tone here is one of grim self-assurance. Even so, at first sight it is hard to understand Wade-Gery's optimistic interpretation (*op. cit.* p. 91): "There have not been too many ages of the world when public opinion could really control governments. . . . From Hesiod through Solon to Aeschylus and Euripides, the Nightingale was a real power in Greek opinion and behaviour, and the Hawk had to listen." But, one protests, the hawk on this occasion does not listen at all; he has things very much his own way. It is only on further examination that we realise that Wade-Gery was, in fact, right, though perhaps not quite in the way he supposed.

The language, significantly, is that of a Homeric ἀγων: as Puelma saw, Hesiod seems to be setting up the ἀοιδός as the proper source of true justice, in contradistinction to the false justice that he fears may be dispensed by the local βασιλῆες.[56] We have here a conflict of principle and of moral authority. Yet we remember that in the *Theogony* (79–97), while ἀοιδοί may belong to the Muses and the βασιλῆες to Zeus, a good βασιλεύς is likewise inspired by the Muses (83, 93) to give "straight judgments" (86). He is, in short, the repository of oral tradition, of accumulated δίκαι. He remembers the oral laws. (Not for nothing were the Muses the daughters of Mnemosyne, Memory.) Hesiod's anxiety in the *Works and Days* seems to be that the βασιλῆες may abrogate their high responsibility—and who but the ἀοιδός can recall them to it? We should also remember that the *Theogony* was delivered before a predominantly noble audience (if, as seems very likely, it was the poem that won the prize at the funeral games of Amphidamas), whereas in the *Works and Days* it is the δῆμος that forms Hesiod's main audience; eulogy is thus predictable in the earlier work, but out of place here.[57]

The real stumbling-block for scholars has always been Hesiod's supposed endorsement of, or at least capitulation to, the hawk's attitude, in a poem which elsewhere consistently advocates the acceptance of Zeus's divine δίκη. It has even been suggested, as an awkward compromise, that Hesiod, while not positively condoning hawkishness, is

55 So schol. 207–12 (Pertusi): τούτων δὲ τῶν στίχων ὁ Ἀρίσταρχος . . . ὀβελίζει τοὺς τελευταίους ὡς ἀλόγῳ γνωμολογεῖν οὐκ ἂν προσῆκον. Goettling and Rzach followed Aristarchus.

56 Puelma, 97: "Der Sänger Hesiod als Volksredner des 'geraden Rechts' gegenüber den Richterkönigen als Sprechern der 'ungeraden Rechtssprüche'—diese Grundsituation des Gerechtigkeitsliedes der Erga (1–285) ist es offenbar, die sich in dem eigentümlich 'homerisch' übersteigerten Rivalitätsverhältnis von Habicht und Nachtigall der Fabel spiegelt."

57 See Catharine P. Roth, "The Kings and the Muses in Hesiod's *Theogony*," *TAPhA* 106 (1976) 331–38; cf. West, *Theogony* 44–45.

simply pointing out the harsh facts of life.[58] But although such stoic resignation would be very much in line with archaic thought, Hesiod does not, in fact, endorse or condone the hawk's action at all: far from it.[59] The paradox, like the earlier court case, turns out to be a mere illusion. The hawk is the exemplar of an ideology diametrically opposed to that of the true ἀοιδός or βασιλεύς, an ideology that Hesiod is determined to pillory through exposure to public contempt. Once we accept the concept of the *Works and Days* as a dramatic monologue, not only does Hesiod's attitude become crystal clear, but the method he employs to drive it home likewise stares us in the face.

What in fact does he say? "Now I will tell an αἶνος for the princes— *they* will understand it well (φρονέουσι καὶ αὐτοῖς)." Whom is Hesiod addressing here? Not, primarily, his readers, let alone modern critics. It is Hesiod's dramatic *persona* rather than Hesiod himself whom we now hear, making a bold bid for sympathy in the crowded *agora*. His words are aimed not so much at princes themselves as at the δῆμος, the crowd; he may be talking *about* those haughty aristocratic authoritarians, but not *to* them. Through his little fable he can show the hawkish βασιλῆες telling the unvarnished truth about the credo to which they privately subscribe, but prefer not to enunciate with quite such chilling clarity—just as modern political murderers are in the habit of talking about the "liquidation of undesirable elements." In symbolic yet transparent terms he is reminding the crowd (and, at one remove, all audiences whatsoever) of the attitude that such judges may be expected to take, of their moral assumptions about life and human relationships and the social order. "He is a fool," says the hawk, "who tries to match himself against his betters; he will be deprived of victory, and suffer the indignities over and above his disgrace." This is the very voice of the Penthelidae, the ruling aristocratic clan of Mytilene, whose idea of dealing with opponents was to club them into submission (Arist. *Pol*.1311b 25); it is Odysseus' instinctive response to a proletarian rabble-rouser like Thersites (Hom. *Il*.2.243–77).

But by Hesiod's day the tide was on the turn: the diffusion of a true, and easily mastered alphabet, the increase of trade, the emergence of the hoplite phalanx, all tended to undercut privileged authority. The nightingale was finding a voice, and, more important, a power-base; the recalcitrant hawk would indeed be forced to listen. Hesiod's audience has just heard this hawk tell his victim, the ἀηδών-ἀοιδός, the nightingale-singer, "You will go wherever I take you, *singer though you are*": the point is driven home past mistaking, what we are shown is violent ὕβρις committed against the sacrosanct mouthpiece of the Muses. Here are the χειροδίκαι against whom Hesiod had earlier delivered his general diatribe.

---

[58] By V. A. Rodgers, "Some thoughts on ΔΙΚΗ," *CQ* 21 (1971) 289–301, esp. 291.
[59] So, rightly, Østerud, 22.

The partisan audience knows what it has to think. And at this precise point, with perfect dramatic control of the scene, Hesiod turns to Perses (213)—we can almost see the theatrical gesture, the stabbing finger—and exclaims: "ὦ Πέρση, σὺ δ᾽ ἄκουε δίκης." The emphasis, and its implications, are unmistakable.

Thus what we have in *WD* 1–285 is the dramatic commemoration of a personal experience, important to Hesiod, and clearly of more than passing interest to his local community. The poem, as he continued to work on it, acquired many other features, paraenetic or proverbial and became, in fact, a holdall for various aspects of his philosophy of life. But the central impulse and core remains his conflict with Perses: that is fundamental. We are often reminded (to revert briefly to Walcot's objections, above, p. 23) that we do not know—which means that we are not specifically informed—whether Hesiod or Perses won the case, or indeed whether a trial was in fact held at all. From a dramatic viewpoint, as I have suggested, this makes little or no difference. At the same time the whole tenor of the *Works and Days* supports a confident answer. That Hesiod based his poem on actual personal experience seems certain: the details are too circumstantial, too idiosyncractic, too involved to suggest—especially ca. 700 B.C.—a sophisticated fiction masquerading as truth. "ἴδμεν ψεύδεα πολλὰ λέγειν ἐτύμοισιν ὁμοῖα," the Muses indeed told Hesiod: but they also added, let us not forget, "ἴδμεν δ᾽ εὖτ᾽ ἐθέλωμεν ἀληθέα γηρύσασθαι." (*Th.*27–28), and surely Hesiod's quarrel with his brother falls into the latter category. And if the case actually took place, that Hesiod won it can scarcely be open to doubt: as Jensen says, "if Hesiod's poem had not been successful we would hardly have had it today."[60] How far, if at all, parts of what we possess originally served—in whatever form—as a forensic plea before that tribunal in Thespiae we cannot tell, nor is it of great importance. What we do know, because we have the text before us, is how skillfully Hesiod recreated and dramatized this important event in his life—as important, in its own way, as his victory at the funeral games of Amphidamas—and how obstinately, for the most part, critics have refused to understand what he was about. I would like to think that in some small degree, after long sharing that blindness, I have helped to set the record straight: παθὼν δέ τε νήπιος ἔγνω.[61]

---

[60] Jensen, 10, cf. Forbes, 85.

[61] This paper was first delivered at a Classics Department colloquium in the University of Texas at Austin, and subsequently, in a revised and expanded version, before the Fellows of the Center for Hellenic Studies in Washington, DC. An abbreviated summary of its conclusions was read in December 1980 at the annual meeting of the American Philological Association in New Orleans. The final version has benefited greatly from discussion and criticism on these various occasions.

GREEK TRAGEDY: WRITING, TRUTH, AND THE REPRESENTATION OF THE SELF

CHARLES SEGAL

I

When tragedy is born in Athens around 500 B.C., the city creates in its midst the civic space in which it can look at itself in the mirror of the ancient myths. *Theatron*, "theater," is a space for beholding, derived from the verb *theaomai*, to behold with wonder. This narrative form is the most vivid possible representation of myth in Greek culture. It is also a form of mythic representation that highlights all the tensions, contradictions, and problems that arise when the Athenians adapt to their new democracy the aristocratic legends of the past: tales about kings and heroes, about ancient families that claim descent from the gods, and about the hereditary curses handed down in the bloodline of these families.[1] But throughout Greece in the course of the sixth and fifth centuries social changes (including the increasing use of writing) and consequent changes in the role of the poet bring concomitant changes in the character and function of mythic narration.[2]

In fifth-century Athens writing enables the democratic polis to see itself in a new perspective and to claim for its contemporary existence, despite its ideology of change and innovation, a patrimony of glorious traditions analogous to the myths of the ancient aristocratic families. The written histories of Herodotus and to a greater degree of Thucydides, as Diego Lanza has recently argued,[3] are analogous to tragedy in that they create for the democracy a mirror in which the Athenians can contemplate the deeds of their city and preserve in memory the words of its leaders. These speeches, now condensed into definitive form and fixed as

---

[1] See Jean-Pierre Vernant, "Tensions et ambiguïtés dans la tragédie grecque," in Vernant and P. Vidal-Naquet, *Mythe et tragédie* (Paris 1972) 24ff.; also Vidal-Naquet's chapters on the *Oresteia* and *Philoctetes* in the same volume, especially 149ff. and 168ff.

[2] For the changing role of the poet in the archaic period see J. Svenbro, *La parole et le marbre* (Lund 1976), with references to earlier literature. For archaic poetry in the perspective of an oral culture see B. Gentili, "Aspetti del rapporto poeta, committente, uditorio nella lirica corale greca," *Studi Urbinati* 39 (1965) 70–88.

[3] D. Lanza, *Lingua e discorso nell' Atene delle professioni* (Naples 1979) 56; also 75f.

part of the history's "eternal possession," are not only the record of what
has impelled the city to its actions but also the verbal expression of its
elusive consciousness, its essential character.

II

The notion of the unity of Greek culture stretching in a more or less
unbroken line from Homer to Aristotle is deeply imbedded in the historical imagination of the modern world, from its early exponents, Lessing,
Herder, and Winckelmann, to the historical synthesizing of Wilamowitz.
But in the last few decades this unitary structure has suffered multiple
fractures. The most recent attack has come from the work of Eric Havelock, whose studies of the implications of literacy and preliteracy over
the last twenty years have forced us to reexamine some of the massive
changes in concerns, outlook, and expression brought about by the transi-
tion from an oral to a literate culture.[4]

Havelock himself has paid remarkably little attention to tragedy and
only recently included it in the framework of his reexamination of the
intellectual history of early Greece.[5] While aware of tragedy's position
between the oral and literate phases of Greek culture, he emphasizes the
continuities of tragedy with the attitudes and style of oral poetry. The
tragedian, on his view, is a late manifestation of the oral poet, conveying
communal and traditional wisdom. My purpose is to give more importance to the tensions inherent in tragedy as a literary form and to allow
more importance to the radical departures from an oral tradition implicit in tragedy.

Tragedy is an oral performance, but one controlled by a written
text.[6] It is performed in the agonistic and ritual setting that characterizes
most of early Greek literature. Unlike oral epic, however, tragedy is not
recreated afresh on each occasion by the improvisatory art of the *aoidos*,
the oral singer. If the plays were acted again after the initial performance at the Dionysiac festival of the Lenaea or the Dionysia (a privilege allowed only to the plays of Aeschylus), they were not re-creations
requiring a fresh inspiration and a new composition for that occasion, as

---

4 E. A. Havelock, *Preface to Plato* (Cambridge, Mass. 1963); *The Greek Conception of
Justice*, (Cambridge, Mass. 1978); *The Literate Revolution in Greece and its Consequences* (Princeton 1982) (collected essays).

5 Havelock, "The Oral Composition of Greek Drama," *QUCC* N.S. 6 (1980) 61–113 =
Literate Revolution 261–313.

6 On tragedy and the development of writing see U. von Wilamowitz-Moellendorff,
Einleitung in die griechische Tragödie (= *Euripides, Herkales*, 1, Berlin 1907) 120–27;
see in general Walter Ong, S.J., *Orality and Literacy* (London and New York 1982) 148f.
Comedy too, though it allows for more improvisation in performance, also depends on a
fixed text; and the development of comedy as a literary form postdates that of tragedy in
fifth-century Athens.

in oral poetry, but the replication of a fixed text.[7] In the fifth century the text serves primarily as the script for a performance. Tragedians do not seem to think of their work as intended for a reading public until the fourth century.[8]

As the creator of a written text destined to be orally performed, the tragic poet, unlike the oral singer, stands in a deferred relation to his work. Instead of the coincidence of composition and performance, there is an intermediate stage, when the work is complete but unrealized. Indeed, a tragedian may have composed plays that were not presented until months or years later. Tragedians might revise a play already presented, as Euripides did with his *Hippolytus Veiled*—a procedure that itself implies heavy reliance on writing in the mode of composition—or might revise a play that would then exist only as a written text, as seems to have happened in the case of Aristophanes' *Clouds*.[9] Admittedly, a choral poet like Alcman composed songs that others would perform later; but such works were far shorter and less complex than a tragedy. The long compositions of Stesichorus that have recently come to light—the "Jocasta" fragment and the *Geryoneis*—are not certainly choral and seem much closer to oral epic in the smooth narrative flow, the simplex and linear movement of the plot, and the elaboration of surface detail.[10]

This division between the two stages in the production of a tragedy— text and performance—may have contributed to the distance from the mythical subject that the conflictual, open-ended, and questioning spirit of Greek tragedy demands. Instead of identifying with a local hero, as in choral lyric, tragedy combines sympathetic participation with the presentation of several different points of view, attitudes, and perspectives, no one of which is necessarily final or "right."[11] Hence Aeschylus can

---

[7] For the difference between oral recreation and exact reproduction see A. B. Lord, *The Singer of Tales* (Cambridge, Mass. 1960) chap. 6. He has reiterated how foreign is the notion of a fixed text in an oral culture in "The Influence of Fixed Text," *To Honor Roman Jakobson* 2 (The Hague and Paris 1967) 1196–1206, especially 1206. See also J. Goody, "Mémoire et apprentissage dans les sociétés avec et sans écriture," *L'Homme* 17 (1977) 29–52, especially 44. For recent discussion, with ample bibliography, see Bruno Gentili, "Oralità e scrittura in Grecia," in M. Vegetti, ed., *Oralità Scrittura Spettacolo* (Torino 1983) 30–52.

[8] Aristotle, *Rhetoric* 3.12, 1413b12ff.; also Albin Lesky, *Greek Tragedy*, ed. 3, trans. H. A. Frankfort (London and New York 1967) 204. See also Aristotle, *Poetics* 26, 1462a11–17 and G. F. Else, *Aristotle's Poetics: The Argument* (Cambridge, Mass. 1957) 635f., 640f.

[9] It is widely agreed that the version of the *Clouds* handed down to us is the revised text of a play that may never have been performed: see K. J. Dover, *Aristophanes, Clouds* (Oxford 1968) lxxxff.

[10] On formulaic elements in Stesichorus see now G. Vognone, "Aspetti formulari in Stesicoro," *QUCC* N.S. 12 (1982) 35–42, who sees in the style an intermediate stage between the oral, rhapsodic tradition and literate poetry. I should say that the former predominates.

[11] On this point see Alvin Gouldner, *Enter Plato: Classical Greece and the Origins of Social Theory* (New York and London 1965) 114; also the essay of Vernant cited above, n. 1.

movingly depict the sufferings of his audience's mortal enemies in the *Persians*, and Euripides can portray with compassion the defeated enemies of the Greeks in plays like the *Andromache, Hecuba*, and *Trojan Women*.

It is also possible—though here we are in a realm of pure speculation—that this two-stage mode of production sensitizes the tragic poet to the two systems of communication and representation, verbal and visual, that his art involves: the power of visualization inherent in the image-making power of the world itself and the concrete act of visualization on the theatrical stage. The coexistence of verbal and visual representation unique to the theater involves, at nearly every point, dichotomy, contradiction, or paradox in the existence of truth. The conflict between appearance and reality, what is seen and what is said, is of course a recurrent theme of Greek literature from its earliest beginning: the external, visual attractions of women's beauty are already dangerous in Hesiod's Pandora; and Homer's Odysseus is a master of lies and disguises. These tensions between the surface world that we see and the hidden truths that we do not are also explored by the philosophers, from Thales and Anaximander to Parmenides and the Atomists. Yet in tragedy the rift between seen and unseen truth acquires a more vivid representation through being enacted before our eyes in the gestures and movements of living men in real space.

In early Greek society the poet is a "master of truth," the speaker of a discourse which derives validity from a set of culturally valid, privileged narratives.[12] Homer invokes the Muses as his source of knowledge about the past (*Iliad* 2.484–87). Hesiod relates how the Muses on Helicon gave him a *skēptron*, a staff, emblem of authority, and breathed into him the power of song, along with the knowledge of its capacity for both truth and falsehood (*Theogony* 26–34).[13] By the late sixth century, however, that authority for truth is secularized and internalized. Oral poetry—and I have in mind the Homeric poems in particular—gives us the sensation of the full presence of events: we feel that we have all the necessary details and that we possess that immediacy of foreground eloquently described by Auerbach in the famous first chapter of *Mimesis*. Tragedy, based as it is on a written text, is full of elusive details, missing pieces, unexplained motives, puzzling changes of mood, decision, or attitude. Instead of the oral poet who tells us in person of "the will of Zeus," we have the absent poet who has plotted out every detail in advance. And we have the feeling, at times, that we have been plotted against, that we are the victims of a calculated counterpoint between

---

12 M. Detienne, *Maîtres de vérité dans la Grèce archaïque* (Paris 1967).

13 For recent discussion of the Muses in Homer and Hesiod see W. Rösler, "Die Entdeckung der Fiktionalität in der Antike," *Poetica* 12 (1980) 294–98, with further bibliography; also P. Pucci, *Hesiod and the Language of Poetry* (Baltimore and London 1977) 8–44.

surface and depth, appearance and reality, seeming and being.

As the basis for bardic authority is reexamined in the critical spirit fostered by writing, authors need to shape another kind of narrative in order to lay claim to a discourse of truth. They need to tell a different kind of story about themselves in order to support the truth that they claim to speak. Such, for instance, is the journey of Parmenides, cast in the traditional form of a Homeric narrative and studded with phrases borrowed from the epic vocabulary.[14] But Parmenides' traditional language only sets off the unique, mysterious quality of his journey and his destination. This poet is going not to a mythical land of Laestrygonians but to a realm of philosophical concepts, Being and Non-being. Such too is Thucydides' new "story" about himself, a story not about gods and Muses but about a "journey" of investigation, inquiry, strenuous examination, *zētēsis tēs alētheias*, "a searching out of truth" (Thucyd. 1.20.3, and in general 1.20–22).

The increasing literacy of the late fifth century, at least in Athens,[15] is one of several interrelated influences that tend to cut the discourse of truth loose from the communal, performative, and agonistic context of the archaic period and thereby to require the poet to reflect consciously on his sources of truth or, in other words, on the kind of story that he has, implicitly, to tell about himself. Later poets, like Callimachus and Theocritus, do this almost as a matter of course and in the spirit of a self-conscious literary *topos*, to distinguish their art from that of their predecessors and contemporaries.[16]

What is the implicit story of the tragic poet? It is no longer a tale of meeting Muses or gods (such as even Pindar could still tell).[17] The tragedian's story perhaps resembles that of Oedipus or Teiresias; it is the story of a double vision or a double language (*dissai phōnai*), of a "backstage,"

---

[14] Parmenides, frag. 28 B1 in H. Diels and W. Kranz, *Die Fragmente der Vorsokratiker*, ed. 6 (Berlin 1952), 3 vols.

[15] For the growing importance of literacy in the last quarter of the fifth century see F. D. Harvey, "Literacy in the Athenian Democracy," *REG* 79 (1966) 585–635; E. G. Turner, *Athenian Books in the Fifth and Fourth Centuries B.C.* (London 1952); A. R. Burns, "Athenian Literacy in the Fifth Century," *Journ. Hist. Ideas* 42 (1981) 371–87; Lanza, *Lingua e discorso* (above, n. 3) 52–84, with the bibliography, 85–87; Giovanni Cerri, *Legislazione orale e tragedia greca* (Naples 1979) 33–45, 65–74; on the limits of imputing too high a degree of literacy to the Athenians, despite the number of inscriptions in the city, see Oddone Longo, *Tecniche della communicazione nella Grecia antica* (Naples 1981) p. 120, with n. 20, p. 125. It is part of Havelock's "oral" thesis that literacy be placed as late as possible in the fifth century, though he admits, rather reluctantly, the high literacy at the end of the century: *The Literate Revolution*, 199ff., especially 203f. (= *New Literary History* 8, 1977, 383ff., 387f.).

[16] Cf. Theocritus 7.123–30, especially 128ff.; Callimachus, *Aitia* I, frag. 1, 21ff., where the status of the fully literate poet is signalled by the presence of the writing tablet on his knees; also frag. 2.

[17] For example, Pindar, *Pyth.* 8.56–60; *Pyth.* 3.77–79, with scholion 137b (Drachmann).

of something hidden *behind* or *beneath*.[18] For Aristophanes, Euripides'
verse, "My tongue has sworn, but unsworn is my mind" (*Hippolytus*
612), became almost a motto of that poet's form of tragedy, the ironic
emblem of his defeat in the *Frogs* (1471). In representing the visually
concrete and physical exterior of the mythical character, tragedy heightens the mystery of his interior life. A self-conscious tragedian like Euripides repeatedly calls attention to the problem of representing, realizing,
and verifying this interior realm.

In the fifth century the "graphic space" of alphabetic writing becomes a convenient metaphor for making visible the hidden realm of the
emotional life, the inner space of the self. As the concretization into
solid, stable, and visual form of the fluid, invisible breath of the voice's
"winged words," writing can represent the process of revealing what lies
unseen within the mind. The most common of these "graphic" metaphors is that of the "tablets of the mind," frequent in the tragedians,
with the concomitant figure of "unrolling" or "unfolding" the interior
secrets of the heart.[19] We may include here too Gorgias' figure of persuasion's "stamp" or "impression" upon the soul (*tēn psuchēn etupōsato*)
and his image of *logoi* that make things to be seen by "the eyes of opinion" (*tois tēs doxēs ommasin, Helen* 13). Immediately afterwards he
speaks of the persuasive power of a *logos* that is "*written* with art" (*technēi grapheis*). Then a few paragraphs later, describing the power of
vision to arouse fear and desire, he uses another metaphor of writing: "So
has vision inscribed (*enegrapse*) on thought the images (*eikonas*) of
actual things seen" (*Hel.* 17). He goes on to speak of painters (*grapheis*)
and sculptors whose work brings pleasure and pain to the eyes. These
visual metaphors, in turn, are intended as analogies for the force of eros
as a quasi-corporeal power that enters the soul through the eyes.

At least two factors aid this association of writing and emotional inter-
iority: the tendency in an oral culture to connect writing with private,
secret, or deceitful communication (particularly of an erotic nature) and
the importance that writing gives to vision, for the Greeks the most powerful stimulus to eros.[20] Gorgias' theory of desire depends on this four-way
association of writing, emotional life, eros, and vision. This graphic space, I
shall suggest later, corresponds to the tragedians' new self-consciousness
about what is going on "behind" and "beneath," about what cannot be
shown visually in the scenic action (the self as inner and hidden) and in the
scenic language (the written text).

It would, of course, be a mistaken exaggeration to attribute to writing

18 Eur., *Hipp.* 925–31; *Med.* 516–19; *H.F.* 655–72. For the "hidden" in human life see
Hipp. 191–97 and the echoes later in Artemis' speech to Theseus, 1287ff.
19 E.g. Eur., *Hipp.* 985; cf. *I.T.* 793.
20 See, for example, Jebb on Soph., *Antig.* 795f.

alone massive shifts of emphasis in Greek society that result from the interaction of many complex factors, economic, social, political, religious, and
so on. The growing individualism of the fifth century, aided by the rationalism of the philosophers and the sophists, the questioning of traditional
values in the various crises of the Peloponnesian war, the gradual evolution
of moral speculation over the past century, including an increasing shift
from "shame-culture" to "guilt-culture," all contribute to this concern with
the "inner" self and the "real" nature of what we are.[21] Nevertheless, the
movement away from the face-to-face exchange of information in a small,
village-type society, where everyone is familiar and defined by multiple
nexuses of relationships, to the more abstractive, intellectual, and less
personal mode of communication of information and ideas inherent in a
literate culture accentuates the problem of self-knowledge and self-
definition.[22] Writing accompanies that increasing acknowledgment of
complexity in the vision of self and world that marks the fifth century. The
self defined by the physical externals of health, beauty, strength, and the
opinion of others[23] is no longer adequate to a world-view aware of irrational, invisible, mysterious forces within the individual and the governance
of the universe.

Along with civic cult, epic and rhapsodic recitation, choral performances, and other rituals of a "dramatic" nature like the Mysteries, drama
depends upon a system of symbols and conventions to effect its mimesis
of reality. The audiences that came to the first tragedies had long been
schooled to a mode of thought that could "see" the Troad or Lemnos or
Egypt in the circular orchestra of the theater or could accept the figure
moving and speaking behind the mask as Theseus, Heracles, or Agamemnon. But phonetic writing gives new force and simplicity of expression to this process of conventionalized, symbolic representation in
everyday life. The increasing alphabetization of Athens in the period
when tragedy develops, along with the critical spirit fostered in a literate
society, sharpens awareness of the discrepancy between the imagined
and the actual objects, just as phonetic writing sharpens awareness of the
discrepancy between the alphabetic conventions and the tactile reality.[24]

---

[21] For some speculation on these social changes see Gouldner 113f., 133f.

[22] For the face-to-face mentality of "village-type," oral societies see Longo, *Tecniche,
della comunicazione* 13ff.

[23] See Gouldner, 98ff., 105ff.

[24] On the importance of phonetic writing as the source of a conventionalized
symbol-system for tragedy see D. De Kerckhove, "Synthèse sensorielle et tragédie:
L'espace dans *Les Perses* d'Eschyle," in *Tragique et tragédie dans la tradition occiden-
tale,* eds. P. Gravel and T. J. Reiss (Montreal 1983) 69–83, especially 75ff., who seems to
me to have isolated and exaggerated the importance of writing. Writing may have contributed to self-consciousness about the conventions, but the conventions themselves have
older, deeper, and more diverse origins. See also his 1979 essay, cited below, n. 28.

Hence the tragedians are interested not only in creating spectacle, but in calling attention to their own *power* to create spectacles, to the system of conventions with which the form itself operates. We are familiar with such self-consciousness about the symbolic system of representation in late Euripidean plays like the *Helen* and *Bacchae*,[25] but the tendency is there even as early as Sophocles' *Ajax*, where the prologue seems to allude to the poet's illusionistic power as a kind of divine *technē* (86), enabling us the audience to be present as if unseen at events acted out before our eyes (83–86):[26]

> *Athena.* He could not see you, do not fear, even if you stand next to him.
> *Odysseus.* How, if he sees with the same eyes?
> *Ath.* I will darken his eyes, even though they see.
> *Od.* Everything may come about with a god's devising craft.

III

Writing provides a fixed point of orientation and organization around which are focussed the mental energies that are more diffused in an oral culture. The new skill appears not merely as an intellectual technique, but as the sheer power of mind and eye (often closely associated by the Greeks, for whom to "know" is to "see," as the two verbs have the same root, *vid-*). Simonides' new "art of memory" at the end of the sixth or beginning of the fifth century seems to have utilized visualization as its main component.[27] Thus the power of memory, instead of being attached to hearing and speech and therefore oriented externally, toward others, is made part of visual experience and is oriented inwardly, toward oneself, toward silence and privacy. The metaphor, frequent in tragedy, of writing on the tablets of the mind identifies memory with something both visual and interior, a kind of interiorized writing (see infra, section VIII). The literate revolution probably played an important role both in emphasizing visualization and in celebrating the power of mind, a recurrent theme in the classical period, from about 460 B.C. to the end of the century.

One of the most famous celebrations of this intellectual power is the *Prometheus Bound* of Aeschylus. Here, I think, we find an important indirect reflection of the new mode of mental organization implied in writing. The Titan, imprisoned and immobilized on his rock in the Caucasus in

---

[25] See below, nn. 75 and 76.

[26] The discovery of Ajax's body at the climax of the play may also be calling attention to the technique of using the eccyclema to make visually powerful what would otherwise remain hidden: cf. 976–78 and 890 with 915–17.

[27] See Cicero, *De. orat.* 2.86.354 and 2.87.357. See Gentili in Vegetti (above, n. 7) 32. See also Kerckhove (next note) 359–61 on Simonides and the "intériorisation d'un espace visuel" (p. 361).

punishment for teaching the arts of civilization to mortals—including the
arts of writing and counting—holds the center of the stage, an object of
magnetic vision to all who approach him.[28] Like the organizing force of a
written text, this figure at the center of the spectacle is the source from
which all the mental energy in the play seems to radiate. He imposes order
and limit by means of his intellectual power—power which consists in the
ordering, presenting, and withholding of knowledge.

At roughly the midpoint of the action, after Prometheus has
enumerated at length his civilizing gifts to mankind, the cow-maiden Io
enters. Zeus' lustful pursuit has driven her over the earth in confused
wanderings. A figure of total disorientation, she utters inarticulate cries,
does not know where she is, and is amazed that Prometheus knows her
name. Their meeting is like the confrontation of oral and written men-
talities. Io is immersed entirely in the immediate present, beyond which
she cannot see. She is surrounded by mysterious voices that drive her
onward, and she is pursued by vague, dreamlike visions of the night that
she can only partially discern and cannot understand. Following a journey that seems to hold neither end nor goal, she lacks the kind of centering and focussing of experience that Prometheus embodies in the play.

When Prometheus urges Io to "write down on the remembering
tablets of her mind" the extent of her future travels (789), he provides
her with both the temporal and the spatial organization that the ordering
of reality by writing makes possible. In clear and well articulated order
he indicates the definite stages in her journey. He orients her according
to the directional marks of north and south, sunrise and sunset (cf. 790f.,
796f.), just as he had oriented mortals by giving them the knowledge of
seasonal limits and by teaching them how to "read" the signs and omens
of the future from the birds (484–99). The verb, "set on a path," *hodoun*,
occurs in both passages (498, 813) and marks the directional, orienting

---

[28] After I had written this section, Professor Froma Zeitlin pointed out to me that a
similar point had been made about the *Prometheus* by D. de Kerckhove, "Sur la fonction
du théâtre comme agent d'intériorisation des effets de l'alphabet phonétique à Athènes au
V siècle," *Les imaginaires, II, Cause commune*, 1979, no. 1, "10/18" (Paris 1979) 345–68,
especially 351–56. Although we both stress the importance of Prometheus' immobility,
Kerckhove emphasizes the effect of "sensory deprivation." In his view this is central to the
reorganization of perceptual reality, for it creates a mode of thinking that is now directed
by the repression of the body and shifts away from oral/aural participation to the more
abstractive processes which he connects with phonetic writing: "Or c'est la tension entre la
répression sensorielle et l'impossibilité de réagir physiquement qui permet à l'énergie de
Prométhée de se concentrer dans une intériorité d' où s'échappe interminablement sa
parole" (353f.). Stimulating as this approach is, it suffers from isolating only one factor in
what is a complex movement toward the conception of an interiorized self in late archaic
and classical Greece. If theatrical space, moreover, is in one sense analogous to the symbolic conventionality of phonetic script, the Greek theatrical performance, with its multi-
media and multi-sensory effects, is far from the abstractive result of sensory deprivation.

nature of the kind of knowledge that Prometheus gives to mortals.

Prometheus' spatial ordering of Io's movements by explaining the route of her wanderings has a temporal equivalent in the future of the places that she traverses. These nameless points, Prometheus says, will become famous in later times, fixed markers in a strange territory, because of her passage (e.g. 732–34, 839–45). He tells her also of the remoter end of her sufferings when she reaches her goal in the land of Egypt, and of another kind of relief in the fact that one of her descendants will be his liberator. In the dimensions of both space and time, then, Prometheus gives her formless world a shape and a form, just as he gives her journey and her experiences a direction and a coherence. He makes available to her the kind of organizing intelligence that comes with writing, coordinating past and future, tracing patterns in the shapeless mass of both space and time, and making patterns visible in the midst of a chaotic mass of unordered detail. He creates for the inarticulate half-human creature of suffering what is virtually a map of where she has been and where she is to go (we recall again that verb of orienting direction, "set on a path," *hodoun*, in 813).

IV

Another great exemplary text of this period has as its central theme the problem of organizing experience into knowledge and moving between different communicative and signifying systems, namely the *Oedipus Tyrannus* of Sophocles. Here even more sharply than in the *Prometheus* the problem of truth has to do with crossing over between aural and visual modes of sorting and preserving information. It is commonplace to observe the importance of sight in the play. But less commonly observed is the interlocking of sight and hearing in many of Oedipus' statements about knowledge. When the primary object of inquiry arises in the prologue, namely the question of the death of Laius, Oedipus describes his knowledge of Laius as follows (105): "I *know* (of him) by *hearing*; for never have I *seen* him." Since *oida*, "I know," is the first syllable of Oedipus' name, the line immediately associates Oedipus' "knowing" with "seeing."

When Oedipus, near the end, blinds himself and returns to the stage, it is as a man returned to the one-dimensional knowledge of an oral/aural culture, reborn into a world dominated by the presence of sound as the primary mode of knowledge (1309f.: "Where in the earth am I borne, miserable? How does my voice fly around me, borne aloft?" *diapotatai phoradēn*). The voice, *phthonga*, becomes something concrete and solid, a separate entity that has a quasi-corporeal reality, a locomotive power, like the Sphinx or like the magical, incantatory "winged word" in an oral culture. When he asks to close off the channels of hearing as of sight

(1386–90), he restates in negative form the double sensory power that consitituted the basis of knowledge in the prologue. In his anger and ignorance he accused the inwardly seeing Teiresias of being "*blind* in his *ears*" as well as in his "mind and eyes" (*Oed. Tyr.* 371). But Oedipus himself is exemplary of tragedy in his determined exploration of the interlocking of visual and auditory knowledge and in his awareness of the doubleness of verbal meanings in man's difficult search for truth. One thinks here too of Sophocles' contemporary, Empedocles, and his concern with the multiple avenues of knowledge thorough the senses.[29]

V

The ambiguity of language as a medium of truthful discourse implied in the *Oedipus* receives perhaps its most pregnant formulation in prose from the rhetorician and sophist Gorgias near the end of the fifth century. In the *Helen* (ca. 13) he evokes the power of language in the oral tradition to give pleasure (*terpein*) and persuade (*peithein*).[30] He distinguishes, however, between the "word written with artful skill," *technēi grapheis*, and the word "spoken with truth," *aletheiāi lechtheis*. A fragment of his *Epitaphios* contrasts the "freshness" and "vitality" of "actions" with the "paleness" and "trembling" feebleness of "letters" (*tremonta kai ōchra*).[31] Gorgias can still play upon *alētheia* as the "truth" communicated in the living interaction of the oral exchange, but with a major difference: he is conscious of being a *scriptor* who has "written" the *logos* of Helen (*grapsai, Hel.* ca. 21) and therefore made a "plaything" or a fiction, a *paignion* (the last word of the *Encomium on Helen*), not a piece of "truth." "I wished to write my discourse," he concludes, "not as an encomium for Helen but as a plaything of my own." His work, then, falls into the category of what is "written with art, not spoken with truth" (*Hel.* ca. 13); he is no longer a "master of truth." As a *writer*, he has a special consciousness of himself as the shaper of his own discourse, with the element of play (*paignion*) that it can exemplify.

Play is also freedom, the new freedom of the writer, detached from the public context of the oral performance, free of the responsibility of transmitting and recording the traditions of his people, able to develop ideas because they interest him alone.[32] He can follow his own path of

[29] Empedocles 31 B3, 9ff. (Diels-Kranz); also B2.7f.
[30] See my remarks, "Gorgias and the Psychology of the *Logos*," *HSCP* 65 (1962) 99–155, especially 106f., 110f., 122ff.; W. J. Verdenius, "Gorgias' Doctrine of Deception," in G. B. Kerferd, ed., *The Sophists and Their Legacy, Hermes Einzelschr.* 44 (Wiesbaden 1981) 121f.
[31] For the text see F. Solmsen, *Hermes* 66 (1931) 249, n. 2 (= *Kleine Schriften* [Hildesheim 1968] 2.159, n. 2).
[32] This play-element has a notable role in Euripides' *Bacchae*: see my *Dionysiac Poetics and Euripides' Bacchae* (Princeton 1982) 266ff.

words and thoughts with an independence not possible for the oral bard
subject to the audience control of the performance. This kind of author
makes no claim to the transpersonal truth beyond himself. Unlike the
oral poet, he knows the moment of his words' origin; he knows that they
arise from within himself, that they are an object that he himself has
fashioned and sees materialized as a text.

We may contrast with Gorgias' self-consciousness of writing the
powerful affirmation of the truth of oral as against written statement a
generation earlier in the Argive King's decree in Aeschylus' *Suppliants*
(946–49), where spoken words have the solidity and tangible presence
conveyed in the metaphor of the firmly fastened "peg" or "bolt" of his
decree (*gomphos*, 945).[33] "These things are not written down on tablets,"
says the King, "nor sealed up in the foldings of scrolls: you hear the clear
words of a tongue and a mouth that speak in freedom." But for Gorgias'
younger contemporary, Thucydides, the relation between the spoken
and the written word is just the other way around. The spoken word
deceives and misleads with its seductive promise of pleasure (*terpsis*) in
the agonistic context of recitation (Thucyd. 1.22.1), whereas the written
word is the result of "effort" (*ponos*) and investigation (*zētēsis*) and
yields "accuracy" (*akribeia*). Writing is surer than speaking in revealing
what is "hidden" (*to aphanes*) behind surface appearances (*phanera
opsis*, 1.10.2; cf. 1.23.3–6).[34]

The division in the philosophers, historians, and the tragic poets,
between surface and depth, appearance and reality, is encouraged by
the special status of the written text in a hitherto oral culture. These
authors have before them two models of mental organization. Oral communication faces outward, to the interactive contextual space between
speaker and audience; written communication faces inward, toward the
personal relation with the hearer. Its concern is syntactics rather than
pragmatics.[35] As Aristotle points out in his discussion of the "graphic"
and the "agonistic" styles, writing fosters the internal subordination of
ideas within the syntax of the sentence.[36] Oral communication, on the
other hand, depends less on the internal logic and structuring of the
ideas than on the repeated assertions of its message, the fullness and

---

[33] On this passage and the solidification of speech as inscribed document see Turner,
Athenian Books, 9; also Longo, *Tecniche della comunicazione* 122f.

[34] On these passages see my essay, "*Logos* and *Mythos*: Language, Reality, and Appearance in Greek Tragedy and Plato," in *Tragique et tragédie* (above, n. 24) 25–27; also B.
Gentili and G. Cerri, *Le teorie del discorso storico nel pensiero greco e la storiografia
romana arcaica* (Rome 1975) 24f.; F. Solmsen, *The Intellectual Experiment of the Greek
Enlightenment* (Princeton 1975) 96f.

[35] See Ong, *Orality and Literacy*, 37f., who cites T. Givón, "From Discourse to Syntax:
Grammar as a Processing Strategy," *Syntax and Semantics* 12 (1979) 81–112.

[36] Aristotle, *Rhet.* 3.12, especially 1413b8–14a7.

copiousness of its style, qualities which take account of the needs and limitations of the listener. The written message is far more enclosed in the autonomy of its own internal coherence. Some of the tensions explored by tragedy may be due to this pull between the inner cohesion of the written text and the other-directedness of the oral medium.

VI

The beginnings of such a tension coincide with the critical reflection on the mythic tradition that writing unquestionably aided. Around the middle of the fifth century, Hecataeus of Abdera, like Thucydides, designates himself explicitly as a *scriptor*, the "composer" of a writing. His new "graphic space" fragments the prior vision of truth into a plurality of modes of understanding the world.[37] In the few fragments that survive of Protagoras' interpretation of Homer, we can see the same processes of distancing and critical examination: the copious flow, the forward-moving impetus, of the oral epic is interrupted after the first words. The fluid linkage of each phrase to the next is broken up into small discontinuous fragments of discourse that can be scrutinized and dissected. It is the same technique that Aeschylus applies to the prologues of Euripides in Aristophanes' *Frogs*.[38]

For Democritus, perhaps at about the same time, even the numinous quality of poetic inspiration is linked to the written word: "Whatever a poet *writes—graphēi*—with inspiration and the holy afflatus is indeed beautiful."[39] The power of a "divine mind" (*theios nous*) lies no longer in the gift of inspiration from the goddesses of Memory but in a ratiocinative capacity, something like "dialogic reasoning."[40] In the oral tradition it is the Muse and the goddess Mnemosyne who endow the poet with the power of lengthy, continuous utterance, made possible by a ready abundance of words and matter. The written word encourages density, concentration, discontinuity. Tragedy, in an intermediate position between orality and literacy, contains both tendencies: the flow of the long messenger speeches and the staccato effect of the dialogue, often marked by the sharp conflict of arguments in *antilogiai* and stichomythia.[41]

---

[37] Detienne, *L' invention*, 138ff., àpropos of Hecataeus fragment 1 (Jacoby); see also Rösler 306.

[38] Aristoph., *Frogs* 1119–1250; cf. Protagoras 80A28–29 Diels-Kranz and my remarks, "Protagoras' *Orthoepeia* and Aristophanes' Battle of the Prologues,'" *RhM* 113 (1970) 158–62.

[39] Democritus 68 B18, Diels-Kranz.

[40] *Dialogizesthai*, Democritus 68 B112, Diels-Kranz.

[41] See Solmsen, *Intellectual Experiment*, 17 and 28ff.; also John H. Finley, Jr., "The Origins of Thucydides' Style," in *Three Essays on Thucydides* (Cambridge, Mass. 1967) 74–82, 110–12.

From the late sixth century on, critical reflection about the traditional tales gains momentum with writing. When variant versions can be fixed in a written text, discrepancies and contradictions are more easily detected.[42] The tragic poets—like Pindar, Hecataeus, and Herodotus—do not merely repeat or retell the myths, but reflect on them in a critical spirit.[43] In the "graphic space" which opens before the tragic poet as the writer of a fixed text, there opens also the autonomous space of the fictional, the possibility of free invention, though obviously within prescribed limits. Instead of being a "master of truth," conveyor of multipersonal norms and values fixed in the conventionalized symbolic system of mythical tales recounted in heavily formulaic language, the poet is on his way to becoming the fabricator of fictions. Younger tragedians like Agathon even experimented with plots of their own invention, though rarely.[44] The task of the tragic poet is now not to unveil reality but to create a self-conscious "imitation" of reality.[45]

The Homeric interpretation of Theagenes of Rhegium at the end of the sixth century is an interesting forerunner of this kind of "imitated" universe of the art-work. Our knowledge of Theagenes is pitifully scanty, but from the extant fragments it seems clear that he wrote a commentary on the Homeric poems, interpreting some of the more troublesome anthropomorphic features of the gods in an allegorical way. In this endeavor he had a predecessor in the Homeric criticism of Xenophanes earlier in the sixth century; but, whereas Xenophanes only criticized, Theagenes seems to have allegorized.[46] To interpret a text, to reflect on it as an object apart from the context of its immediate performance is to imply a second plane of truth. As a writing, such poetry no longer opens to a public world, fully visible to all and immediately comprehensible in the shared values that it utters and endorses. Instead, as a text, the poem reveals a hidden world that becomes visible only as we scrutinize the words as an object of contemplation. Its surface has to be lifted away or penetrated to reveal the "deeper" levels; it contains a

---

[42] See J. Goody and I. Watt, "The Consequences of Literacy," in *Literacy in Traditional Societies*, ed. J. Goody (Cambridge 1968) 27–68, especially 44ff.; see also Svenbro 15.

[43] Detienne, *L' invention*, chaps. 3 and 4; also Svenbro 173–212.

[44] Aristotle, *Poetics* 1451b19–26.

[45] See Rösler 309ff.; J.-P. Vernant, "Le sujet tragique: historicité et transhistoricité," *Belfagor* 34 (1979) 639f. and "Naissance d'images," in *Religions, Histoire, Raisons* (Paris 1979) 111; Verdenius (above, n. 30) 123f., who points out the generally negative attitude toward poetry as fiction in early Greek literature.

[46] The little that is handed down about Theagenes can be found in Diels-Kranz 1. 51f. (no. 8). If the tradition is reliable, he is a contemporary of Aeschylus and Pindar, and he "wrote" his comments down (*grapsas*, frag. 2, ad fin. and frag. 4). Something at least survived in writing for Hellenistic scholarship to pass on to late antiquity, from which come our only notices of his work. For Theagenes' Homeric interpretation and the implications of literacy see Detienne, *L' invention*, 130.

thought that lies "beneath" the visible meaning (*hypo-noia*), or, in later terminology, says something "other" than its overt statement (*allēgoria*).[47] With a written text, it becomes possible to distinguish a first level of meaning from a second; and there enters a critical distance which does not exist in a traditional society whose truth is firmly ensconced in the memory of its members. With the practice of writing, the true meaning of the traditional wisdom is hidden and invisible, something to be reached by that effort of intellect and abstraction that writing makes possible.

This is the kind of search in which Thucydides is also engaged, far more self-consciously. He rejects the fluid surface of Herodotus' discourse, still oriented to the oral context,[48] in favor of the more strenuous examination of evidence, comparison of divergences, abstraction and inferences that all go along with writing. For the atomists Democritus and Leucippus the phenomenal world itself is a "text," a surface of appearances that has to be analyzed into its permanent but invisible "truth" of atom and void, the *stoicheia*, "elements," "letters," of its invisible atoms.[49] To reach truth one must distance oneself from the "human lifeworld" and plunge beneath this surface "into the depths" (*buthos*).[50] Such, mutatis mutandis, is also the investigative procedure of Thucydides: he seeks to recover the hidden causes which are *aphanes*, invisible, hidden behind the *phanera opsis*, the "visible appearance" (cf. 1.10, 1.22–23).

VII

In a preliterate society conflicts are acted out in social situations of encounter and exchange.[51] So too values are embodied in concrete, externalized objects, solid and visible points of reference for everyone.[52] With its distancing of experience and its removal from the necessity of face-to-face exchange in communication, writing encourages the internalizing of experience and the exploration of the private, the self-consciously

---

[47] The term *hyponoia* is probably pre-Platonic; *allēgoria* is late: see Svenbro 113–15.

[48] For the predominance of the "oral code" in Herodotus see Longo, *Tecniche della communicazione* p. 72, n. 26.

[49] Leucippus 67 A9 (Diels-Kranz) (= Aristotle, *De gen. et corr.* 1.315b6ff.) and Lucretius, *De rerum natura* 1.197f., 823–29, 2.688–99 are also evidence for the atomists' use of the letters of words as analogous to the atoms of things.

[50] Democritus, 68 B117, Diels-Kranz. On the notion of truth in things beneath the surface and compounds of *buthos* in archaic poetry, see Svenbro 119–21.

[51] See J. Russo and B. Simon, "Homeric Psychology and the Oral Epic Tradition," *Journ. Hist. Ideas* 29 (1968) 483–98.

[52] See L. Gernet, "La notion mythique de la valeur en Grèce," in *L'anthropologie de la Grèce antique*, ed. J.-P. Vernant (Paris 1968) 93–137.

personal.[53] The realm of the private, the personal, begins to appear. Conflicts are interiorized, and the whole inner world of the emotional life opens up. Phaedra's refusal to speak of her love, her reluctance to enter into dialogue with the Nurse and the women of Troezen, is symmetrical with the ambiguous silent speaking of the written tablets that she leaves for her husband.

The further development of writing increases the duplicitous potential of language. The gap between word and thing, *logos* and *ergon*, between what one says and what one is, becomes ever more evident and more problematical: compare Theseus' complaint of the deceptive discrepancy between men's "voices" (what they say) and their characters (what they are) in *Hippolytus* 925ff. Language now is no longer the fullness of ready, serviceable stories that flow from the generous gifts of the goddess Memory, but becomes an ambiguous series of signs, traces, and absences.[54] Sophocles' Oedipus confronts language as a difficult "track" (*ichnos*) which he must follow out to the unknown end, like a hunter following the spoor of his prey (*Oed. Tyr.* 108–111; cf. *Ajax* 5–10). *Muthoi* and *logoi*, what men say to one another, lead no longer to an open road but to a narrow and difficult path. Parmenides' route is "outside the track of men."[55]

The first reference to writing in Greek literature assigns to it the quality of ominous mystery as a sign. Such are the *sēmata lugra*, "baleful markings," that Bellerophon bears in the folded tablets intended to lead him to his doom (*Iliad* 6.168ff.). Yet even into the fourth century writing is the distillation of the deceptiveness of language and the difficulty of communication. It can be a mark of prestige and a guarantor of accuracy and truth.[56] But a culture that still privileges face-to-face contact and immediate sensory experience also regards writing as an object of suspicion, the characteristic tool of guile and treachery. In Thucydides' account of the Spartan Pausanias' illicit dealings with the Persian King, letters are the mark of his secrecy; but the ephors, to whom he is betrayed by letters, are convinced of the man's guilt only when they see and hear for themselves.[57]

Sophocles' *Trachiniae* and Euripides' *Hippolytus* (as well as the latter's lost *Stheneboea*) associate writing, trickery, concealed love, female desire as all related distortions of truth. In tragedy writing often serves as

---

[53] See Ong, *Orality and Literacy*, 178f.

[54] This point becomes explicit apropos of written language in Plato's famous myth about writing in *Phaedrus* 274c–276a. Building on Plato, Derrida works back from writing to all language as a proto-writing.

[55] Frag. 28 B1. 27, Diels-Kranz: *ektos patou*.

[56] E.g. Hdt. 1.125 or 3.128; Thuc. 7.8; see Longo, *Tecniche della comunicazione* 61f., 66f.

[57] Thuc. 1.133. On this passage see Longo, *Tecniche della comunicazione* 62f.

a motif or a figure around which the poet can crystallize the ambiguous attitudes of the culture toward the female and especially toward female desire.[58] In the *Hippolytus* writing appears as a duplicitous silent speaking that can subvert the authority of King and Father. As a concentrated form of seduction and persuasion, such "female" writing is doubly a threat to the masculine ideal of straightforward talk and forthright action.[59]

In the *Trachiniae* the letters that Heracles leaves behind for his family serve the father's goal of assuring the disposition of the patrimony after his death (46f., 156ff.; cf. also 1166–72). But there is another kind of writing, the metaphorical bronze tablet that describes Deianeira's memorization of Nessus' instructions about what she believes to be a love-charm (680–84). The metaphor deepens the theme of communication and exchange in this portion of the action, for the robe on which she smears the drug is sent to Heracles as her message of fidelity, a sign of "faith of words" (*logōn pistis*, 623).[60]

This metaphorical writing essential to the transmission of the robe, along with the sexual charm that it supposedly contains, is a continuation of the Centaur's deceptive speech. It expresses in a visual metaphor Deianeira's susceptibility to his ambiguous "persuasion," with its erotic magic (710; cf. 660–62). The tablet speaks a language of her unknown or unacknowledged self. As a silent remnant and record of the last words that Nessus addressed to her on the banks of his river, it shows Deianeira to herself as the exemplar of destructive female sexuality. It reveals the monstrous power of sexual desire that she can see in Heracles, Nessus, and Achelous but not recognize in herself.

In the interior space of the *oikos*, the woman's world, the open violence of the Centaur's masculine lust is transformed into feminine guile, persuasion, and seduction; and its murderous force operates through characteristically feminine arts.[61] This baneful and mysterious power of female desire works not on the open, visible surfaces of the body, but on the inner organs (1053–57). Its effects in these lines are described in metaphors of ingestion and digestion, processes involving the body as interior space, hollow or vessel. It uses enclosure, enfolding, and immobilization rather than penetration (cf. 1057). Heracles explicitly contrasts

---

[58] We may recall here Gorgias' *Helen*, discussed above, which probably draws on tragic material (cf. frag. B23).

[59] On women and writing as a joint object of suspicion, cf. Menander, frag. 702K, on which see Harvey, "Literacy," 621; also Susan G. Cole, "Could Greek Women Read and Write?" *Women's Studies* 8 (1981) 137 and 155.

[60] For the theme of communication and exchange in the *Trachiniae* see my remarks in *Tragedy and Civilization: An Interpretation of Sophocles* (Cambridge 1981) 94ff.

[61] For some implications of the tablet see Longo, *Tecniche della comunicazione* 65f.; Page duBois, *Centaurs and Amazons* (Ann Arbor 1982) 98f.

the wounds inflicted on him by the robe with the masculine weapons of war, the spear and the sword (1058, 1063).

The metaphorical tablet is not only the negation of the patriarchal order implicit in Heracles' letters but is also the dark counterpart of the robe's intended message of wifely fidelity (492–95). It conveys a different message about the nature of women. Its perverted speech utters the feared and suppressed truth that the chaste wife is also a lustful female, that the bride of Heracles is also the woman who yielded to the Centaur's "persuasion"/seduction and might yield to the more overt sexuality of his animal nature. These themes extend far beyond the implications of the "writing of the brazen tablet" in 683; yet the implicit transformation there from speech to writing, voice to silence, force to guile, male to female desire is a focal point for the inversions of the social codes that tragedy often explores.

It is part of the multiple and shifting meaning that writing can have in this period that men can also send deceitful and death-bearing messages (Agamemnon in *Iphigeneia at Aulis*), and letters by women can bring salvation (Iphigeneia in the Taurian *Iphigeneia*; Andromeda in Euripides' lost play of that name.)[62] In the political sphere written laws are a safeguard against tyranny and the guarantee of fairness and equality under the Athenian democracy (Eur., *Suppl.* 429–37); yet the "unwritten laws" still enjoy the prestige of ancient tradition and sacral usage (Soph., *Antig.* 450ff.; cf. Thuc. 2.37.3).[63] The combination of the practical, day-to-day utility of writing with its relative unfamiliarity and perhaps its Near-Eastern origins doubtless encouraged such ambiguous, even contradictory meanings.

On the rational side, the practice of writing gradually transforms the invisible, quasi-magical power of the spoken word into a familiar, material object, a well defined, clearly delimited human creation.[64] This concretization of language into writing gives an impulse to the study of language and communication per se.[65] Indeed one finds a fascination with the origin and nature of language throughout this entire period, in the Sophists, in Thucydides, Herodotus, and the tragedians. All of the

---

[62] Euripides is probably more open to these ambiguous associations of writing than Sophocles: see Longo, *Tecniche della comunicazione* 66.

[63] On the relation of literacy and orality to the debate between written and unwritten law in the fifth century see Cerri, *Legislazione orale*, especially chaps. 4 and 5; also Fabio Turato, "Seduzioni della parola e dramma dei segni nell' *Ippolito* di Euripide," *BIFG* 3 (1976) 181f.

[64] See J. Goody, *Literacy in Traditional Societies*, Introduction, p. 1, "Its [writing's] most essential service is to objectify speech, to provide language with a material correlative, a set of visible signs . . ."

[65] See in general Longo, *Tecniche della comunicazione*, chaps. 2 and 3; Lanza, *Lingua e discorso* (above, n. 15) chap. 1, with the bibliography, pp. 50f.

tragedians speculate on the origins of language and the origins of writing. A curious fragment of Euripides' lost *Theseus* shows a fascination with the physical form of letters (a character describes the shape of the letters that make up the name "Theseus"); and the popularity of the passage is indicated by the fact that it was closely imitated by two of Euripides' younger successors, Agathon and Theodectes. All three are interested in the physical form of letters as visual signifiers of the spoken word.[66] Such passages are indications of the new consciousness of the textuality of the work, operating at the microcosmic level of the basic act of composing shapes into language.

Instead of disappearing into the collective memory once the performance is over, being absorbed back into the communal voice, the written word of the poet has an autonomous existence apart from the spoken utterance which realizes it. The literate poet becomes even more aware than the archaic bard that his words are the component parts of an artistic product, a crafted object. His work is no longer a memorial to others' deeds, as in Homeric epic or even the archaic encomium, but a distinctive entity of his own, the guarantor of his own skill, not his patron's eternal fame.[67] Of the extant tragedians, Euripides most frequently utilizes this metaphorical crystallization of poetry as a monument or an artifact[68]— and also as a text.

VIII

In tragedy, where the poet never speaks in his own person, this kind of self-conscious textuality can only work implicitly, behind the dramatic spectacle. To see how it may function, even where the play seems relatively unselfconscious about its own poetics, I shall examine briefly the climactic events in Sophocles' *Oedipus Tyrannus* (1237–96). The main actors are absent from the stage; and the dramatic enactment of the events is suppressed in favor of a long narrative account, in the third person, by an outsider, a new arrival, the second Messenger who tells the tale. The Messenger begins by pointing out that he tells of things that were and are not seen: "There is [was] no vision present" (*opsis ou para*, 1238). He thereby sets off by contrast the distinctive quality of the telling that takes place through the visual representation onstage. As a correlative of this absence

---

[66] Eur. frag. 382; Agathon, frag. 4; Theodectes, frag. 6 (Nauck); see Harvey, "Literacy," 603f.

[67] See Svenbro 186ff., on Simonides. Contrast passages like Ibycus 282.47f. (Page) or Theognis 237–54 with passages like Pindar, *Ol.* 1.111ff. or *Ol.* 6. 1–4 or *Pyth.* 6.7–18. For recent discussion of the poetics of sixth-century singers see Gentili in Vegetti (above, note 7) 53–76, especially 62ff., with the bibliography, 75f.

[68] See, for example, *Alcestis* 962–71; *Medea* 190–203; *Hipp.* 1125ff., 1428–30; *Ion* 1143–65; *H.F.* 673–95; see in general, P. Pucci, "The Monument and the Sacrifice," *Arethusa* 10 (1977) 165–95; also my *Dionysiac Poetics* 318ff.

of the physical action in the theatrical spectacle, his recited tale also emphasizes the importance of memory. "There was no vision present," the Messenger says; "and yet as far as lies in my memory you will learn the suffering of that unhappy woman" (1238–40).[69] Memory is here correlative with vision, a kind of non-visual seeing, just as writing is a non-oral speaking. It is also an interiorized seeing, and we may recall here the implications of the metaphorical writing on the mind's tablets.

The Messenger's tale not only presents the visual contents of memory, but is also an emblematic account of memory's inner vision, for it consists in the gradual penetration to increasingly interior and hidden spaces (1239–96). This memory of the Messenger conducts us, verbally, inside the gates of the palace, where Oedipus rushes around in wild despair. Then it shows us the interior space of Jocasta's marriage-chamber, the scene of her suicide and Oedipus' self-blinding. The narration, however, permits us to glimpse these most important events only in fragments, by significant absence rather than through the full presence of the actors or the enacted events. By calling attention to the fact that he is withholding the visual appearance of his chief protagonists in favor of a purely verbal narration, the poet also reveals his self-consciousness of the theatrical spectacle as a special form of narrative, mediating between external and interior vision, between visible, physical acts and the emotional world which they reveal.

The Messenger ends his long narrative with the words, "For these gates of the palace are opening; soon you will see a *spectacle* (*theama*) such that even the one who loathes it will feel pity" (1295f.). The theatrical action, the visible opening of the outer doors of the palace, now mirrors the Messenger's verbal account. That recited narrative, based on a carefully structured *text*—words set down in advance to be delivered exactly as the poet has planned—has its own mode of revealing what is kept hidden. Its climactic moments too are the acts of closing and opening doors (1244, 1261f.; cf. 1287, 1294f.), but these acts take place entirely in the unseen, interior space within the palace.

Sophocles uses the conventional device of the messenger-speech with a new self-consciousness of the relation between the poet's text and the dramatic (visually enacted) events. He stresses the parallelism and the contrast between verbally describing the unseen events behind the palace and bedchamber doors and theatrically showing Oedipus as a "spectacle" on the stage. Oedipus now emerges through the palace doors as the center of all attention and the object of pitiable *sight* to all. "O suffering fearful for men to *see*," is the immediate response of the chorus

---

[69] Recent translators somewhat obscure the meaning by making the stark "There was no vision present," into a more colloquial, personal, and active construction: "You did not see the sight" (Grene); "You did not see it. I did" (Berg and Clay); "You never had to watch . . . I saw it all" (Fagles).

(1298). The terms for vision, spectacle, and the opening of gates shift between the narrator and the events he describes, the hideous violence that takes place behind closed doors.[70] Sophocles thus calls attention to the double mode of narration going on before us. He implies thereby the self-consciousness of the text which has plotted out the story in advance of the performance. The spectacle onstage has behind it a narrative of actions in which "there is no vision present" (*opsis ou para*, 1238). The Messenger's purely verbal tale is like the stage-business before our eyes: it too is a way of "opening doors" to the hidden events that arouse our terror and our pity.

This textual self-consciousness, I suggest, owes much to the transitional moment of the form between oral and literate. This concern with the hidden, private, inner space, here and elsewhere in Greek tragedy, points to a poet-writer whose frame of reference is *both* the physical, public space of the oral performance in the theater *and* the graphic space of the text. By the conventions of Greek drama, this interior space of house or palace is not represented on the stage but is always implicit behind the action. The poet composes for a stage which shows only the outside, but that exterior face of the represented world has a depth of meaning which derives in part from its hidden interior scene. That inner scene corresponds both to the emotional life of the characters and to the graphic space of the poet whose act of composition takes place before and apart from the public appearance in the theater where his words are given full realization.

The hiddenness of the tragic poet's text in the performance is the negative sign of something always hidden from view, on the other side of the palace wall, which is also the side of the Other. As a poet/writer who manipulates real bodies in real space on the stage, the dramatist becomes sensitized both to the invisible graphic space of his text and to the hidden, interior space of the self. What is concealed behind doors and gates—the gates of the palace, of the mouth, or of the body— becomes the problem of his writerly art. Greek tragedy has no word for the self. As John Jones, arguing from Aristotle's *Poetics*, maintains, it concentrates on exterior forms and events, on *mythos* as a concatenation of actions, *pragmata*.[71] Yet the sense of a self, of a complex inner life of motives, desires, and fears, is everywhere implicit. How does the tragedian make the inner life of the self visible? Where does it appear? Not on the stage, but in the behind-the-stage implied by the invisible text;

---

[70] E.g. 1238, 1253, 1261, 1265, 1271, 1287, 1294.
[71] *Poetics* 6. 1450a 2ff. John Jones, *On Aristotle and Greek Tragedy* (London 1962), especially 24ff., 35ff., 41ff. I am not advocating return to post-Romantic psychologism, but rather suggesting a way of looking at the vexed issue of character in Greek drama through posing the self as problem. Here, as elsewhere, the Greeks raise the fundamental questions of representing "reality" in art with exceptional clarity.

something *there* but not representable, or representable only as a tension between the seen and the unseen. This interplay between interior and exterior space parallels the increasing awareness of the interior realm of the *psychē*, the individual personality, that develops in late fifth-century thinkers like Socrates and Democritus.

Euripides is more explicit than Sophocles about the operations of this new textual awareness and the interior life that it implies. The *Hippolytus* is perhaps his most interesting work in this respect. This play, so concerned with the dichotomies of visible and invisible, inner and outer purity, "tongue" and "heart," also makes an explicit correlation between what is hidden behind the "gates" of the mouth and the "gates" of the palace, and furthermore connects this movement between inner and outer with writing.[72] The silent speaking of Phaedra's written tablets, left in the interior chamber where she hangs herself, proves to be more persuasive than the spoken utterances of face-to-face confrontation between Theseus and Hippolytus.

When the absent king returns to Athens, the scenic action stresses a double contrast between interior and exterior space and between the silence of written speech and the sounds of words cried out in pain or anger. Theseus is surprised at the "shouting" and "heavy cry" from within (790f.), and he is indignant that "the house does not deem it worthwhile to open the gates and address me joyfully" (792f). Told of Phaedra's death, he gives orders to open the "enclosures of the gates, in order that I may *see* the bitter *sight*" (808ff.; cf. 792f.). But when that inner scene is exposed (through the stage machinery of the eccyclema), it reveals the ambiguous speech-in-silence of the woman's tablets inside her chamber. Theseus responds (877–81): "The tablet shouts, shouts things not to be forgotten. How shall I flee the weight of woes? For I am gone, utterly destroyed. Such a song, alas, have I seen crying forth through the writing." His repeated allusions to the barrier of communication between himself and the unspeaking corpse (e.g. 826f., 842) set off this anomalous "speaking" of the tablet (cf. 856–65). This utterance is something "not endurable, not speakable" (847 and 875).

The spatial movement between inner and outer through the gates of the palace (793, 808) now shifts to a metaphorical movement between oral and written in words that pass or do not pass through the "gates of the mouth" (*stomatos pulai*, 882). As a speech that does not pass through "the gates of the mouth," writing is an ambiguous mode of communication; but here that stifled form of utterance does in fact "shout out" (877) with full communicative power. When Theseus first saw the tablet, he

---

[72] I have touched on the interior/exterior contrasts in my "Shame and Purity in Euripides' *Hippolytus*," *Hermes* 98 (1970) 278–99 and on possible connections with writing in "Tragédie, oralité, écriture," *Poétique* 50 (1982) 148f.

described it as "showing" and "saying" (*sēmēnai*, 857; *lexai*, 865); now its oral force intensifies. In reply, Theseus cannot contain his cry of grief (882–86): "I shall no longer hold down in the gates of the mouth this thing of ill passage outside, a destructive evil. O city! Hippolytus had dared to touch my bed by force, dishonoring the holy eye of Zeus." The passage continues the collocation of visual and oral that pervades the scene (e.g. 865, 879). In contrast to the woman's enclosed chamber of the "unspeakable" crime stand the speaking out and showing forth of revealed crime to the public space overseen by the eyes of father Theseus and Father Zeus (886). As in the *Oedipus*, the Other Scene, the son's violation of the most sacred and most forbidden of interior spaces, is presented as a series of recessive movements to a closed interior; and here that interior is explicitly identified with the ambiguous graphic space between utterance and silence, concealment and revelation, containment and ejaculation.

As in the *Trachiniae*, writing is a metaphor for the deviousness that female sexuality brings into the world. Communication between Phaedra's realm of feverish desire inside the house and the males outside is by indirection. She addresses Hippolytus only by the intermediary of the Nurse,[73] and she addresses Theseus only through the silent speech of her writing. In her famous speech resolving to die early in the play, she laments the confusion that surrounds the two forms of *aidōs*, "shame" or "modesty," two meanings spelled with "the same letters" (386–88).[74] Here, as in the case of her tablet, writing is the model for the ambiguities of language, for the possibility of error and deception as opposite meanings slide into one another. From this source flows a whole series of confusion in the lives of the characters and in the value systems that impinge upon them. Instead of the clearly delineated roles and stable, univocal meanings of a traditional, aristocratic society, with its emphasis on face-to-face contact, words and modes of behavior become paradoxical, and familiar boundaries no longer hold. Hippolytus is both bastard and well born (cf. 1454f.); Theseus is the source of domestic and political order and also of violence, bloodshed, and impurity (cf. 34f.); Phaedra is both noble in her fame (*eukleia*) and shameless in her passion (cf. 1299ff.; also 715ff.).

The last phase of Greek tragedy, the late plays of Euripides, shows another kind of awareness of tragedy's power as a medium that doubles the mimetic capacity of the word by the physical mimesis of deeds acted out by three-dimensional figures on the stage. In his last play, the *Bacchae*,

---

[73] In the first *Hippolytus*, however, presumably followed in this respect by Seneca in his *Phaedra*, there was a face-to-face interview between the queen and Hippolytus.

[74] For the *grammata* of 387 in relation to the problem of signs and language in the play see Turato (above, n. 63) pp. 163f. with n. 25.

Euripides weaves the madness of Pentheus into a complex texture of illusionistic effects and places it in a precarious balance between seeming and
being, hallucination and reality, that reflects the paradoxical status of the
theater itself. Amid the visible presences and tangible actions every event is
also a form of illusion.[75] The god's visitation of madness upon his mortal
victim becomes part of this tension between a subjective, distorted, private
view of the world and the objective reality of the god's supernatural power.

The *Bacchae* problematizes the mask as the symbol of the god's
power. In so doing it also problematizes the power of the theatrical spectacle to represent the hidden reality of the interior life, the sub-surface
beneath the mask. Dionysus in the play appears not only as the god of
wine and religious ecstasy, but also as the god of the mask and of the
theatrical illusion embodied in the mask.[76] The crisis of knowledge (and
self-knowledge) is now framed as a theatrical crisis, i.e., as a form of the
question, How much and what kind of reality is contained in the fictional construction of the spectacle? Is there a truth hidden beneath the
mask and beneath the act of wearing masks? Or further back still, what
kind of truth can be claimed by a discourse whose origins are no longer
sacred, no longer derived from the inspiration of the Muses, but lie
entirely in the writer himself as the fabricator of a text whose very mate-
riality attests to its human creation? The increasing pressure of these
questions follows with that inexorable logic that pervades early Greek
culture and is perhaps one of the factors responsible for the demise of
tragedy as a creative form.

The *Bacchae* is among the last of these tragedies. A generation earlier, in Sophocles' *Oedipus Tyrannus*, the god, however mysterious,
retains his Olympian otherness, the objective reality of his mysterious
power. In the *Bacchae* the god enters the subjective play of disguise and
role-playing on the tragic stage and is himself a kind of externalized
projection of human phantasies, fears, desires.[77] At its most optimistic,
the last phase of Greek tragedy celebrates its power to create fictions.
This more optimistic mood pervades the *Helen* of Euripides.[78] At its
most pessimistic, it calls attention to the airy bubble of its imagination,

---

[75] See my *Dionysiac Poetics*, 215–71. On this concern with appearance and reality in
Greek thinking about art, see Vernant, *Religions, Histoires, Raisons*, 128ff.

[76] See my *Dionysiac Poetics*, 215ff., 223ff., 260ff.

[77] For these concerns of late fifth-century drama see Helene Foley, "The Masque of
Dionysus," *TAPA* 110 (1980) 107–33; Froma Zeitlin, "The Closet of Masks: Role-playing
and Myth-making in the *Orestes* of Euripides," *Ramus* 9 (1980) 62–77 and "Travesties of
Gender and Genre in Aristophanes' *Thesmophoriazusae*," *Critical Inquiry* 8 (1981)
301–27, especially 309ff. I take a rather different view of the mask from Jones, *On Aristotle*, 43ff., 59f.

[78] See my study, "The Two Worlds of Euripides' *Helen*," *TAPA* 102 (1971) 553–614,
especially 610ff.; also my *Dionysiac Poetics*, 340ff.

floating precariously in a world which no longer knows what reality is. In the terms of the *Bacchae*, the mask is an extension of the god's power, the sign of his ambiguous presence among men, forcing them to choose between illusion and ultimate reality; but it is also a human creation, the sign of man's power to shape fictions which may be only an emptiness behind the illusionist covering.

IX

In a preliterate society you know what you can recall. What is useful, appreciated, valued, and therefore relevant is preserved and lives on the lips of men. The "winners" are remembered; the losers fade away.[79] The effect is what anthropologists like Goody have called homoeostasis, a tendency to maintain the current values and modes of behavior by a kind of natural selection of what supports them.[80] When Herodotus undertakes to preserve in writing what would otherwise become *exitēla* (1.1), that is, vanish into the detritus of the forgotten, he marks a new stage in Greek culture. When the tales about the past, the myths, genealogies, wise sayings, proverbs, laws, instructions can be fixed in the definitive form of writing, they can be scrutinized and criticized for discrepancies or contradictions. In a purely oral culture all the variants are "true," that is, have a claim to be heard simply because they are told, because they are living tales through which the society expresses its consciousness of itself. When men have the unsorted multiplicity of such tales crystallized in writing beneath their eyes, truth or accuracy becomes something to be adjudicated among conflicting or contradictory claims. Hecataeus may smile at the plurality of tales that he sets down in writing (*graphō*, 4F1 Jacoby), as Detienne recently points out,[81] but, in the more serious mood of tragedy, conflicting claims on truth involve life and death.

While Hecataeus and Herodotus and to a far greater extent Thucydides are fixing in writing, for critical examination, the events of the recent past, the tragedians fix in writing, for another kind of examination, the myths, the tales of gods and remote heroes, whose overt content is the distant past. Contemporary subjects, like Phrynichus' *Capture of Miletus* or Aeschylus' *Persians*, are rare; and even such events gain a certain aura of mythical remoteness through the elevated language, the close presence of the gods, and the intervention of the supernatural in ghosts, omens, prophecies, and the like. Tragedy resembles the poetic narrations of an oral culture in that its concern is the present relevance of the myths it uses. These tales are remade to fit a homeostatic present,

---

79 See Ong, *Orality and Literacy*, 47f.
80 Goody and Watt 31–34; see Rösler 304.
81 Detienne, *L'invention*, 138.

with little concern for historical depth. Yet the quality of that mythical narrative is determined by the spirit of criticism fostered by writing. The myths told by tragedy are no longer the myths of an oral society, clear exemplars of a received truth or accepted communal values.

Innovation in mythical narration is the stock-in-trade of Greek poets, beginning with Homer. In tragedy, however, that innovation is more drastic, less predictable, and cuts more radically to the heart of the story's meaning. Attending a tragic performance, one could never be certain just how a given myth would be told. The surviving tragedies about Iphigeneia, Electra, and Orestes and what we know of Oedipus or Philoctetes in the three tragedians show how divergently a myth could be handled. And even a single tragedian could present quite different versions of the same subject, as Euripides does with the tales of Hippolytus and Phaedra, Orestes, Iphigeneia, and Helen.

Mythology, Marcel Detienne has recently argued, comes into being only with the crystallization of oral tales into the written form that fixes them as "fictional stories," *muthoi plasthentes*, as Plato calls them.[82] For Plato, whose battle against the mentality of the oral culture Havelock has eloquently traced in *Preface to Plato*, truth should be the property of the philosopher who enunciates the values and norms that had previously been in the hands of the poets. The philosopher is a writer; Plato, with whatever elaboration and malaise, writes down the conversations of Socrates. The philosopher rethinks and rebuilds from the ground up what had been diffused in the scattered tales, maxims, sayings, paradigms handed down orally from generation to generation, without critical examination. From this perspective, which is the perspective that the historical development of Greek culture has bequeathed to us moderns, myth appears as something remote and primitive to which we look with nostalgia and wonder, a mode of expression untampered with by the secondary elaboration of writing.

The oral culture of early Greece is mediated to us by writing, and the search for the pre-literate substratum may be another form of Western man's perpetual longing for a primordial world of innocence and simplicity.[83] When writing becomes the major force not only in recording, but also in creating and reshaping myth, we may be dealing with "l'illusion mythique" rather that with the genuine, first degree myth of an oral culture; and access to a realm of "pure" myth, uncontaminated by the reflective and distancing processes of recording them, becomes ambiguous, uncertain, and paradoxical.[84]

---

[82] Plato, *Republic*, 2.377b; Detienne, *L'invention*, 180.

[83] D. Wesling, "Difficulties of the Bardic," *Critical Inquiry* 8 (1981) 73 warns against the modern "myth" of the Bardic, which is part of "print culture's nostalgia for oral culture."

[84] Detienne, *L'invention*, 226.

Our own interpretation of Greek culture curiously recapitulates the experience of the Greeks themselves at the end of their great tragic age. As we take account of the controlling and reshaping power exercised by writing in forming the versions of the myths that come down to us as literature, as letters and by virtue of being preserved in letters, with all the absences that letters imply, we too are inevitably involved in the demystification and demythification of the mythical. We too become not merely hearers or even readers, but interpreters, confronted with the paradox of a text that is forever fixed and forever elusive. The tragedians also, as writers, are not only mythicizers, but the self-conscious interpreters of myth. It is important to recognize the complexities implied in their textual production and not idealize them, following Nietzsche's "myth" of tragedy's Dionysian music and fusion with nature, as participants in the immediacy of oral vitality and the living, spontaneous power of primordial myth.[85]

[85] I met Karl Hulley in Boulder when I delivered a public lecture at the University of Colorado about a decade ago. I carried away an impression of lively intellectual inquiry, and in that spirit I offer this contribution to his memory. A French version of some parts of this essay, in a different form and with a different emphasis, will appear as the introduction to my *La musique du Sphinx: structure, mythe, langage dans la tragédie grecque* (Maspero, Paris, forthcoming). I thank the John Simon Guggenheim Memorial Foundation for a Fellowship in 1981–82, which supported the research for this study. I am grateful to Professor Froma Zeitlin of Princeton University for friendly criticism and advice.

MALE INTRUDERS AMONG THE MAENADS:
THE SO-CALLED MALE CELEBRANT

ALBERT HENRICHS

"Maenadism is women's business," noted Louis Gernet pointedly some three decades ago.[1] In other words, when Greek women left the traditional confines of house, family and city for a limited time every other year to go "to the mountain" (εἰς ὄρος) and to practice maenadic rites in a state of ritual madness that was very different from their normal behavior, they went by themselves and without male companions. A pioneer in the social study of Greek religion, Gernet had a particularly keen eye for the various and often separate roles that Greek religion assigned to different age groups as well as to the two sexes. Most modern students of Dionysus would agree that Gernet's definition of maenadism as "chose féminine" or "une forme de la vie féminine" is fundamentally correct. While appealing to men and women alike, Dionysus offered each sex a different attraction—to men the gift of wine and its ritualized consumption on a variety of social occasions such as wine-festivals and symposia; to women the "blessings of madness" within the institutional limits of ritual maenadism.[2] Wine and maenadism, the two major provinces of Dionysus, were kept strictly separate: wine-drinking maenads are as unheard of in real life and actual cult as male maenads. Not even in the *Bacchae* of Euripides, with its extremely ambiguous portrayal of maenadism, do the maenads drink wine or mingle with men: both charges, though repeatedly made by Pentheus, are refuted by the first messenger, an eyewitness (*Ba.* 686ff.). Nor do Cadmus and Teiresias, who carry thyrsi and wear fawnskins without donning women's clothes (176f. and 249ff.), ever join in the rites of the real maenads on the mountain.[3]

---

[1] Gernet, "Dionysos et la religion dionysiaque," *REG* 66 (1953) 377–95 at 383 = *Anthropologie de la Grèce antique* (Paris 1968, partial reprint 1982) 72 (repr. 94).

[2] For details see A. Henrichs, "Changing Dionysiac Identities," in B. F. Meyer and E. P. Sanders (eds.), *Jewish and Christian Self-Definition III: Self-Definition in the Graeco-Roman World* (London 1982, Philadelphia 1983) 137–60 (text), 213–36 (notes), cited below as Henrichs 1982.

[3] Since the two men learned of Pentheus' fate only after their return βακχῶν πάρα (*Ba.* 1222–24), they could not have witnessed the maenadic rites on Cithaeron, even though they must have reached the mountain; cf. J. Roux, *Euripide, Les Bacchantes*, II (Paris

Pentheus alone goes farther. Induced by Dionysus, he becomes a maenadic transvestite and spies on the maenads but pays for his sham maenadism with his life. Euripides pushed the concept of the maenad to its
very limits, yet in doing so he confirmed the exclusive nature of maenadic rites, participation in which was generally confined to female
worshipers of Dionysus.

Ritual maenadism was practiced over a period of at least 800 years,
from the time of its earliest attestation in archaic epic poetry to its gradual disappearance in the second or third century A.D.[4] It is a priori
unlikely that the social conditions for maenadism, including the relationship between the two sexes, remained always the same. In fact changes
in ritual practice did occur, but it is difficult to determine their significance in a given case. Indispensable though it is, the diachronic study of
maenadism is beset with uncertainties which are due to the wide discrepancy between the mythical conception of the maenad in literature
and art as opposed to the ritual reality of maenadism that emerges from
historical authors and the epigraphical record; to the complete lack of
direct information concerning the practice of maenadism prior to the
Hellenistic period; and to the widespread tendency, especially in Hellenistic and Roman art, to merge the mythical with the cultic sphere.
Despite such difficulties, the available evidence suggests very strongly
that the sexual barriers separating male and female followers of Dionysus began to break down in the late classical period. By the third century
B.C., joint participation in non-maenadic Dionysiac rites by men and
women alike must have been the norm rather than an exception. Ongo-
ing changes in social attitudes even affected the practice of maenadism
proper, so much that M. P. Nilsson throughout his work felt the need to
differentiate between the "old orgia" which were "savage" in origin and
which admitted only women, and later forms of Bacchic cult associations
which were indifferent to the sex of their members.[5] Mixed *thiasoi* of

---

1972) 605 *ad loc*. Whether or not they actually met the maenads Euripides does not say,
but he does imply that they did not attend their rites (*pace* G. Norwood, *Essays on Euripidean Drama* [Berkeley, London and Toronto 1954] 38, who concludes that Euripides is
inconsistent).

[4] See A. Henrichs, "Greek Maenadism from Olympias to Messalina," *HSCP* 82 (1978)
121–60 (cited as Henrichs 1978); Henrichs (1982) 143–48, 218–26; J. Bremmer, "Greek
Maenadism Reconsidered," *ZPE* 55 (1984) 267–86.

[5] Nilsson, "En marge de la grande inscription bacchique du Metropolitan Museum,"
Studi e materiali di storia delle religioni 10 (1934) 1–17, esp. 3–8 = *Opuscula Selecta* II
(Lund 1952) 526–32; *Geschichte der griechischen Religion*, I (3d ed., Munich 1967)
568–78, 614f.; *The Dionysiac Mysteries of the Hellenistic and Roman Age* (Lund 1957)
4–8 (pages that contain several errors). Other discussions of sex roles in Dionysiac cult
include L. R. Farnell, *The Cults of the Greek States*, V (Oxford 1909) 159–61; R. S.
Kraemer, "Ecstasy and Possession: the Attraction of Women to the Cult of Dionysus,"
HThR 72 (1979) 55–80; Henrichs (1982) 147f.

men and women under female leadership, which had their roots in
maenadic rites, are attested for Magnesia ad Maeandrum in the third
century B.C. and for Rome in 196 B.C.[6] In Hellenistic Miletus, the chief
maenad would not only lead maenadic *thiasoi* of women to the mountain but also conduct Dionysiac processions attended by the whole citi-
zen body on other ritual occasions.[7]

At this point it is important to notice that regardless of the changes
that occurred in the composition of Dionysiac groups, women remained
indisputably in charge of strictly maenadic congregations as well as
mixed *thiasoi* founded by a female leader. For example, around the
middle of the third century B.C. three Theban maenads were imported
by the city of Magnesia who organized (συνήγαγον) three local *thiasoi*,
at least one of which included male participants; the three founding
maenads were held in high esteem even after their death.[8] In nearby
Miletus women presided over the various maenadic *thiasoi*, both public
and private, and the chief maenad Alkmeionis led her fellow maenads to
the mountain (εἰς ὄρος ἦγε) around 200 B.C.[9] In the case of the Italian
Bacchanalia, both before and after their suppression by the Roman senate in 196 B.C., female votaries provided the dominant element from
which the leadership was recruited under the title of "priestesses."[10] And
finally, Plutarch's lady friend Klea, who was in charge of the Delphic
Thyiads at that time, held the office of "first maenad" (ἀρχηίς).[11] Chief
maenads are also found in myth, which thus reflects cultic practice. In
the *Bacchae*, for instance, Agaue, Autonoe and Ino each lead (681 ἦρχε)
one of the three Theban *thiasoi*.

It should be clear by now that any scholar who chooses to ignore or
dispute the fact that maenadic colleges were led by women must be either
blind to the evidence presented above, or in possession of new information
that would effectively contradict this evidence. E. R. Dodds put the modern study of maenadism on a new foundation, but he often went much
beyond the facts in the interest of his theoretical suppositions, which were
inspired by comparative anthropology and clinical psychology. A case in
point is the so-called "male celebrant," a new figure on the Dionysiac scene

---

[6] Henrichs (1978) 132–36, (1982) 151–55.

[7] Below, n. 9.

[8] O. Kern, *Die Inschriften von Magnesia am Maeander* (Berlin 1900) no. 215, with
Henrichs (1978) 123–37.

[9] The evidence comes from two Hellenistic inscriptions discussed by Henrichs (1978)
148–52, cf. "Die Maenaden von Milet," *ZPE* 4 (1969) 223–41.

[10] Henrichs (1978) nn. 42 and 44.

[11] Plut. *De Is.* 35, 364E (ἀρχηίς), with *Fouilles de Delphes* III 6 (Paris 1939) 3f. and J.
G. Griffiths, *Plutarch, De Iside et Osiride* (Univ. of Wales Press, 1970) 430; cf. Plut. *Qu.
Gr.* 12, 293f. (ἀρχηγός). An epitaph from Tusculum commemorates a nine-year old girl
who participated in Bacchic *thiasoi* as [ἡγ]ήτειρα σπείρης, or "leader of the Dionysiac
group" (R. Merkelbach, *ZPE* 7 [1971] 280).

which Dodds introduced into the scholarly discussion of Greek maenadism in 1940. Dodds concluded from two passages in Gilbert Murray's text of the *Bacchae* that the only men not excluded from maenadic rites were "male officials of the cult," in particular "one male celebrant, who is identified with the god."[12] A few years later he repeated in his immensely influential commentary on the *Bacchae* that maenadism "was originally a women's rite with a single male celebrant" and that "the male leader of the ὀρειβασία is in the sacrament identified with the god."[13] Dodds never explained to his readers how the maenads could be led at the same time by a "male celebrant" (according to his own theory) as well as a chief maenad (according to Euripides and the epigraphical record).[14] The contradiction is glaring, yet hardly anybody has taken issue with Dodds.[15] The vast majority of scholars, including R. P. Winnington-Ingram, Walter Burkert, George Thomson, and Ross S. Kraemer, have accepted the "male celebrant" without further scrutiny.[16]

The time has come for students of maenadism to face the facts and to realize that the notion of the "male celebrant" is an ill-conceived modern construct that must be given up. Dodds based his far-reaching conclusions

---

[12] Dodds, "Maenadism in the Bacchae," *HThR* 33 (1940) 155–76 at 170 n. 71.

[13] Dodds, *Euripides, Bacchae* (Oxford 1944, 2d ed. 1960) 82f. on *Ba.* 115; cf. 85–88 on *Ba.* 135, 136, 141 and 144–50 (quoted below, n. 60).

[14] Cf. *Ba.* 680ff. (three *thiasoi*, each of which is led by one of Cadmus' three daughters). Dodds *ad loc.*, in a discussion of the evidence for the "triple organization," takes female leadership for granted, without reference to the "male celebrant." R. P. Winnington-Ingram, *Euripides and Dionysus: An Interpretation of the Bacchae* (Cambridge 1948) 155 n. 2, while adopting the "male celebrant" from Dodds (below, n. 16), tried to get around the dual leadership by arguing thus: "For the Stranger seems to be the ἔξαρχος [*Ba.* 140] of the Theban Bacchanals also. In his absence Agave naturally takes the lead." If true (and it is true only as a gross oversimplification), this explanation would reconcile the male and female leadership only for the *Bacchae*. But what about the actual cult? When did male and female leaders take similar turns in maenadism as actually practiced? The contradiction becomes intolerable only if one goes beyond the *Bacchae* and into actual cult (as Dodds clearly does).

[15] I objected on several occasions, to no avail; see *ZPE* 4 (1969) 230 n. 24, Henrichs (1978) 133 n. 40, (1982) 224f. n. 98.

[16] Winnington-Ingram (above, n. 14) 37 n. 3 and 155 ("the god in the person of the celebrant" who is the "male leader" of the maenads); Burkert, *Griechische Religion der archaischen und klassischen Epoche* (Stuttgart 1977) 434f. ("doch können auch Männer zum Berg ziehen, ja der Anführer des Thiasos ist ein Mann," with reference to the *Bacchae*); Thomson, "The Problem of the 'Bacchae'," *Epistem. Epeter. Philos. Schol. Aristot. Panepist. Thessal.* 18 (1979) 424–46 at 424 ("led by a male priest [ἔξαρχος]," which reflects Dodds's interpretation of *Ba.* 141); Kraemer (above, n. 5) 69–72 (esp. 71 "there is a clear suggestion of identification of the male celebrant [ἔξαρχος] with Dionysus, which in turn suggests that groups of Bacchic women were led by an actual male celebrant or leader, who at certain times during the ritual identified with the god himself"). See below, n. 61.

about male participation in maenadic rites on a questionable text of Euripides that has been abandoned by more recent editors, and on the dubious assumption, ultimately rooted in Romantic tradition, that followers of Dionysus identified themselves with their god at the height of the ritual. In an effort to refute Dodds and to remove the male intruder from the company of the maenads, I will first discuss the two crucial passages from the parodos of the *Bacchae* that led Dodds astray; other evidence adduced by Dodds in support of the "male celebrant" will be reviewed next; in the third section, some comments on shifting and mistaken identities in the *Bacchae* serve as a reminder that human and divine roles are left in limbo by Euripides, whose conscious ambiguities have added to the confusion; and finally, in the same section, I will trace the alleged identity of god and human celebrant in Dionysiac rites back to its intellectual roots in late nineteenth-century scholarship, especially to the fascinating but highly speculative theories of Erwin Rohde and, ultimately, Friedrich Nietzsche.

I. The Subject of *Ba.* 115 and 135ff.: God or Man?

In several recent editions of the *Bacchae* (including those by J. Roux and E. C. Kopff) the two passages in question appear uniformly as printed below, if we discount various differences in spelling, punctuation and colometry that are of no consequence for our present argument.

Ba. 114ff.		. . . αὐτίκα γᾶ πᾶσα χορεύσει,	
	115	Βρόμιος εὖτ᾽ ἂν ἄγῃ θιάσους	
		εἰς ὄρος εἰς ὄρος . . .	
		115 εὖτ᾽ ἂν ἄγῃ Elmsley: ὅτ᾽ ἄγῃ L; P : ὅστις ἄγει	
		Demetrius Triclinius in L	
Ba. 132ff.		ἐς δὲ χορεύματα	
		συνῆψαν τριετηρίδων,	
		αἷς χαίρει Διόνυσος.	antistrophe B ends
	135	ἡδὺς ἐν ὄρεσσιν ὅταν	epode begins
		ἐκ θιάσων δρομαίων	
		πέσῃ πεδόσε, νεβρίδος ἔχων	
		ἱερὸν ἐνδυτόν, ἀγρεύων	
		αἷμα τραγοκτόνον, ὠμοφάγον χάριν,	
		ἱέμενος ἐς ὄρεα Φρύγια Λύδια·	
	141	ὁ δ᾽ ἔξαρχος Βρόμιος, εὐοῖ.	
		135 ὅταν Demetrius Triclinius in L; P : ὃς ἂν Robert	
		Gompf 141 ὅδ᾽ ἔξαρχος Kamerbeek, Roux	

For the past 150 years the text of lines 115 and 135 in particular has attracted much critical attention. The textual problems presented by these two lines are different in each case and are best discussed separately, even though many critics have assumed some kind of connection between them and treated them in conjunction.[17] Before we turn to a discussion of the nature of the problem and of the solutions adopted by successive generations of editors, it will be helpful to chart the shifting currents of critical opinion with the help of the following tabulation. The patterns and trends which emerge from it are directly relevant to the question of the "male celebrant."[18]

Text	115		135	
	relative	temporal	temporal	relative
Musgrave 1778	ὅστις ἄγει		ὅταν	
Elmsley 1821, ²1822				
Text	"		"	
Notes		ὁπότ' ἂν ἄγῃ or εὖτ' ἂν ἄγῃ	" "	
Hermann 1823	"			ὅς τ' ἄν
W. Dindorf				
Text 1833		ὅταν ἀγάγῃ	"	
Notes 1840		εὖτ' ἂν ἄγῃ	εὖτ' ἄν	
Fix 1843	"		ὅταν	
Schöne 1851, ²1858	"			ὃς ἄν
Nauck ²1857 (1860)		εὖτ' ἂν ἄγῃ	"	
Paley 1858, ²1874		"	"	
Kirchhoff 1867		"	"	
Nauck ³1871 (1889)		"	εὖτ' ἄν	
Tyrrell 1871, ²1892		"	"	
Wecklein 1879		"	" .	
Sandys 1880, ⁴1900		"		"
Bruhn 1891		"		"
Wecklein 1898		"		"
Dalmeyda 1908		"		"
Murray 1909, ²1913	ὅστις ἄγῃ		ὅταν	
Dodds 1944 [Notes]	"	["]	"	

[17] P. Elmsley, *Euripidis Bacchae* (Oxford 1821, Leipzig 1822) on *Ba.* 115, who printed ὅστις ἄγει while expressing a preference for εὖτ' ἂν ἄγῃ, noticed a structural and conceptual similarity between lines 115 and 141 but not between lines 115 and 135 (the latter of which he considered extremely difficult and possibly corrupt). W. Dindorf, *Annotationes ad Euripidem*, III (Oxford 1840) 698f., was inspired by Elmsley's εὖτ' ἄν (115) to change ὅταν (135) to εὖτ' ἄν for metrical reasons. Several editors, including Nauck (in the third edition of his Teubner text), Tyrrell and Wecklein (1879), followed Dindorf and printed εὖτ' ἄν in both places. The majority of the more recent editors of the *Bacchae* also prefer a temporal clause at 115 as well as 135 (see chart), thus interpreting the two passages implicitly along similar lines.

[18] Although I did not have access to every edition of the *Bacchae*, my survey is sufficiently representative to support the conclusions that I have drawn from it.

Dodds [2]1960 (Notes)		εὖτ᾽ ἂν ἄγῃ		ὃς ἂν
Roux 1970		"	ὅταν	
Seeck 1977		"	"	
Ebener 1980		"	"	
Kopff 1982		"	"	

The chart shows that the text of both lines remained on the whole fairly stable between approximately 1840 and 1880, a crucial period during which the textual criticism of Euripides reached new heights. Most editions of the *Bacchae* that appeared during this interval adopted Elmsley's εὖτ᾽ ἂν ἄγῃ at 115 and printed the manuscript reading ὅταν, or Dindorf's substitute εὖτ᾽ ἂν (inspired by 115), at 135. The same trend has again prevailed in more recent times. Since Roux's edition of 1970 editors have universally preferred a text which introduces a temporal clause in lines 115 as well as 135. The first major departure from what had become the vulgate text took place in the 1850s when F. G. Schöne replaced the manuscript reading ὅταν (135) with Gompf's conjecture ὃς ἂν, thus turning the second temporal clause into a relative clause. Schöne's example was followed by Sandys, Bruhn and Wecklein (1898), whose editions dominated the philological world from 1860 to at least 1909. In his Oxford edition of the same year, Gilbert Murray departed from the text of his immediate predecessors in both places by admitting a relative clause at 115 and a temporal clause at 135. It was Murray's text which formed the basis for Dodds's commentary and which, as we shall see, influenced his theory of the "male celebrant."

What is wrong with the transmitted text? At 115, the manuscript reading is metrically corrupt, as is shown by comparison with the corresponding part of the antistrophe. What is needed is a glyconic or "prosodiac" of the type ⏑⏑⏑–⏑⏑–⏑⏑–.[19] The corruption lies in the phrase ὅτ᾽ ἄγη as given in LP, which falls short of the characteristic "choriamb" that forms the center of the colon. Two conjectural remedies are available, Demetrius Triclinius' ὅστις ἄγει[20] (whence Murray's ὅστις ἄγῃ) or Peter Elmsley's εὖτ᾽ ἂν ἄγῃ. Elmsley's conjecture has been the overall favorite since the middle of the nineteenth century; only Murray returned to Triclinius' text. On the syntactical level, the difference between Elmsley's text and that of Triclinius is merely one between a temporal and a relative clause. In terms of substance, however, the choice is between Bromios (i.e. the god Dionysus) as leader of the *thiasoi* (if Elmsley's temporal clause is adopted) or an unidentified leader (man or god?) who is equated with Bromios (if one reads ὅστις ἄγει with Triclinius). With the exception of Murray, editors

[19] See A. M. Dale, *The Lyric Metres of Greek Drama* (2d ed., Cambridge 1968) 166 n. 2 on the meter of *Ba.* 112/127 = 115/130; M. L. West, *Greek Metre* (Oxford 1982) 116.
[20] The hand of Triclinius in L was identified by A. Turyn, *The Byzantine Manuscript Tradition of the Tragedies of Euripides* (Urbana 1957) 242ff.

following the Triclinian text always assumed that ὅστις stands for ὅς and that "it is Bromios who leads the *thiasoi*."[21] As long as it is Dionysus who leads the maenads, the problem of the "male celebrant" (who is, according to Dodds's own definition, a man, not a god) does not arise. The god himself is often imagined as present among the maenads in both myth and cult; in one inscription he is explicitly invoked as "the leader of the swift maenads."[22] It was Murray, though, who substituted a male *human* leader, ultimately to be identified with Dionysus, when he rendered 115 Βρόμιος ὅστις ἄγῃ θιάσους as "Bacchus fit quicumque ducit thiasos"[23] in the critical apparatus of his Oxford text.[24]

Line 135 presents a different and more intricate problem which has been discussed more than once in recent years.[25] The transmitted text, though syntactically sound, is not above suspicion.[26] Even where the text of

21 S. Musgrave's edition of Euripides (Oxford 1778) 404 on *Ba.* 115: "Non significat *quicunque* sed *simpliciter qui.* . . . Sensus est: *Bacchus*, Bacchus revera est qui thiasos in montem ducit." Musgrave's explanation was adopted by Elmsley (above, n. 17) and G. Hermann. On ὅστις preceded by a definite antecedent in tragic diction see most recently A. C. Moorhouse, *The Syntax of Sophocles* (Leiden 1982) 265f.

22 *Brit. Mus. Inscr.* 902.1 (Halicarnassus, 3d century B.C.) addresses Dionysus poetically as θοᾶν ληναγέτα Βακχᾶν. Cf. Aesch. *Eum.* 25 ἐξ οὗτε Βάκχαις ἐστρατήγησεν θεός and Eur. *Ba.* 566ff. Εὔιος . . . μαινάδας ἄξει. According to Diod. 4.3.3 cultic maenads celebrated τὴν παρουσίαν τοῦ Διονύσου (see below, n. 32); cf. Soph. *Ant.* 1149ff. and *OT* 211f.

23 Echoed by A. W. Verrall, *The Bacchants of Euripides and Other Essays* (Cambridge 1910) 42 n. 4: "Whosoever leads the companies is a Bromios" (adduced by Verrall to support the notion of a human "leader" as well as "the mystic assimilation of the worshipper to the god," a clear anticipation of Dodds's view). Cf. G. S. Kirk, *The Bacchae of Euripides, Translated with an Introduction and Commentary* (1970, repr. Cambridge 1979) 39 on the implications of the two alternatives at 115 (ὅστις versus εὖτ' ἄν): "If '*whoever* leads the bands is Bromios' (that is, Dionysus), then the chorus is asserting that any human leader actually becomes the god as a result of his exaltation—a very remarkable idea. '*Whenever*' gives a less startling sense and a better sequence of thought: the whole land will dance whenever Dionysus leads his band to the mountain. Here the god is envisaged as the real leader, as indeed will be stated at 141."

24 In his translation of the *Bacchae*, which appeared several years before his edition, Murray still read εὖτ' ἄν ἄγῃ at 115: "when Bromios his companies shall guide hillward, ever hillward" (*Euripides Translated into English Rhyming Verse* [1902, 3d ed. London 1906] 84).

25 J. C. Kamerbeek, *Mnemosyne* IV.6 (1953) 192f.; C. W. Willink, *Class. Qu.* N.S. 16 (1966) 31–35; Roux's commentary (above, n. 3) 290; H. Oranje, *De Bacchae van Euripides: het stuk en de toeschouwers* (Diss. Amsterdam 1979) 155–59 (made available to me by J. N. Bremmer), revised as *Euripides' Bacchae: The Play and its Audience.* Mnemosyne Suppl. 78 (Leiden 1984) Appendix 4 (*non vidi*); W. J. Verdenius, *Mnemosyne* IV.34 (1981) 307–10.

26 The original scribe of L ended line 135 with ὄρεσιν (*sic*). It was Triclinius who added ὅταν, and the complete line was then copied by the scribe of P (G. Zuntz, *An Inquiry into the Transmission of the Plays of Euripides* [Cambridge 1965] 117). It is unlikely that ὅταν represents nothing more than Triclinius' own conjecture. If ὅταν were conjectural, however, Gompf's ὅς ἄν (which presupposes ὅταν as a genuine manuscript reading) would

the epode makes good sense, its meter is so unreliable that metrical considerations offer no guidance to the textual critic.[27] Not surprisingly, therefore, several scholars have tried to improve the overall meaning and coherence of the passage by rewriting it.[28] I shall ignore most instances of excessive deviation from the manuscript text of the epode,[29] not only because I consider them unjustified but because they are irrelevant to the discussion of the "male celebrant." The problem of line 135, if there is one, has to do not with the text as such but with its interpretation within the larger context of lines 135–41.

Who is the subject of 135–40? Is it Dionysus himself (who was last mentioned in 134 and reappears as Bromios in 141); or a single "male celebrant," as Dodds suggested in the 1940s; or (with ὃς ἄν instead of ὅταν) any of the human followers of the god, including the maenads of the chorus? Each of these mutually exclusive interpretations has had its advocates since G. Hermann first raised the question in 1823. He felt that if Dionysus were understood as subject of 135–40, it would then be intolerably awkward to have the god contrasted with himself in 141 (ὁ δ᾽ ἔξαρχος Βρόμιος).[30] Hermann's objection is subtle, too subtle, I think. It makes too much of the δέ in 141, whose force need not be adversative.[31] Given the emotional and hectic tone of the epode, it is surely wrong to look

---

lose its sole raison d'être, and so would its synonym ὅστις ἄν, which Oranje (preceding note) restores, unconvincingly, for metrical reasons.

[27] Cf. Dale (above, n. 19) 126: "The strange medley of metres in the rushing epode 135–69 is so complicated by difficulties of text and interpretation that I have not attempted its analysis here." In other words, meter takes second place in this case, and the business of establishing a text that is intrinsically plausible comes first. It is misguided, under the circumstances, to use metrical considerations as an excuse for a conjectural text, as Oranje does (above, nn. 25–26).

[28] Among the principal offenders are Wilamowitz, who moved line 141 before 135 (*Griechische Verskunst* [Berlin 1921] 577–80); Willink (above, n. 25), who completely rewrote lines 136–37 by supplying the human subject which he thought was missing in 136 and by inserting line 141 after πεδόσε in 137; and Oranje (above, nn. 25–26), who changed ὅταν to ὅστις ἄν because in his view line 141 presupposes a human celebrant as the subject of 135–40, thus excluding the god.

[29] Including Peter Dobree's suggestion to replace ἡδὺς ἐν ὄρεσ(σ)ιν ὅταν . . . πέσῃ with ἡδύ γ᾽ ἐν ὄρεσιν ὅταν . . . πέσῃς, which leads nowhere. Dobree's ἡδύ γ᾽ was adopted by W. H. Thompson (*ap.* J. E. Sandys, *The Bacchae of Euripides* [Cambridge 1880, 4th ed. 1900] 117), E. Bruhn (edition of 1891), G. Dalmeyda (edition of 1908), and H. Grégoire (Budé edition of 1961).

[30] Hermann, *Euripidis Bacchae* (Leipzig 1823) 26: "Ac primo, non esse de Baccho sermonem, ostendit, quod paullo post scriptum est, ὁ δ᾽ ἔξαρχος Βρόμιος εὐοῖ. Non enim, si de ipso dicebatur, ipse sibi opponi potest." He concludes that lines 135–40 must refer to worshipers of Dionysus in general (below, nn. 32, 36, and 38).

[31] Of the many δέ's that occur in lines 142f. (thrice), 144, 145, 151 and 165, not a single one is adversative. Without exception, they are "continuative," to use J. D. Denniston's term (*The Greek Particles* [2d ed., Oxford 1954] 162ff.).

for strictly logical progression.[32] If lines 135–40 are a description of Dionysus as leader of the maenads, we envisage the god exhausting himself in the performance of the maenadic ritual, to the point where he "falls to the ground" (137).[33] Such a scene is indeed vivid and bold, but it is far from inconceivable.[34] Once we reach line 141, the god is still the central figure, as he is in subsequent lines. But the focus has shifted and Bromios is back on his feet, ostensibly rushing to the mountains of Phrygia and Lydia: "And leading the way is Bromios, euhoi!" More and more editors seem prepared

[32] Once the chorus has set its eyes on Dionysus (134), the focus shifts from the god's exemplary role in the ritual (135–40) and from Bromios as leader of the *thiasos* (141) to Dionysiac miracles (142f.) and back again to "the Bacchic One" (145 ὁ Βακχεύς, i.e. Dionysus) who rallies his followers (146ff.). The swift movement culminates in a line in which Dionysus refers to himself in the third person (155 μέλπετε τὸν Διόνυσον, with Dodds's note on 151). Scholars who explicitly recognize the omnipresence of Dionysus in this epode (his ritual παρουσία according to Diod. 4.3.3 [above, n. 22]) include Wilamowitz (above, n. 28, 578) and J. Roux (in her translation and commentary). By contrast, most British and American commentators seem to disagree. Several of them (most notably Tyrrell, Paley, and I. T. Beckwith [in his edition of the *Bacchae*, Boston 1885]), while reading either ὅταν or εὖτ᾽ ἄν at 135, nevertheless take the unexpressed subject of the temporal clause to be not the god of 134 but "the followers of the god" (Paley) or "any wearied Bacchant" (Paley) or "the Bacchant" (Tyrrell, Beckwith) in general (cf. *Ba.* 73ff. for this unmarked use of the masculine; below, n. 38). To add to the confusion, Tyrrell, Paley and Beckwith identify ὁ Βακχεύς (145) as the human "bacchant-leader" (Beckwith), in keeping with their interpretation of 135ff., but grant divine status to the ἔξαρχος Βρόμιος (141). Finally, Dodds brings about a complete fusion of human and divine roles when he describes ὁ Βακχεύς (145) as "the god temporarily incarnate in the celebrant" (on *Ba.* 144–50).

[33] The interpretation of line 137 is controversial. First, who "falls to the ground"? Is it (A) the god, or (B) his human follower? Second, why does he fall? Is it (a) "through fatigue" (Paley), or (b) owing to a trance-like state (Dodds), or (c) while swooping down on his prey (Roux)? The following answers have been attempted: Ab (Verdenius [above, n. 25, 310]); Ac (Roux, *ad loc.*); Ba (Paley, Sandys and Bruhn, *ad loc.*); Bb (Dodds, *ad loc.*). I prefer Aa, with Wilamowitz, who paraphrased: "Er, der Führer der Schwärmenden, ist freundlich, wenn er sich vom Schwärmen Atem zu holen auf den Boden niederlässt" (*Verskunst* [above, n. 28] 578; cf. *Griechische Tragödien übersetzt*, IV [Berlin 1923] 167). "Gods are not fatigued" (Dodds) is hardly a valid objection (cf. *Il.* 14.352f.), especially when the god's behavior is modeled on that of his maenads, who are often represented as exhausted, either sitting or lying on the ground, in literature as well as art. Artemis too is tired by the hunt, at least in Ovid (*Met.* 2.454, 3.163).

[34] Scholars who found it difficult to envisage Dionysus as a practitioner of σπαραγμός and ὠμοφαγία include Kirk (above, n. 23, 41) and Oranje (above, n. 25, 156). Yet the active ritual role assigned to Dionysus in lines 135ff. finds support elsewhere (cf. Roux [above, n. 3] on *Ba.* 139; Verdenius [above, n. 25] 308–10): Dionysus was ὠμηστής ("Raw-Eater") in certain cults (Henrichs [1978] 150–52); on two Attic vases, the god himself is shown tearing animals (F. T. van Straten, *Lampas* 9 [1976] 66 with figs. 15–16; cf. J. Harrison, *Prolegomena to the Study of Greek Religion* [3d ed., Cambridge 1922] 450 fig. 137; *La cité des images. Religion et société en Grèce antique* [Lausanne 1984] 144 fig. 205).

to accept this scenario, and rightly so.[35]

Hermann's own solution was to introduce a subject other than Dionysus by replacing the manuscript reading ὅταν with a relative pronoun and a connective particle (ὅς τ' ἄν).[36] Several editors followed in his footsteps and changed ὅταν to ὅς ἄν (thus dropping τε). The scholar responsible for this dramatic change was apparently Robert Gompf, an obscure schoolteacher at the Gymnasium of Torgau near Leipzig in the early 1830s.[37] Gompf did not live to witness the success which his conjecture was to enjoy later, after its adoption by F. G. Schöne and J. Sandys in their respective editions of 1851 and 1880. If ὅταν is rejected in favor of ὅς ἄν, Euripides' description must refer to followers of Dionysus in general, regardless of their sex.[38] In his Oxford edition of 1909 Murray took exception to Gompf's

---

[35] Including J. Roux, *Euripide, Les Bacchantes*, I (Paris 1970) and E. Chr. Kopff, *Euripides, Bacchae* (Teubner edition, Leipzig 1982), the two most convenient editions available at the present time. Roux should not have adopted Kamerbeek's "elementary expedient" (thus Dodds, who rejects it) who tried to solve the alleged problem by writing ὅδ' ἔξαρχος Βρόμιος (above, n. 25, 192). Kamerbeek may not have realized that he had been anticipated by the Greek editor of the Aldine edition of 1503.

[36] Hermann (above, n. 30) 26f. His unfortunate conjecture was inspired by a grotesque misunderstanding of the phrase πέσῃ πεδόσε (137), which he paraphrased as "*quum in aequore campi venatur.*" He thus assumed *two* locations, syntactically connected by τε, where worshipers of Dionysus would enjoy (ἡδύς) their rites, the mountain (135) as well as the plain (137).

[37] Gompf (1807–1836) taught at Torgau (a small town more prominent in the history of warfare than in the annals of philology) from 1833 until his untimely death, according to the short notices in *Neue Jahrbücher für Philologie und Pädagogik* 7 (1833) 108, 17 (1836) 80, and 18 (1836) 358. I do not know where Gompf published his conjecture (if it is his), nor do any of the editors of the *Bacchae*, who either ascribe ὅς ἄν to Gompf without quoting their source (Wecklein [1898], Murray and Kopff), or give the credit for it to Schöne (Sandys), or suppress it altogether (Roux, among others). Schöne himself, the first editor to print ὅς ἄν, noted laconically: "ὅς ἄν st(att) d(er) Vulg(ata) ὅταν" (F. G. Schöne, *Ausgewählte Tragödien des Euripides*, I [Leipzig 1851] 32 on *Ba.* 140 [= 135]). Gompf published very little, if the standard reference works are a reliable guide (F. A. Eckstein, *Nomenclator philologorum* [Leipzig 1871, repr. Hildesheim 1966] 202; W. Pökel, *Philologisches Schriftsteller-Lexicon* [Leipzig 1882, repr. Darmstadt 1966] 98; E. Hübner, *Bibliographie der klassischen Altertumswissenschaft* (Berlin 1889, repr. Hildesheim 1973] 246). In his two known publications (*Sicyoniacorum specimen primum* [Berlin 1832] and *Sicyoniacorum specimen secundum* [Torgau 1834]), both of which deal with the history, the topography and the antiquities of Sicyon, he makes no reference to the *Bacchae*. It is hardly important to know which scholar suggested ὅς ἄν for the first time, but one would like to know the reason that prompted his departure from the transmitted text and his adoption of a conjecture that is so very reminiscent of Hermann's misguided suggestion (preceding note). (I am grateful to Professors Susan G. Cole and Rudolf Kassel for bibliographical help in connection with the elusive Gompf.)

[38] Sandys, Bruhn and Dalmeyda point out that ὅς ἄν equals ἐάν τις. Professor Kassel refers me to R. Kannicht's review of the second edition of Dodds's commentary (*Gymnasium* 69 [1962] 97; emphasis mine): "135 nimmt D(odds) jetzt Gompfs ὅς ἄν auf, *das freilich der Rechtfertigung mit der Teilnahme von Männern an der* ὀρειβασία *kaum mehr bedurfte*: das Masc(ulinum) bezeichnet lediglich die allgemeine Gültigkeit der Aussage

ὃς ἄν by noting "sed unus tantum vir," and reinstated the ὅταν of the manuscripts. In Murray's view, the "unus vir" who forms the subject of the
temporal clause is the effeminate and "sweet" (135 ἡδύς) Lydian stranger
(i.e. Dionysus in human disguise) described in *Ba.* 235–38. Murray never
reconciled his comment on 135 with his previous one on 115.

It was Dodds who in 1940 combined Murray's two separate and, conceivably, unrelated comments on 115 and 135 when he concluded from
135 that there was "only one male celebrant, who is identified with the
god."[39] Dodds's phrase "only one male celebrant" clearly echoes Murray's
"unus tantum vir," and his identification of that "human celebrant" with
Dionysus recalls Murray's interpretation of 115. In fact Dodds in his commentary of 1944 justified the striking conclusion that he had drawn from
135ff. with a mere reference to Murray's interpretation of 115. Whereas
Murray did not force the obvious meaning of Euripides' text when he took
the subject of 135ff. to be Dionysus in human disguise, Dodds went significantly beyond the printed text of Euripides and the stated intentions of
Murray by reversing the relationship between human and divine identities,
thus making the subject a "human celebrant" identified with Dionysus. As
far as the *Bacchae* was concerned, Dodds thus rested the case for the "male
celebrant" on Triclinius' conjectural text of 115 and on Murray's controversial interpretation of it. This would have been an extremely shaky foundation even if Dodds had been absolutely confident about Murray's text. But
he was not. He admitted that he actually preferred Elmsley's temporal
clause at 115.[40] As for 135, he said, "I feel no certainty about the passage."[41]
We are left to wonder why Dodds was at pains, at least in 1944, to wring a
dubious "male celebrant" from a text in which he had no real confidence.
Did he know of other evidence, outside the *Bacchae*, that would have lent
support to his conclusions?

---

und entspricht dem Gebrauch meist pluralischer (also verallgemeinernder) masculinischer
Participien für Frauen." In other words, even if Gompf's ὃς ἄν were read, the masculine
relative pronoun should be understood in a generalizing sense (see W. S. Barrett, *Euripides Hippolytos* [Oxford 1964] 366), without any implication about the actual sex of the
worshipers.

[39] Dodds (above, n. 12) 170 n. 71, discussed in section II below.

[40] Dodds (above, n. 13) 83 on *Ba.* 115. According to Dodds, Murray concluded in 1940
"that he no longer thought ὅστις right."

[41] On *Ba.* 135. Dodds wrote the above sentence before he became attracted to Gompf's
ὃς ἄν. He changed his mind between 1944 and 1960 after K. J. Dover had convinced him
"that ἡδύς can be applied to the worshipper as 'well pleasing' to the god" (86 n. 2). Dodds
never doubted, however, that ἡδύς makes equally good or even better sense when applied
to Dionysus himself, who is ἡδύς in the eyes of his worshipers and who receives this epithet several times in Greek poetry (see Roux [above, n. 3] 290 *ad loc.* for a selection of
relevant passages).

II. The Silence of the Maenadic Inscriptions

Dodds's published views on male participation in maenadic rites evolved in three successive stages over a period of twenty years. As the years went by, his views became progressively more dogmatic. He did not realize until 1960 that the evidence which he cited in support of his conclusions, and which he augmented with each new treatment, failed to bear him out. In his landmark article on maenadism, published in 1940, he still followed Nilsson and concluded "that this was originally a women's rite, and that the exclusion of men, other than male officials of the cult, was maintained to the end at Delphi, and down to Hellenistic times elsewhere also."[42] This is essentially right, apart from the intrusive reference to "male officials of the cult," and more detailed studies of maenadism undertaken in recent years confirm Nilsson's main point.[43] But who are these "male officials"? Dodds mentions two, the γυναικονόμος and the "male celebrant" (Dodds's own term, for which there is, not surprisingly, no Greek equivalent).[44] For the γυναικονόμος he refers to a well-known Hellenistic inscription from Methymna, according to which a local official called γυναικονόμος was in charge of a Dionysiac παννυχίς which was celebrated by women and from which all other men were excluded.[45] Despite its fragmentary condition, the text from Methymna makes it virtually certain that the γυναικονόμος himself was also barred from the παννυχίς. He was a "male official of the cult" in a very limited and passive sense only. During the Hellenistic period γυναικονόμοι kept a watchful eye on women's rites, Dionysiac or otherwise, in many city-states.[46] The Methymnaean inscription provides a

---

[42] "Maenadism in the Bacchae" (above, n. 12) 170, with reference to Nilsson, "En marge de la grande inscription bacchique" (above, n. 5) 3 = Op. Sel. II 52: "Les vieux mystères bacchiques étaient réservés aux femmes." Nilsson never mentions a "male official of the cult," let alone a "male celebrant," but states emphatically that "les hommes étaient exclus." Several decades later, however, Nilsson concluded from the late Lemmatist's title for A.P. 7.485 = Dioscorides XXV Gow-Page that "the leader of the orgia is a man" (Dionysiac Mysteries of the Hellenistic and Roman Age [Lund 1957, repr. New York 1975] 6 and, along the same lines, Geschichte der griechischen Religion, II [2d ed., Munich 1961] 100). The title ὀργιοφάντης does not mean "the man who performed the rites of the orgia," as Nilsson thought, but "one who reveals the orgia," i.e. hierophant (Henrichs, ZPE 4 [1969] 229 n. 21).

[43] Above, n. 4.

[44] "Maenadism in the Bacchae" 170 n. 71.

[45] IG XII 2.499 (4th century B.C.) = L. Ziehen, Leges Graecorum sacrae II (1906) no. 121 = F. Sokolowski, Lois sacrées des cités grecques (Paris 1969) no. 127. Cf. M. P. Nilsson, Griechische Feste von religiöser Bedeutung mit Ausschluss der attischen (Leipzig 1906, repr. Darmstadt 1957) 282f. (who thought that the gynaikonomos was present during the women's rites, an interpretation which was based on a misguided reading of the stone, as Ziehen showed); Henrichs (1978) 159.

[46] On gynaikonomoi and their role in Greek society see C. Wehrli, Mus. Helv. 19 (1962) 33–38 and C. Vatin, Recherches sur le mariage et la condition de la femme mariée à

welcome illustration not of male participation in maenadic rites, but of
the degree of male supervision to which maenadism, or what was left of
it, was made subject in the fourth century B.C.

From the γυναικονόμος Dodds turned to the "male celebrant,"
whom he found in the *Bacchae*: "Euripides in his description of the normal rite (Bacch., 135ff.) appears to recognize only one male celebrant,
who is identified with the god; he corresponds to the Μιμαντοβάτης at
Erythrae."[47] Dodds's approach to *Bacchae* 135ff. was evidently inspired
by the peculiar interpretations of Tyrrell, Murray and Verrall, who
introduced the human "leader" of the *thiasos* into the parodos of the
Bacchae.[48] As we have seen, the Euripidean passage does not support the
notion of "only one male celebrant," no matter what one's Greek text.[49]
Ultimately Dodds's case for the "male celebrant" rests solely on the term
Μιμαντοβάτης in an Erythraean inscription of the third century A.D.
and on Dodds's questionable interpretation of that term. The inscription
honors T. Flavius Aurelius Alexander, a high-ranking local official who
had accumulated numerous honorific titles, including those of λει-
τουργός, Μιμαντοβάτης, ἱερεὺς θεοῦ Ἀλεξάνδρου, ἀγωνοθέτης τῶν
Διονυσίων, and ἱερεὺς τῆς Ἰωνίας.[50] That Aurelius Alexander had
climbed Mt. Mimas (a mountain range in the area[51]) in an official capacity and, more specifically, in observance of a local ritual custom is a
conclusion which is hard to escape. It is not so obvious, however, that the
cult in question should have been Dionysiac, let alone maenadic. As
Dodds himself admitted, "that the title is Dionysiac is not certain."[52] In
at least one instance, ritual mountain-climbing was performed by Greek
men for a deity other than Dionysus: in Magnesia ad Maeandrum

---

l'époque hellénistique (Paris 1970) 254–61, who make no reference to the inscription from
Methymna. See also B. J. Garland, *Gynaikonomoi: an Investigation of Greek Censors of
Women* (Diss. Johns Hopkins University, 1981; *non vidi*).

[47] Loc. cit. (above, n. 44).

[48] Above, nn. 23 and 32, and section III below.

[49] Above, section I.

[50] *IGRR* IV 1543 = H. Engelmann and R. Merkelbach, *Die Inschriften von Erythrai
und Klazomenai*, I, Inschriften griechischer Städte aus Kleinasien I (Bonn 1972) no. 64,
who adopt a Dionysiac interpretation of *Mimantobates* without mentioning Dodds. More
recently, M. Blech, *Studien zum Kranz bei den Griechen*, Religionsgeschichtliche Ver-
suche und Vorarbeiten 38 (Berlin 1982) 205 explicitly follows Dodds.

[51] On Mt. Mimas see J. Keil, *RE* 15 (1932) 1713f.; F. Bömer on Ovid *Metam.* 2.222; R.
Renehan, *Greek Lexicographical Notes*, Hypomnemata 45 (Göttingen 1975) 140; *ZPE* 38
(1980) 150 = *SEG* 30 (1980) 1327.5. If Aurelius Alexander had climbed Mt. Mimas for
pleasure, for example to enjoy the view from the top (D. Fehling, *Ethologische Untersuchungen auf dem Gebiet der Altertumskunde*, Zetemata 61 [Munich 1974] 52–58 dis-
cusses the ancient evidence on "Fernsicht"), his pastime would have hardly been recorded
in an offical inscription.

[52] "Maenadism in the Bacchae," 156 n. 5 = *The Greeks and the Irrational* (Berkeley/
Los Angeles 1951) 278 n. 4.

so-called ἱεροὶ ἄνδρες "leapt from precipitous rocks" and "pulled up giant trees" in honor of Apollo of Aulai.[53] Even if one assumed, for the sake of argument, that the Μιμαντοβάτης at Erythrai was a worshiper of Dionysus and that his ὀρειβασία was in fact Dionysiac, it would not follow at all that he was a "male leader" of maenads in the sense postulated by Dodds. Most likely he would have been attached to a mixed *thiasos* of any number of men as well as women who went together εἰς ὄρος as members of a Dionysiac club. In Locrian Physkos, for instance, the male and female members of a Dionysiac "*thiasos* of Amandos," which was named after its founder and flourished in the second century A.D., were obliged to pay a fine if they failed to convene εἰς ὄρος.[54] Inscriptions of this type reflect the ultimate decline of maenadism, and it is futile, to say the least, to try to solve textual and interpretative problems in the *Bacchae* with recourse to epigraphical evidence for Dionysiac cult, including the Μιμαντοβάτης of Erythrai (if he belongs here), that postdates Euripides by more than five or six hundred years.

Neither the *Bacchae* itself nor the numerous Dionysiac inscriptions found in the Greek world contain any reference to a human "male celebrant" who could have acted as the "leader" of local maenads. Yet Dodds proceeded in his commentary on the *Bacchae* as if the "male celebrant" were an established fact. What had started in 1940 as a casual suggestion became a major article of faith in the edition of 1944, which was reprinted in 1953 and, with some additional footnotes that contain "substantially modified views," again in 1960.[55] Without mentioning the Μιμαντοβάτης in his commentary, Dodds referred to his earlier treatment and to the auhority of Nilsson (who said the exact opposite[56]) for the view that the ὀρειβασία "was originally a women's rite with a single male celebrant."[57] This statement echoes that of 1940, cited above, except that the "male celebrant," who had been confined to a footnote as well as to the *Bacchae* in the earlier version, has replaced the "male officials of the cult." He is thus recognized as a major figure of maenadism as actually practiced. But Dodds went even further. While commenting on the alleged identification of the human Βάκχοι and Βάκχαι with Dionysus, he adds: "The organization would be like that of a witches' coven, where the single male leader was known to his congregation as 'the devil'."[58] Understood as Dionysus

---

[53] Paus. 10.32.6 in P. Levi's Penguin translation of 1971; cf. L. Robert, *BCH* 101 (1977) 77–88 and 102 (1978) 538–43, who considers the rite an "oribasie" for Apollo and tries, less convincingly, to connect it with the Magnesian cult of Dionysus as well.

[54] *IG* IX 1².3.670 = Sokolowski, *LSCG* (above, n. 45) no. 181; cf. Henrichs (1978) 155f.

[55] Above, n. 13. The quotation is from the Preface to the revised edition of 1960.

[56] Above, n. 42.

[57] Dodds (above, n. 13) 83 on *Ba.* 115.

[58] Reference as in preceding note. On the "male celebrant" as an incarnation of Dionysus, see section III.

incarnate, the "male celebrant" has finally become the Greek equivalent of the devil incarnate of medieval witchcraft, and the comparative method, inherited by Dodds from J. G. Frazer and the Cambridge school and conspicuous throughout *The Greeks and the Irrational*, is invoked to clinch the argument in favor of the "male celebrant."

In both editions of Dodds's commentary the "male celebrant" makes his first appearance in the note on *Ba*. 115, as "the most natural explanation" of Triclinius' text Βρόμιος ὅστις ἄγῃ θιάσους, even though Dodds himself rejects this text the moment he turns from *Religionsgeschichte* to textual criticism (in that order!) later in the same note.[59] In subsequent notes this celebrant and his special status are taken for granted.[60] Created for the sole purpose of explaining *Ba*. 115 and 135, the "male celebrant" has unfortunately become a celebrity of sorts who continues to attract the interest of classicists and non-classicists alike.[61] He would have been retired more than two decades ago, if users of the revised edition had paid attention to Dodds's second thoughts. In an addendum to his note on *Ba*. 135, which is his last word on the matter, Dodds reversed himself completely: he returned to Gompf's ὃς ἄν and renounced the "male celebrant." Reminding us that "men were admitted to the ὄργια," he now concluded that while "true of the situation on Cithaeron,"[62] the single "male celebrant" did *not* exist in actual Dionysiac cult, which either excluded men

---

[59] Dodds (above, n. 13) 83.

[60] Dodds (above, n. 13) 86 on *Ba*. 135 ("the god *in the person of his* ἔξαρχος or celebrant priest"), 87 on *Ba*. 136 ("the celebrant falls unconscious and the god enters into him") and on *Ba*. 144–50 ("the god temporarily incarnate in the celebrant").

[61] B. Simon, *Mind and Madness: the Classical Roots of Modern Psychiatry* (Ithaca 1978) 257: "Dionysus, a male god, understands the feeling and needs of women. In this sense, the god (in myth) and the cult leader (in reality) correspond to the physician in the treatment of the hysterical woman" (I refrain from comment); L. Feder, *Madness in Literature* (Princeton 1980) 55: "It is generally agreed that the worship of Dionysus 'was originally a women's rite with a single male celebrant' [with reference to Dodds on *Ba*. 115], although there is evidence of later male participation in such rites" (an unobjectionable summary of the *communis opinio* created by Dodds's commentary; as usual, his later rejection of the "male celebrant" is ignored). On the adoption of the "male celebrant" by classicists and historians of religion, see above, n. 16. Some interpreters of the *Bacchae* are undecided; cf. Kirk (above, n. 23) 6 ("led by an imagined god or his human priest"), and C. Segal, *Dionysiac Poetics and Euripides' Bacchae* (Princeton 1982) 23 ("the subject of 135ff. is ambiguous, but probably the god is meant") versus 145 ("the fall of the celebrant in the parode").

[62] As opposed to the situation envisaged in the parodos. Dodds thought that the parodos is a "description of the normal rite" or "white" maenadism, i.e. actual maenadic ritual, whereas the two messenger speeches describe "black" or mythical maenadism ("Maenadism in the Bacchae" 159 n. 19 [= *Irrational* 279 n. 18] and 170 n. 71). Even Dodds acknowledged that Euripides' access to maenadism as practiced was at best very limited ("Maenadism" 169ff.). For criteria which will make it easier to differentiate between mythical and cultic elements in the maenadic record, see Bremmer's recent discussion (above, n. 4).

altogether or admitted more than one man.[63] With that decision, the debate over line 135 had come full circle, and Dodds left students of the *Bacchae* exactly where their predecessors had been over a hundred years earlier, except for the "celebrant priest," who is kept alive against Dodds's explicit wish by his readers and whose presence adds an unwanted third party to the two protagonists of the epode, Dionysus and his maenads.

III. Ritual Identification with Dionysus in the *Bacchae*?

Dodds's change of mind reflects a fundamental truth, which he apparently learned very reluctantly—the truth that myth and ritual are never exactly the same, and that even though maenadic myth as portrayed in the *Bacchae* does indeed recognize a special "male celebrant," namely Dionysus himself who leads the maenads in human disguise, maenadism as actually practiced did not.[64] The Dionysus of the *Bacchae* who hides his divine identity behind a human mask is essentially a conventional figure who acts out his dual role within the traditional perimeter of Greek religion and Attic drama. Gods in human disguise can be found already on the pre-Euripidean stage as well as in archaic myth.[65] In one of Aeschylus' lost plays, Hera appeared as a begging priestess in the service of certain Argive nymphs in order to bring about the downfall of Semele.[66] More to the

[63] Dodds (above, n. 13) 86 n. 2. For male participation in Dionysiac ὄργια Dodds refers to Herod. 4.79 (the initiation of the Scythian king Skyles in Olbia, a colony of Miletus) and to the celebrated inscription from Cumae (c. 450 B.C.) which marked the burial place of a Bacchic congregation (F. Sokolowski, *Lois sacrées des cités grecques, Supplément* [Paris 1962] no. 120 = L. H. Jeffery, *The Local Scripts of Archaic Greece* [Oxford 1961] 239 οὐ θέμις ἐνταῦθα κεῖσθαι εἰ μὴ τὸν βεβακχευμένον, in standardized spelling). The Bacchic rites in Olbia and Cumae were not maenadic, and it is not known whether or not women participated in them (cf. M. L. West, *ZPE* 45 [1982] 17–28 esp. 25ff.). It is surprising, therefore, that this particular evidence prompted Dodds to abandon his theory of the "male celebrant." He never understood the difference between maenadic and non-maenadic types of Dionysiac cult.

[64] The presence of Dionysus in maenadic rites was often assumed (above, nn. 22 and 32) but never enacted with the help of a male "leader" (above, p. 71). Dodds connected "the coming of Dionysus in the *Bacchae*" with the reception of the Phrygian cult of Sabazios in Athens ("Maenadism in the *Bacchae*" 173–75; *Euripides, Bacchae* xxiiif.), and like Sandys, he compared *Ba.* 141 (Dionysus as ἔξαρχος) with Dem. 18.260 (Aeschines as ἔξαρχος καὶ προηγεμών of women's *thiasoi* in the cult of Sabazios). This may well be relevant, but the bulk of his evidence points to the 360s, at the earliest.

[65] Cf. A. P. Burnett, "Pentheus and Dionysus: Host and Guest," *Class. Philol.* 65 (1970) 15–29 esp. 24f.

[66] Aesch. fr. 355 Mette = fr. 279 Lloyd-Jones (Appendix to the Loeb Aeschylus, vol. II); cf. N. Robertson, "Greek Ritual Begging in Aid of Women's Fertility and Childbirth," *TAPA* 113 (1983) 143–69 esp. 153–62 (who connects the plot with the Proitids). On ritual ἀγερμός see, apart from Robertson, L. Gernet, *Anthropologie de la Grèce antique* (Paris 1968 [partial repr. 1982]) 56ff. [76ff.]; K. Latte, *Kleine Schriften* (Munich 1968) 484; E. Fraenkel on Aesch. *Ag.* 1273; R. Merkelbach in K. Meuli, *Gesammelte Schriften*, II (Basel 1975) 1059 n. 3.

point, in the *Edonians* Aeschylus introduced Dionysus as an effeminate Lydian stranger who is not recognized by Lycurgus, Pentheus' mythical double.[67] Dionysus in disguise makes excellent theater because he is an unfailing source of dramatic irony; Ovid's clever imitation merely confirms his success.[68] In the case of the *Bacchae*, only the poet and the audience, apart from Dionysus himself, know who the stranger really is. Not even the Asiatic maenads of the chorus recognize the true identity of their "human" leader. It would have been out of character for the chorus to know more than the other human parts. But illusion and irony in the *Bacchae* are, characteristically, of two opposite kinds, designed to reinforce the fundamental dichotomies that run through the whole play.[69] As used by Dionysus in his successive dealings with Pentheus, dramatic irony is, in the eyes of the audience, a deadly weapon which disintegrates the king's identity long before the physical σπαραγμός occurs offstage. The ironic effect is reversed, however, and ignorance enlightened by faith has its immediate rewards when the pious chorus, which is unaware of the god's presence, implores him to leave his distant haunts and to come to the rescue of his own disguised self, and when moments later, after the palace miracle, the stranger appears onstage to complete the divine epiphany.[70] Far from being an end in itself, the human appearance of Dionysus throughout the *Bacchae* only serves to bring his divinity into sharper focus. As *deus praesentissimus*[71] he reveals his divine nature to believers and non-believers alike, but only those who recognize the god in him benefit from his presence.[72]

On this reading, the boundaries between divine and human states would seem to be firmly drawn by Euripides. At no time does Dionysus cease to be a god, and the audience knows it. Yet modern interpreters have blurred this essential distinction between god and man time and again. The rationalist tendency to play down the physical presence of Dionysus as a divinity in the *Bacchae*, especially in the parodos, and to reduce the god to a mere human figure who is no god at all, or who attains divine status only

---

[67] Aesch. frs. 72–74 Mette.

[68] Ovid *Metam.* 3.572ff. Ovid's Acoetes is Bacchus in human disguise (H. Herter, "Die Delphine des Dionysos," *Archaiognosia* 1 [1980] 101–33 disagrees). The Ovidian conflation of the *Homeric Hymn to Dionysus* with *Ba.* 434ff. is replete with allusions to Euripides' Dionysus in disguise, which are ignored in Bömer's commentary on *Metam.* (cf. *Metam.* 3.575 and *Ba.* 437; 3.582 and *Ba.* 438f.; 3.583 and *Ba.* 464; below, n. 71).

[69] This key aspect of *Ba.* has now been treated exhaustively in C. Segal's monograph (above, n. 61).

[70] *Ba.* 545ff., 576ff., and 604ff.

[71] Cf. Ovid *Metam.* 3.658f. *nec enim praesentior illo* (sc. Baccho) *est deus* (with Bömer's note *ad loc.*) and *Ba.* 500ff. The irony of having the god in disguise refer to his own presence is in both cases the same.

[72] *The Homeric Hymn to Dionysus* exhibits the same aretalogical structure. The classical study is still A. D. Nock, *Conversion* (Oxford 1933).

at rare moments of ritual exaltation, or who personifies a psychological condition inherent in his worshipers or in human nature as such, has been particularly rampant among British and Irish scholars. In 1871 Tyrrell set the tone of the subsequent debate when he took the masculine subject of *Ba.* 135ff. to be a male *human* being, the leader of the maenads of the chorus, whom he recognized in the Βακχεύς of *Ba.* 145.[73] Tyrrell's separation of the human leader, who is present among his maenads, from the god, who is not, was adopted in the commentaries of Paley (1874) and Beckwith (1885).[74] In 1908 Gilbert Norwood, who was much attracted by A. W. Verrall's rationalist criticism of Euripides, launched a full-scale attack against the literal veracity of the *Bacchae* and the divinity of its Dionysus.[75] Not only did he deny the dramatic reality of the miracles that take place in the *Bacchae*, what is more, he suggested that Euripides never intended his Dionysus as a god but as "a man masquerading as a god masquerading as a man," in other words, as an impostor whose mission was to mislead the audience.[76] In 1909 Murray, who was less interested in the divinity of Dionysus than in that of his worshipers, turned the Dionysus Βρόμιος of *Ba.* 115 into a *human* leader of the maenads who is ritually identified with the god;[77] three years later he described the alleged relationship between the worshiper and the god more fully: "A number of difficult passages in Euripides' *Bacchae* and other Dionysiac literature find their explanations when we realize how the god is in part merely identified with the inspired chief dancer, in part he is the intangible projected incarnation of the emotion of the dance."[78] In 1910 Verrall himself, in response

---

[73] R. Y. Tyrrell, *The Bacchae of Euripides, with a Revision of the Text and a Commentary* (London 1871, 2d ed. 1892) on *Ba.* 141: "Βρόμιος is described as Exarch, not as being really present with them, but as supplying the orgiastic furor; their actual leader is the Bacchant, v. 145, the pretended servant of Dionysus, whom, of course, the Chorus do not suspect to be the god himself." I am indebted to Miss Lucia Athanassaki of Brown University, who took my *Bacchae* seminar in the fall of 1982, for the observation that the "male celebrant," or at least his earliest ancestor, makes his first appearance in Tyrrell's commentary.

[74] Above, n. 32.

[75] G. Norwood, *The Riddle of the Bacchae. The Last Stage of Euripides' Religious Views* (Manchester 1908) 80–125. Almost a lifetime later Norwood recanted in his *Essays on Euripidean Drama* (above, n. 3) 52 n. 2: "I now discard the belief that he [i.e. the Stranger of the *Bacchae*] is a human prophet."

[76] Norwood as summarized by Dodds (above, n. 13) xlix. Dodds's seminal article "Euripides the Irrationalist" (*Class. Rev.* 43 [1929] 97–104 = *The Ancient Concept of Progress and Other Essays on Greek Literature and Belief* [Oxford 1973] 78–91) was a response to Verrall's *Euripides the Rationalist* (Cambridge 1895). Although Dodds condemned the rationalist Euripides created by Verrall and Norwood, his own attempt to substitute a human celebrant for the Dionysus of *Ba.* 115 and 135ff. reflects a similar rationalism, which goes hand in hand with his more obvious borrowings from the Cambridge school.

[77] Above, at n. 23.

[78] G. Murray, *Four Stages of Greek Religion* (Oxford 1912) 43 = *Five Stages of Greek*

to Norwood, confirmed the human nature of "the stranger" or "adept" in the three central episodes of the play, even though he acknowledged the divinity of the Dionysus of prologue and *exodos* (the "Man-God," as he called him).[79] Following Murray, Verrall regarded the Βρόμιος of *Ba.* 115 as a human incarnation of the god; but unlike any other scholar before him, he also assigned the same human status to the ἔξαρχος Βρόμιος of *Ba.* 141.[80] It seems to follow from this brief review of scholarly opinion that the human leader of the maenads, who duplicates Dionysus, was born in England between 1908 and 1910 out of a serious misunderstanding of Dionysus' role in the *Bacchae*. When Lewis Richard Farnell published the last volume of his monumental survey of Greek cults in 1909, in which much space is given to Dionysus, the alleged human leader of the maenads had not yet come to his attention.[81]

Dodds's "male celebrant" is nothing less than the ultimate product of this whole tendency to replace Dionysus with human surrogates. Like Murray, Dodds took the Triclinian text of *Ba.* 115 as his principal excuse for substituting a male leader for the god; like Verrall, he applied the same concept to *Ba.* 141; and finally, he adopted Tyrrell's interpretation of *Ba.* 145. The one text that influenced Dodds most is Murray's version of *Ba.* 115. He made it one of the cornerstones of his overall conception of Dionysiac religion, and referred to it as early as 1929 in a memorable passage:

> Euripides is dealing here with something based neither on reason nor on Homeric tradition, but on an immediate personal experience—an experience in which 'the heart is congregationalized' (*Bacchae* 75, the rendering is Verrall's), so that the worshipper is made one with his fellow worshippers, one also with the wildness of brute nature (726), and one with Dionysus, the spirit of that wildness (115 Βρόμιος ὅστις ἄγῃ θιάσους. I accept Murray's reading and interpretation of the line).[82]

Religion (Oxford 1925 [3d ed. 1951]) 44 [27]. Murray did not say which passages he had in mind; *Ba.* 115 must have been one of them.

[79] Verrall, *Bacchants* (above, n. 23) 1–160.

[80] *Bacchants* 42: "The mystic assimilation of the worshipper to the god, of the *bacchos* to the *Bacchos*, is asserted expressly only of the leader of the company, but it is doubtless to be understood of all in due degree" (with references to *Ba.* 141 and to Murray's version of *Ba.* 115). Housman deplored the "baleful influence" of Verrall on Murray's Oxford text of Euripides (in H. Maas, *The Letters of A. E. Housman* [Cambridge, Mass. 1971] 404, quoted with approval by H. Lloyd-Jones, *Blood for the Ghosts* [London 1982] 201f.). Verrall's approach to *Ba.* 115 is a revealing example of an equally baleful influence in the other direction. Verrall's influence on Murray was confined to textual matters; it would never have occurred to Murray to believe with Verrall that only "the pious, the indifferent, and the ignorant" among Euripides' audience would have taken the *Bacchae* at face value (*Bacchants* 17).

[81] L. R. Farnell, *The Cults of the Greek City States*, V (Oxford 1909) 85–344, esp. 159–61 on "the prominence of women in the ritual."

[82] "Euripides the Irrationalist" (above, n. 76) 102. While a student at Oxford, Dodds heard Murray's lectures on the *Bacchae*, which made a lasting impression on him; when he succeeded Murray as Regius Professor of Greek in 1936, he was already working on his

In this passage as well as in his commentary, Dodds takes far greater pains than his immediate predecessors to impress upon his readers that the human celebrant "is in the sacrament identified with the god," that "the god enters into him," or that "the god is temporarily incarnate in the celebrant."[83] Now this is doubtless the most peculiar part of Dodds's theory. For Dodds, the "male celebrant," and he alone, is by definition an incarnation of Dionysus, a view which derives its sole support from Murray's interpretation of *Ba.* 115. But upon reflection it should be obvious that ritual identification with Dionysus and the existence of the "single male celebrant" are in reality two very separate issues. Already Verrall, with infallible logic, saw that the concept of "mystic assimilation to the god," if true, must apply to *all* worshipers.[84] Farnell, who had never heard of the "male celebrant," believed firmly that in certain Dionysiac rituals the priest "temporarily incarnates the god."[85] Dodds alone linked the two issues. He first misused the methods of textual criticism and philological interpretation to remove Dionysus from two passages of the parodos of the *Bacchae*, thus creating the "human celebrant." He then proceeded, as a historian of Dionysiac religion, to confer divine status upon this celebrant, thus returning Dionysus, if only in a roundabout way, to his proper place.

Like Murray before him, Dodds was ultimately more interested in the concept of ritual identification with divinity than in the question of the "male celebrant." This explains why he could give him up so perfunctorily in 1960. Once he had divested himself of Murray's interpretation of *Ba.* 115 and of the "male celebrant," he continued to believe that *every* worshiper could be "made one with Dionysus." This view, which is shared by most modern interpreters of the god, goes back, as is well known, to Harrison and Frazer, and ultimately to Rohde and Nietzsche, whose works Dodds had already read as a student.[86] The following excerpts from the two German scholars, who are not usually remembered in this connection, may serve as a convenient reminder:

> Die dionysische Erregung ist imstande, einer ganzen Masse diese künst-
> lerische Begabung mitzuteilen, sich von einer solchen Geisterschar
> umringt zu sehen, mit der sie sich innerlich eins weiss. . . . Hier ist

---

Bacchae commentary (Lloyd-Jones [above, n. 80] 289f.). But when he reprinted his article on Euripides in 1973, he added, in reference to "Murray's reading and interpretation" of *Ba.* 115: "I now doubt both: see my commentary ad loc." (*The Ancient Concept of Progress* [above, n. 76] 87f.). Dodds's second thoughts are discussed above, end of section II.

83 On *Ba.* 115, 135, 136, 141, and 144–50; above, n. 60.

84 Above, n. 80.

85 *Cults*, V (above, n. 81) 105f. and 168.

86 For further details, I refer to my "Dionysiac Identities" (above, n. 2) 143–46, 159f., with nn. 51–54, 79, 83, 134, 216, and to "Loss of Self, Suffering, Violence: The Modern View of Dionysus from Nietzsche to Girard," *HSCP* 88 (1984) 205–40.

bereits ein Aufgeben des Individuums durch Einkehr in eine fremde Natur. (Nietzsche)[87]

Am Hauptfesttag ist der Priester der Repräsentant seines Gottes und geht ein mystisches *Eins-werden* mit ihm ein. Am Jahresfest der Stiftung, wo die Geschichte der Entstehung *dargestellt* wird, ist der *Priester der Gott selbst.* Er hat die Kleidung seines Gottes an. . . . Aus allem ergiebt sich die ursprüngliche Auffassung des *Priesters als einer zeitweiligen Inkarnation des Gottes.* (Nietzsche)[88]

Der Gott ist unsichtbar anwesend unter seinen begeisterten Verehrern. . . . Und die Feiernden selbst, im wüthenden Ueberschwang der Begeisterung, streben ihm zu, zur Vereinigung mit ihm; sie sprengen die enge Leibeshaft ihrer Seele; Verzauberung packt sie, und sie selbst fühlen sich, ihrem alltäglichen Dasein enthoben, als Geister aus dem Schwarm, der den Gott umtost. Ja, sie haben Theil an dem Leben des Gottes selbst. . . . Der mit dem Gotte in der Begeisterung eins gewordene heisst nun selbst Sabos, Sabazios. (Rohde)[89]

Der Priester tritt an die Stelle des Gottes, erleidet, was nach den von ihm celebrirten δρώμενα der Gott erleidet: so geschieht es ja vielfach. (Rohde)[90]

Rohde followed Nietzsche to the letter, but added the savage Thracian ambience. Dodds read Nietzsche through the anthropological spectacles of Rohde, Frazer and Harrison. In the final count, the modern interpretation of the Dionysiac mood has, on the whole, not advanced beyond the views of Nietzsche and Rohde, as sanctioned by Dodds. I do not wish to suggest for a moment that their views are wrong, although I happen to believe that the ancient "identification" with Dionysus, as with other gods, was less internal and less psychological than Rohde thought, and had more to do with external imitation of the god's mythical image through ritual action.[91] What is wrong, however, is to read their insights

---

[87] *Die Geburt der Tragödie aus dem Geiste der Musik* (1872), section 8.

[88] "Der Gottesdienst der Griechen" (lecture course, winter 1875/76), in *Nietzsche's Werke*, vol. XIX (part 3, vol. 3), *Philologica*, edited by O. Crusius and W. Nestle (Leipzig 1913) 85 and 87.

[89] *Psyche. Seelencult und Unsterblichkeitsglaube der Griechen* (2d ed., Freiburg 1898) II 12 and 14 (English trans., London 1925, 258).

[90] *Psyche* II 118 n. 2 (English trans. 353 n. 35).

[91] The external imitation of Dionysus was most conspicuous when Mark Antony, dressed in Dionysiac garb, entered Athens, Ephesus and Alexandria in triumphal procession as Neos Dionysos (Henrichs 1982, 157f.). Plutarch (*Ant.* 24) reports that he was escorted into town by Ephesian men, women and children posing as maenads, satyrs and Pans, and the Elder Seneca makes a similar point about Antony's entry into Athens (*Suas.* 1.6 *nam cum Antonius vellet se Liberum patrem dici et hoc nomen statuis subscribi iuberet, habitu quoque et comitatu Liberum imitaretur, occurrerunt venienti ei Athenienses cum coniugibus et liberis et* Διόννσον *salutaverunt*, a remarkable passage brought to my attention by Professor W. M. Calder III). In both cases, the religious context is ruler cult, not maenadism, and Mark Antony is not an incarnation of Dionysus, but a self-declared replica of

back into the *Bacchae* and its parodos, at any price, as Dodds did. In the end, Dodds realized his mistake and corrected it. Let us hope that modern students of Dionysus will finally take his word and drop the "male celebrant" once and for all.[92]

him. The psychology of ruler cult is complex, but not as complex as the modern notion of the "male celebrant" and his identification with Dionysus.

[92] The argument of section II has been much improved by the keen comments of Professor Jeffrey Rusten. Dr. James Diggle, who gave me the benefit of his opinion on section I, favors Gompf's conjecture at *Ba.* 135.

THE SADDLE-CLOTHS OF ALKIBIADES

BENJAMIN D. MERITT

It is an honor to offer in memory of the late Professor Hulley a brief note on a new reading of an old Greek noun in an epigraphical context. An item in the list of the property of Alkibiades which was sold in 414/13 B.C. has been taken to mean "horsehair ropes" and referred to his bedroom furniture: [κ]άλο ἱππεῖο δύο.¹ The fragment of Attic inscription on which this item appears (Fig. 1) was first published by Adolf Wilhelm in 1903.² He read it as [κά]λο ἱππεῖο δύο. In 1912 this text was repeated by Charles Michel and in 1915 by Wilhelm Dittenberger³ with the same reading. The horsehair ropes were in the text but only by courtesy of restoration. When Hiller von Gaertringen came to Athens in the 1920s to verify texts for the new publication of the Attic inscriptions before Eukleides⁴ he—even with impaired vision at that time—was able to see part of a letter to the left of the lambda. He took this to be part of the alpha which Wilhelm had restored, and he read [κ]άλο ἱππεῖο δύο. The horsehair ropes were now entrenched and have continued to remain until this day. The first systematic study of the stone in its relation to the other fragments which record the list of confiscated property in 414/13 was made by W. K. Pritchett;⁵ he cites the photographs in his bibliography but makes no change in the text of previous editors. Somewhat later an edition of this inscription was published by Gerhard Pfohl⁶ which also retained the reading of [κ]άλο of earlier editors, and *IG* I³ 421, line 187 makes no change.

But this is an incorrect reading. The second letter of the line is an undoubted upsilon. The upper right diagonal stroke is preserved entire, and there is still enough of the surrounding surface above and below to guarantee that the letter in question could have been only an upsilon

---

¹ *IG* I² 330, line 19, as explained by W. K. Pritchett, *Hesperia* 25 (1956) 293.

² *JOAI* 6 (1903) 238, fig. 130.

³ C. Michel, *Recueil d'inscriptions grecques, supplement* (Paris 1912) 75, no. 1511; W. Dittenberger, *Sylloge Inscriptionum Graecarum*,³ no. 102.

⁴ *Inscriptiones Graecae, Inscriptiones Atticae Euclidis Anno Anteriores* (Berlin 1924).

⁵ *Hesperia* 22 (1953) 225–99, especially 243, line 214; 25 (1956) 293.

⁶ *Griechische Inschriften als Zeugnisse des privaten und öffentlichen Lebens* (Munich 1966) 99, no. 99, line 214.

Figure 1. *IG* I² 330 showing line 19 = line 187 of *IG* I³ 421

(Fig. 1). Alpha is definitely out of the question. The line, therefore, must be read as [τ]ύλο ἱππείο δύο. This can all be seen quite clearly also in the photograph which I published in *Hesperia* 3 (1934) 49. I was not publishing a new text of *IG* I² 330 but was using the document to illustrate the script of new pieces of the sale of confiscated property as they were found in the excavation of the Athenian Agora. I was able, however, to place correctly the two fragments of *IG* I² 330 and to note the join between them.[7] It was not until much later that I noticed the correct reading of the second letter as upsilon which is also visible somewhat less clearly but just as certainly in the photograph published by Wilhelm in 1903.

The clue to the meaning of [τ]ύλο ἱππείο δύο is to be found in J. K. Anderson's book *Ancient Greek Horsemanship*, published at Berkeley in 1961. Anderson devotes a chapter to Saddle-cloths, Dress, and other Accessories (pp. 79–88). Saddle-cloths were a luxury not known in mainland Greece in the fifth century, but enjoyed along the coast of Asia Minor as an inheritance from Persia. Anderson gives illustrations (see especially his plate 13b from Xanthos in Lycia) to show some of the more elaborate specimens. There are no representations of saddle-cloths even in vase painting or sculpture of mainland Greece before the end of the fifth century. Cavalrymen on the mainland in the fifth century rode their horses bareback as illustrated in the frieze on the Parthenon. Alkibiades was ahead of his time in having saddle-cloths in his wardrobe, but they accord well with his fondness for luxury and extravagance, and imports from Asia Minor are listed among his possessions.[8] But by the early fourth century we know from Xenophon that there were the two possibilities of bareback or the use of saddle-cloths for cavalrymen. Xenophon refers to the alternative to bareback as ἐφιππίου with the accompanying noun understood: ἐπειδάν γε μὴν καθίζηται ἐάν τε ἐπὶ ψιλοῦ ἐάν τε ἐπὶ τοῦ ἐφιππίου (Περὶ Ἱππικῆς 7.5). This passage with its contrast between riding bareback and riding on something on which the rider sat leads to the interpretation of what Anderson calls the saddle-cloth.

There is a passage from the comic poet Eupolis, a contemporary of Alkibiades, in which he links the word τύλη with the word κεκρύφαλοι.[9] κεκρύφαλος can mean a woman's hair net or the headstall of a bridle. Clearly a woman's hair net is nothing we need to concern ourselves with here; the linking of the word with τύλη suggests a meaning for both of the words with something to do with horsemanship. The meaning of

---

[7] *Hesperia* 3 (1934) 49.

[8] E.g. the Milesian-made beds recorded in lines 202 and 206 of *IG* I³ 421 closely associated with the saddle-cloths of line 187.

[9] Th. Kock, *Comicorum Atticorum Fragmenta* I, 305, no. 170.

τύλος = τύλη[10] is "*any swelling or lump*, especially a porter's *shoulder which has grown round and callous* from carrying weights" as the Boeotian says in Aristophanes, *Acharnians*, line 860. From this comes easily the second meaning of a "pad for carrying burdens on." A further meaning is clearly "a pad for sitting on" upon a horse, for the horse to carry the burden of a man, in other words the saddle-cloth, still an imported luxury in the time of Alkibiades for which there may well not yet have been a word in common use. When used with ἱππεῖος, as in the inscription, τύλος must mean a saddle-cloth. The noun understood in the passage in Xenophon may well have been equivalent to that τύλη linked with κεκρύφαλοι by Eupolis and in fact the τύλος of the inscription recording the property of Alkibiades. The words of the inscription give a very clear and simple translation "saddle-cloths for horses two."

If it be objected that these items of the inscription are in the context of Alkibiades' bedroom furnishings, it may be noted that such luxury items as these saddle-cloths would very reasonably be stored with his bedroom linens in his domestic quarters. In any case the word must surely be τύλο and τύλο must just as surely mean saddle-cloths when it is [τ]ύλο ἱππεῖο as it is in *IG* I[3] 421, line 187.

[10] *LSJ ss. vv.*

AN UNRECOGNISED DATE IN CICERO'S TEXT?

E. BADIAN

Cic. *Att.* I 16,13: *Lurco autem tribunus plebis, qui magistratum simul cum lege alia iniit, solutus est et Aelia et Fufia ut legem de ambitu ferret, quam ille bono auspicio claudus homo promulgauit. ita comitia in a.d. VI Kal. Sext. dilata sunt.*

Early in July 61 B.C., in a long letter giving Atticus assorted news from Rome, Cicero casually and jocularly mentions the *ambitus* bill of Lurco,[1] which the Senate must have thought important, but which (as far as we know) never became law. The relative clause near the beginning of this passage has caused immense difficulties. Watt, whose OCT may be consulted for an apparatus, obelizes *simul . . . alia* and commends *Aelia* for *alia* (an anonymous comment on the Mediceus and in a minor manuscript): clearly an early learned conjecture, or perhaps even just a scribal error in one of the two cases, based on the word *Aelia* that follows soon after. On purely technical grounds, this would not be a reason for approving of that reading. Some of the numerous conjectures are listed by Tyrrell–Purser;[2] with the exception of one by Clark, Shackleton Bailey brands them as making practically no sense. I see no reason to disagree, and shall not discuss them here.

Clark's suggestion, accepted by Shackleton Bailey, was *qui magistratus simultatem cum lege Aelia iniit.* Shackleton Bailey (pp. 159–60) translates it as follows: "Lurco the Tribune, an office at declared enmity with the Lex Aelia, has been dispensed from its provisions and those of the Lex Fufia too. . . ." It is, of course, quite close to the transmitted text, and if it made perfect sense, would be well worth considering. But I cannot see that it does.

First, the translation offered is not a particularly precise one; it is more in the nature of an explanation, and it considerably improves on the suggested Latin: *qui magistratus simultatem cum lege Aelia iniit* does not look particularly close to "an office at declared enmity with the *Lex Aelia.*" It does not attempt to render *iniit.* I do not know how common *simultatem*

---

[1] Probably M. Aufidius Lurco: see D. R. Shackleton Bailey, *Cicero's Letters to Atticus* 1 (1965) 323.

[2] See Tyrrell–Purser, *The Correspondence of Cicero* 1 (1904) 444.

inire is in Latin prose, though, of course, *magistratum inire* is very common indeed. In any case, a meaning can be found, and should be. Perhaps the sense would be closer to the original (while still somewhat improving on it) if we rendered, e.g., "who entered upon an *ex officio* feud with the Lex Aelia." The key word *iniit* at least appears in all its oddity in this rendering. It must denote a positive step voluntarily taken and can hardly (as is suggested by Shackleton Bailey's translation) be regarded as negligible, so that the whole phrase can then describe a mere accidental concomitant of Lurco's office. If correct, it must mean that he at least "took upon himself" the feud inherent in the office which he happened to hold. The common phrase *proelium inire* may give some guidance as to the kind of sense needed here.

Once this has been made clear, it cannot be at once rejected. We must, however, at least ask what sort of positive step Lurco might have taken in order to be thus described as having taken that feud upon himself. An answer could no doubt be suggested, if we accept the question as valid. The implication might be that Lurco proposed (or perhaps, rather, that he announced his *intention* to propose) his *ambitus* bill, even though it was clearly contrary to the *lex Aelia*: that he was so eager to pass it that he proposed it after the elections had been announced. It would then have to be added that the Senate, sharing his eagerness, rescued him from patent illegality by dispensing him from the law (and from the *lex Fufia* as well).

This seems a good deal to construct in order to bolster a conjectural phrase. What is more, it lacks conviction. If the Senate was so eager to pass that bill, surely Lurco would have found out about this earlier and not have got himself into a situation where he appeared to be about to break the *lex Aelia*? In other words, the reconstruction necessitated by proper attention to the conjecture seems historically otiose. Yet I have not thought of anything significantly less complex that would still be compatible with the sense offered by Clark's phrase.

Let us, however, for the sake of argument accept this reconstruction, so that sense emerges for the conjecture. How good is that sense in other respects? Was there indeed a *magistratus simultas* which Lurco could be said to have taken upon himself? Of course, the *leges Aelia et Fufia* are frequently cited by Cicero as bulwarks of the *res publica* against tribunician demagogy. They were clearly a *restraint* upon the tribunate.[3] But it takes two to make a *simultas*. And although one might *expect* tribunes to be *ex officio* hostile to these laws,[4] this expectation is

---

[3] Cicero's references to them are particularly frequent in connection with Vatinius' failure to observe them and P. Clodius' alleged abolition of them. A representative passage (*red. Sen.* 11) is quoted by Shackleton Bailey, l.c.

[4] *Prima facie*, of course, equally to both of them. There is no reason why the *lex Aelia*

not borne out by scrutiny of the facts. Indeed, as soon as we examine the passages where Cicero chooses to elaborate upon his general statement regarding these laws, we find that his point is precisely that tribunes had always unquestioningly *obeyed* these laws, not that they had fought against them. See, e.g., *Vat.* 18: *lex Aelia et Fufia, quae leges saepenumero tribunicios furores debilitarunt et represserunt, quas contra praeter te* [i.e., Vatinius in 59 B.C.] *nemo umquam est facere conatus.* Clearer still, ibid. 23:

> *tu qui . . . sanctissimas leges, Aeliam et Fufiam dico, quae in Gracchorum ferocitate et in audacia Saturnini et in colluuione Drusi et in contentione Sulpici et in cruore Cinnano, etiam inter Sullana arma uixerunt, solus conculcaris.*

We could not have a more explicit statement of Cicero's opinion that, right down to 59 B.C., these laws had been universally respected by dogmatic tribunes no less than by ruthless dictators. No inkling of any feud can be discerned.

This makes it very difficult to assume, as Clark's suggestion leads us to do, that in 61 B.C., two years before the events of Vatinius' tribunate which Cicero so flamboyantly rehearses, he was already implying—and implying in a casual and offhand way, as something generally known—that tribunes had an *ex officio* feud with these laws that restrained them. Quite the contrary: it seems that no tribune had ever thought of attacking or even defying them. And in that case it becomes even more difficult to believe that Lurco—not notorious in the series of exteme demagogues—not only took such a feud upon himself, but was about to defy those laws (for the first time in Roman history), had not the Senate rescued him from his own action. Clark's conjecture, if properly scrutinised and carefully analysed, in fact makes no real sense in the context of Cicero's own words and thoughts, even though it produces Latin that can be translated.

What remains to be done? I would suggest that we might try to take the text as it is transmitted. The text of *Ad Atticum* is no model of accuracy, as is well known; but we must nonetheless first see, in each suspect instance, whether it does not perhaps yield sense to patient reading.

If we take this passage as it stands, Cicero is telling us, in a humorous figure of speech, that Lurco entered upon his magistracy "simultaneously with a different law" (i.e., different from the Aelia and Fufia soon

---

should be specified, without reference to the *lex Fufia*, as the one attracting peculiar tribunician hostility. We do not know, and it seems impossible to establish, what distinctions there were between the two laws. (See A. E. Astin, *Latomus* 23 (1964) 443ff., refuting an attempt by G. V. Sumner to find such distinctions.) In fact, in one case (and there are not many where one law is named by itself, without the other) where we find a tribune contravening one of them, it is precisely the *lex Fufia*, not the *lex Aelia*: in 54, C. Cato was prosecuted (and acquitted) on that charge (Cic. *Att.* IV 16,5; 15,4). That, of course, was several years after 59, let alone 61 (the date of the letter here discussed).

to be mentioned). This could be taken as a typical piece of allusive Ciceronian wit, on the assumption that Atticus would know a key fact: that on the day when Lurco entered upon his tribunate (December 10, 62) another law—one different from the two next mentioned—was passed. In principle, the assumption is surely credible, provided the law was of some importance: in that case, every Roman interested in politics would remember the date, a few months later.

That a law was passed on that day is also technically possible. December 10, the day before the Agonalia, was a *dies comitialis*.[5] In fact, since not many more than half the days of the Roman year were by now *comitiales*,[6] and several of them had to be reserved for elections, while others would be lost because of bad weather; since (moreover) a great deal of routine legislation had to be passed, as we can gather from the legal sources, and we do not even hear of most of it—in view of all this, the chance that a law was passed on any given available comitial day must have been quite high.

However, we still need to probe the precise point of Cicero's cryptic reference. Why should he (if we accept the text) be jocularly referring to a *lex alia* other than the Aelia and Fufia, and expect Atticus to pick up the reference, without saying more than that it was passed on the very day when Lurco entered upon office? There would be no point to the joke, if that law were a mere piece of routine legislation, or of no political importance. In fact, neither Atticus nor anyone else was likely to remember the numerous dates when such legislation was passed. We must look for a law different from the Aelia and Fufia, yet to be thought of in association with them, and of political significance similar to theirs.

There is also a further, purely technical, point to be borne in mind. Most routine laws, of course, were passed by tribunes. This, indeed, was the chief constitutional function of the tribunate in the middle and late Republic. However, December 10, though a *dies comitialis*, did not permit of tribunician legislation. A new board of tribunes was just assuming office, and there had been no time for the *promulgatio* required under the laws we have been discussing. December 10, therefore, was available only for consular or praetorian legislation.

Once we are aware of all this—of the kind of law, both in technical nature and in substance, that we must look for—a law that would be a perfect fit comes to mind. Some time in 62 (we are nowhere told in what part of the year), the consuls D. Iunius Silanus and L. Licinius Murena[7] passed a law dealing with legislative procedure. As usual, alas, we do not

---

[5] See A. K. Michels, *The Calendar of the Roman Republic* (1967) figures 3 and 4.

[6] See Michels (cit.) 35, finding 195 *dies comitiales* at this time.

[7] See *MRR* II for sources: the order of the consuls' names is given differently even, at various times, by Cicero himself.

know precisely what it contained, though at least one important part of it was a provision requiring that proposals of laws be given proper publicity. Schol. Bob. 140 St., commenting on Cic. *Sest.* 135, tells us that law *cauebat ne clam aerario legem ferri liceret, quoniam leges in aerario condebantur.* What precisely the scholiast meant by this cannot be known for certain. The phrase *clam aerario* suggests the prepositional use of *clam* (roughly, "without the knowledge of the *aerarium*"), but the figure is admittedly odd. Halm proposed *inferri* (a minimal change) for *ferri*—an easy guess, giving a totally different meaning, and quite possibly right. However, for an odd figure it substitutes an odd picture: a secret procession in the middle of the night, silently opening the locks on the *aerarium* and carrying tablets in for storage rather as thieves might have carried out treasure. The transmitted text has also found wide acceptance,[8] though I cannot find serious discussion. It can be defended by reference to Cic. *Phil.* 5,7f., where in a context of complaints that laws were passed without the legally required public notice, the *lex Iunia et Licinia* is mentioned together with the *lex Caecilia et Didia*:

> *quid? non ante lata quam scripta est? quid? non ante factum uidimus quam futurum quisquam est suspicatus?*

And this reference to publicity before the vote (and not secret storage after) gets further support from Cic. *leg.* III 11, on the process of legislation: *promulgata proposita in aerario cognita agunto*—a text which has, in this case quite irresponsibly, been obelized or emended, though it makes perfect sense, and the sense required. (The *tricolon* may be translated, roughly, "They shall put to the vote bills promulgated, put up on the *aerarium*, and known.") Here it is quite clear that what Cicero had in mind is not secret storage of laws voted, but proper and lawfully required publicity: the bill is presumably to be affixed to the outside of the *aerarium*, so as to be read in detail by anyone interested.

If this was the main import of the *lex Iunia et Licinia*, it is not surprising that in Cicero's mind it was associated with the *leges Aelia et Fufia* and is mentioned together with them (thus the only two references in the Letters: *Att.* II 9,1; IV 16,5). It completed and secured proper fulfillment of their requirement of promulgation. A cryptic allusion to this law in connection with a dispensation from the Aelia and Fufia would not be at all surprising.

If the text, and the interpretation here suggested, can be accepted as sound, the *lex Iunia et Licinia* becomes perhaps the only law transmitted to us in a purely literary tradition of which we know the precise date of passage.[9]

---

[8] See, e.g., Mommsen, *RStR* II[3] 546; Rotondi, *LPPR* 383; *TLL* I 1058.

[9] I should like to thank Professor Shackleton Bailey for looking at this note. As usual, the opinions expressed and errors committed are entirely my own.

MAIOR NASCITUR ORDO

Of all the episodes in ancient literature that which ends the *Aeneid* has recently generated the most impassioned responses. No one, at least no critic of the *Aeneid*, remains indifferent to Aeneas' slaying of Turnus, for it challenges some of our deepest feelings about justice and mercy. That is as it should be, for if the *Aeneid* is a great work of literature it ought to engage our mind and our emotions. Two major responses exist: condemnation of Aeneas for destroying Turnus, a response usually coupled with the belief that Aeneas is a dull creature with no will of his own, a man driven by fate; or acceptance of the deed but with a feeling of repugnance at its necessity, and this response is usually connected with an implicit conviction that the modern world, i.e., ours, orders things better than did the ancients.[1] We can despise Aeneas or we can tolerate and deplore him, but we cannot admire him, let alone approve or like him. Yet neither response does justice to what Vergil has achieved in the final scene of his epic. Indeed if we accept such views about the last scene, we call into question our understanding of the whole *Aeneid*.

But a close examination of the final scene may result in the resolution of these interpretations and in a demonstration that Aeneas is neither villain nor dupe, and even an admirable hero. In that final episode the actors see and speak, and one becomes angry and acts. Anger and action have captured the attention of critics to the neglect of the other two, yet speech and sight are inextricably bound to the anger and action. These four topics deserve exploration, but it will be well to indicate briefly my presuppositions.

The first, and most obvious, is that Vergil is a self-conscious artist, one who knows what he is doing and does it for a purpose. To assume any less about an artist is critically unsound. As an artist Vergil presents a concrete, detailed world in his poem. He is not writing a philosophical tract, but he is explaining, among other things, the relationship of the

---

[1] The debate will no doubt continue. Even now the bibliography is quite extensive, but summaries as well as references are conveniently found in W. R. Johnson, *Darkness Visible* (1976), esp. pp. 156–57 and in the annual bibliographies published by A. G. McKay in *Vergilius*.

divine and the human. The world of the *Aeneid* is a human world in which men and women think, feel, respond, and act. The divine world appears but to a great extent the divinities of the epic act in response to the will and actions of men.

Furthermore, the world, the cosmos, assumed in the *Aeneid* is a determined one, for it depends upon strict causality, and whether the actual cosmos has such an organization is beside the point. Only one character in the poem, Jupiter, perceives and understands the fact of causality; everyone else, gods as well as human beings, fails to take it into account. If such is the world of the *Aeneid*, what place then does "free will" have in the epic? Almost none it might be answered, but such a response would be somewhat off the mark, for even if the cosmos is determined there still exists the freedom, meager though it may seem to be, to act or not to act. No coercion upon the individual exists; he is free to do or not to do. But in either case consequences ensue. It follows, then, that the world Vergil constructs in the *Aeneid* presupposes that living men not only act but must act; the *Aeneid* does not suppose a world where the value of pure contemplation is an end in itself. This presupposition is in harmony not only with the familiar belief of the ancient world that men are judged by their actions as well as by their intentions, but more importantly, with life itself, for human existence is primarily a process from birth to death, one which requires that men respond and act at every step of the way. Implicit in the world of the epic is also the idea that some actions are successful and others not; some acts bring about death and others not.

One further point needs comment, and it has to do with the artistic presentation of the epic: the use of point of view. Who sees, hears, and interprets events is as important as what he sees or hears; but in addition how he sees, hears, or interprets is just as important, for he thereby reveals his character. In reading and pondering the *Aeneid* one needs to observe constantly who says or does what and with what degree of perception, for one needs to make judgments about the characters of the poem, if one is to understand what Vergil has achieved. Vergil no more than any other great writer wants his audience to accept everything at face value. But like any great writer he gives his reader indications and clues whereby a judgment can be formed which is both accurate and independent of the character who either speaks or acts. If one reads attentively, it becomes apparent that not everything is to be given the same credence. For example, one cannot always believe that Aeneas is telling Dido's court the full story of the fall of Troy; he stresses one aspect, the violence of the Greeks, but in his narration he reveals that more than Greek violence ruined Troy.

To return to the final scene; both Turnus and Aeneas see and speak, and Aeneas becomes angry and acts. The entire scene is a composite, but first it will be helpful to examine how speech is used and what the act of speaking itself signifies in the course of the epic.

Speech is first of all insubstantial. When Iulus gives Nisus and Euryalus instructions to carry to his father, his words are borne away by the breezes into nothingness: *sed aurae/ omnia discerpunt et nubibus inrita donant* (IX. 312–13).[2] Their lack of substance renders words ephemeral. Speech is sound striking air and reverberation on the ears of the listener. But not all sounds nor all words are speech. For example, in order to rescue Turnus from encountering Aeneas Juno devises a cloud which has the appearance of the fully armored Trojan hero. To foster Turnus' belief in the illusion, she gives the cloud *inania verba, sine mente sonum* (X. 639–40). It is evident that what is needed for words to become speech is *mens*, which may reasonably be translated as "intelligence," which must necessarily organize the sounds so that they become bearers of meaning.

Repeatedly in the *Aeneid* the shades or ghosts of the dead speak; in fact shades can do almost nothing other than speak. The connection between the ghosts and speech emphasizes the insubstantial quality of speech (it is like the shades of Creusa and Anchises which Aeneas tries in vain to embrace, II. 792–94, VI. 700–2) and it also emphasizes that ghosts and speech are signs. Just as the shades of Creusa and Anchises are incorporeal shapes of what they were in actual life, so speech is the symbolic shape of reality imagined or actual, for there is no absolutely necessary connection between sign and the thing signified. Because speech is independent of physical process yet in some way parallel to it, it indicates man's ability to associate and connect different planes of reality. Man alone in the animal world is able by speech to parallel or model external events and thereby to construct a world of perceptible signs which cohere. But in order for a speaker to speak meaningfully to another, both must agree on the set of symbols used. However, if both agree on the set of symbols, the speaker has only the obligation to present what he hopes will be a convincingly coherent recital of events; he need not concern himself with a true presentation of reality, so long as his listener can be persuaded that it is. To the listener, then, falls the necessity for testing the validity of what the speaker says. It behooves one who listens to have a keenly developed sense of critical awareness. But it is at this point that trouble begins. An acute critical awareness is a difficult accomplishment for men, yet without it disaster can too easily ensue. In the *Aeneid* Sinon's speeches to Priam and the Trojans vividly and disastrously for the Trojans illustrate what happens when critical awareness is suspended (II. 77–104, 108–43, 154–94). The Trojans from an unwillingness or an inability to test the tale of the Greek suffer

---

[2] All citations are from the Oxford Classical Text edited by R. A. B. Mynors (1976).

destruction.[3] As Aeneas' words suggest, all the proof seducing them into believing Sinon is ambiguous, including the interpretation of the appearance of the serpents which destroy Laocoon and his sons. But critical awareness not only tests the falseness of a speaker's words, it also proves their truth. If one hears but cannot discern the truth, he endangers himself. The Latins fail to realize that Latinus speaks the truth about the Trojan's arrival in Latium, so they rush headlong into war (VII. 259–73, 591–600). Of all the human actors in the *Aeneid* only Aeneas ever develops his critical awareness, and in his case the process is a slow, painful education which starts at his lowest point, the last night of Troy. As he develops his ability to test the speech of others, he also learns to speak as accurately as possible.

The motives which prompt the characters to speak are the same as those observable in everyday life: love, hatred, patriotism, glory, security, whatever. But what is more interesting is the degree to which the speakers speak in conformity with reality, and what is worth noting is that the lesser the degree of conformity with reality, the lesser the chance for successful persuasion. Sinon's speeches appear exceptional to this generalization, but it is impossible to tell, for of all the speeches in the *Aeneid* his are the only ones which cannot be tested by other data. One may want to believe a great number of things from what Aeneas says Sinon said, such as that he is a liar, that Odysseus never plotted against him, but given the evidence of the poem verification is impossible. No attempt is made by Priam or the other Trojans to prove Sinon's words, and so Dido, Dido's court, and even the reader is swept into a sympathetic, even pitiable attitude towards the Trojans. That attitude is part of Vergil's strategy in preparing the audience for the denouement, that unproven sympathy is sentimental and ultimately destructive. The demonstration is begun in book II and ends in book IV with Dido's death.

In the same second book Aeneas reveals how little he understood about the connection between speech and reality, for it is speech which almost destroys him as it does destroy his companions. Hector has told him that Troy is finished and that he should flee (II. 289–95); Panthus reiterates that Troy is finished (II. 324–35). But nevertheless Aeneas persuades a band of Trojan youths to fight on behalf of the city (II. 348–54). But as the episode ends speech itself, the very sound of words, betrays them and brings about the destruction of the band (II. 420–30). The exhortation to the Trojan band and its result, in the history of Aeneas his first utterance in the epic to other men, reveal a pattern observable throughout the poem. No matter what the motive for speaking, by as much as the speech conforms to the way things are, i.e., to

---

3 Note the use of the plural verbs at II. 145 and Priam's action and speech, II.146–51.

reality, by so much is it ultimately successful. The dialogue between Juno and Aeolus shows the same pattern (I. 65–80). Juno stirs up the winds in order to destroy the Aeneadae, but she fails to overwhelm Aeneas and the Trojan remnant; she succeeds only in delaying them. Though she knows the facts of fate, the facts of reality, she tries again and again to bend those facts to her will. On each occasion she uses speech, and on each occasion she is ultimately unsuccessful. Even Venus suffers in the same way, for her speech to her son in North Africa (I. 335–70, esp. 387–401) indicates that she has only a limited grasp of what Jupiter has just told her (I. 227–96), for her conversation with Aeneas, while in no detail false, encourages him to go forth to what will prove extremely dangerous both for himself and his companions.

Of all the things speech can do, it cannot change the real situation; it cannot coerce reality into a different configuration; it may persuade others to believe what is not true, but that does not alter reality; what it alters is the response of human beings. The point can be illustrated in Iarbas', Amata's, and Juno's allusions to Aeneas as a second Paris.[4] Iarbas and Amata may have some justification for believing in such an analogy, for Aeneas is a Trojan, he does come sailing to a new land, and he becomes involved with a woman. Iarbas, piqued by the scorn with which Dido rejected his suit in preference for Aeneas, vents his rage to Jupiter by labelling Aeneas as yet another Trojan adulterer. So too Amata, angered that Turnus is not to be her son-in-law, is convinced that Aeneas is only another rapist bent on destroying her daughter. But both Iarbas and Amata have incontrovertible evidence that such is not the case; Aeneas has come neither to Carthage nor to Latium to steal the most beautiful woman in the world as a reward for having judged Venus the most beautiful goddess. But Juno, a goddess who knows the truth as she says, has not the slightest justification for her accusation of Aeneas as another Paris. Her sense of outrage at what she esteems an act of *lèse majesté* impels her to the same false charge. Anger and frustration elicit from all three the same response, but the fact remains that Aeneas is not a Paris. The labelling of Aeneas as such points up the danger of analogy. Iarbas and Amata assert that the analogy between Aeneas and Paris is total and then act on their belief, and in Amata's case she persuades others to believe as she does. Seduced by her own words Amata reveals that she conceives of the present as an exact repetition of the past. Such a conception denies the possibility of change and so denies the future. Past and present are the same; what has been is what is. Pursued further, this attitude precludes the redemption of the past through the understanding by remembrance, for if the past is always present, it cannot be remembered. To believe as Amata does is to be in bondage to chaos,

---

[4] IV. 215–17 (Iarbas); VII. 321 (Juno); VII. 361–64 (Amata).

and, for the human being, to death. Amata's words betray her at the same time that they reveal her. Juno is in a similar plight: Paris' decision is forever present to her, and therefore her hatred is forever present. Juno's enslavement to hatred is comparable to Amata's bondage to death, and hatred is a kind of living death: hatred permits no change, and only by allaying hatred can change occur.

Dido suffers a similar bondage as her speeches reveal: hers is the wound of love which turns to hatred. The transformation is not hard to understand for the love she felt for Aeneas had little foundation in the reality that was Aeneas. Dido's speech to Anna at the opening of book IV indicates that Dido has not listened with a critical awareness to what Aeneas has told her about the fall of Troy and his wanderings, for she has absorbed only the fact of his suffering (IV. 9–14). As a result she constructs through her own words an image of Aeneas as suffering hero, and with this image she falls in love. He is as much an image, an artifact, to her in book IV as the simile describing her first revelation to him suggested (I. 586–93). Confronted by the actual Aeneas, who must leave for Italy, she gives way to anger because he does not conform to her view. In her passion the more she speaks the more enmeshed she becomes in her belief in her own words so that at last she can only see death as a release. If her words have not persuaded Aeneas, they at least have persuaded her.

These illustrations demonstrate clearly enough how often speech is used without regard for reality but only to incorporate a sentimentality which frequently results in death. But there are speeches in the *Aeneid* which do conform with reality. The best example is that of Jupiter (I. 257–96). In order to allay Venus' concern for her son he lays open to her the future of the race Aeneas is to found. In the *Aeneid* only Jupiter speaks clearly with full knowledge of past, present, and future, and he alone consistently speaks the truth. But others, too, speak with knowledge, and they are not believed. Mention has been made of Latinus and Hector both of whose speeches essentially concern the future, and for that reason they are not understood. To speak truthfully of the future, or to prophesy, presents enormous problems to men, as book III explores. Aeneas has been told he must go westward to found a city. He originally conceives of his mission as one to refound Troy or as close an approximation as possible. But this proves impossible in Thrace, disastrous in Crete, and he at last realizes that "city" and "Troy" are not to be equated. Buthrotum proves him right. But still his mission is murky. When Mercury greets him in Carthage Aeneas has become a Carthaginian, as the description of his dress indicates (IV. 259–64). He has forgotten the prophecies of Creusa, the Penates, and Helenus, and this forgetfulness permits his taste for dalliance to flourish. But why should he forget? The power of a voluptuous self-indulgence would not have worked so effectively had it not been for the very character of prophetic speech. No human being can understand the future, no matter how clearly it may be told to him and how receptive he is, for speech about the future cannot be tested or proved. We cannot know the future until it is present, and even then we may not understand it until it is past. Aeneas at Carthage is no different. To speak to him of Hesperia, a western land, could reasonably enough signify a city in North Africa. Even when he realizes that Troy is not to be refounded Aeneas still does not understand what *condere urbem* means. Does it mean a city of walls, houses, temples? So at first it does to Aeneas and the Trojans, and so it will to the Latins. Aeneas learns only in the underworld that it means a race of people. His failure to comprehend comes from his inexperience, his lack of understanding of the idea of the future, and Mercury at Carthage recalls him to his mission in the only way which could be meaningful to Aeneas, by referring to Ascanius, Aeneas' only tangible link with the future (IV. 272–76).

If speech needs testing what can one do then with speech about the future? Exactly what Aeneas does when the Penates first speak to him at Crete (III. 154–71) or Mercury at Carthage: go on in ignorance until something proves the truth or falsity of the speech. The acceptance of the unknowable future (note that Aeneas sails into a black storm when he leaves Crete, III. 192–95) and the ability to act provisionally are the hall-marks of the adult, and perhaps the hardest task placed upon human beings, for it means risking all without guarantees of success. Aeneas' education involves not only his apprehension and testing of the validity of words but also his willingness to accept speech provisionally. Aeneas begins his career by rejecting speech which is rooted in reality and has present application; he learns the pragmatic value of testing the utterance of others; and although he does not know (nor does he ever learn) how to test speech which concerns the future, he nonetheless is willing to move forward until such evidence comes to him. In the underworld he hears Anchises' explanation of the cosmos and the destiny of the race he is to found, but he does not know whether or not what Anchises says is true. But by his descent he signifies his acceptance of the possibility of the future, and this he can do because he has come to terms with his past. He can live in the present with remembrance of the past and what it has to teach him. The way in which Vergil allows the audience to perceive this fact suggests that Vergil's insight into human psychology was one of the most penetrating the world has known. He arranged his poem so that Aeneas first sees his past and fails to profit from it (in Dido's temple to Juno, I. 453–97), and then Aeneas tells his past, and in the act of telling it reveals the very lessons of it. To articulate the past is the only way to comprehend it, to make it coherent, for it is chiefly by words, by speech that one is able to construct a coherent view of the world. By contrast the erotic experience of Dido is directly presented; there is no attempt by the protagonists to recall it in words.

Only when he gazes at the Daedalian doors on the temple of Apollo (VI. 14–33) is there the faintest suggestion that Aeneas is viewing an analogy to his own erotic life. For what the experience of Dido looses in Aeneas is his own adult sexuality which for the rest of the *Aeneid* is never absent. Eros once awakened is never again dormant; it is unmediated reality whether we know it or not.

Aeneas, unlike Dido or Amata, is not held in bondage to death or to chaos. The career of Aeneas furthermore demonstrates that after his descent into the underworld he never again calls on the gods for reassurance about the future nor does he ever misuse speech, for he has learned not to rely on the false security of either. But it is only Aeneas who achieves this degree of tranquillity. Trojans and Latins alike continue to believe in deluded security, for they never learn how to test speech much less how to cope with the possibility of the future. When Aeneas is absent from the Trojan camp in Latium his companions show themselves all too eager to believe in unproven words, as the night action of Nisus and Euryalus illustrates. And so do the Latins who are described in book IX in the language used of the Trojans on the final night of Troy (IX. 164–67, cf. II. 265–67). But it is Turnus whose use of language needs now to be considered, for Turnus' use of speech tests all that has so far been said.

Judged by the criteria of meaningful adult speech as the history of Aeneas testifies to, speech which accords with reality and in so far as possible is verifiable by reality, Turnus fails to measure up. From his very first appearance he displays an unwillingness to listen attentively. In fact his insulting remark to Allecto disguised as Calybe hinges on his belief that old women cannot speak the truth (VII. 436–44). Lamentably for Turnus they often do. What Turnus failed to do, namely consider the remark and test its validity without regard for the speaker, is emblematic of his whole attitude toward speech. His preconceptions about truth, about its possibility as well as its utterance, deafen him to any voice other than that which he wants to hear. His attitude is evident in his interpretation of the metamorphosis of the Trojan fleet (IX. 126–58). Wanting to destroy them, he considers the goal accomplished in his terms when he witnesses their transformation.

Repeatedly Turnus boasts of his strength. The boasting is ostensibly designed to encourage his followers, but lurking behind his words is a desire to convince himself. He wants to believe his own words, to believe that they accord with reality. So long as he does not confront any challenge by an equal or a greater man he succeeds. His vaunts to Pallas and to the Trojans appear justified (X. 439–509). But Turnus is at his mightiest only when he knows Aeneas is away from battle. His exultation when the wounded Aeneas limps away (XII. 324–28) leads him to savagery against the Trojans, for he can only live up to his own estimation in the wholesale slaughter of those weaker than himself, and in this he is not so very different from Euryalus who fights only when the odds favor him.[5]

Turnus uses words only to persuade for his own ends, and his chief purpose is to soothe and flatter his own esteem. His address to Juturna explicitly reveals his preoccupation with glory (XII. 631–49), but when he at last faces the fact that he must fight Aeneas if his own glory is to be justified in even the smallest way, he still cannot admit that he was in any way at fault. He reproaches Juturna as the one responsible for keeping him from combat with Aeneas. But this is clearly not the case; nothing except his own desire prevented him from putting Juturna aside sooner than he does. The point is borne home in his final speech to his sister when he asserts that he will engage in single combat with Aeneas and follow wherever *Fortuna* leads (XII. 676–80). It is no longer Juturna on whom he can fasten blame; nor is it Fortune; he himself is guiltless of fault; he is a victim of chance. When one reflects but a moment one realizes that Turnus' blame of Fortune is the reasonable consequence of the belief that words can shape reality, that they are merely counters to be played with at will. As a result of such an attitude, such a person must, whenever his conviction is proved wrong, blame an agency outside himself, for in this way he preserves the illusion of his own prowess and soundness.

On the last day of battle both Aeneas and Turnus refer to Fortune. Turnus' reference has been noted. A bit earlier Aeneas had used the same word when in arming himself to go forth to fight Turnus he told Ascanius to learn virtue (*virtus*) and true labor from him, but fortune from others (XII. 435–40). Aeneas, who has proved himself a man, has no need to rely on the notion of chance as the source of good or bad fortune in life. The ways in which the two men use the word in book XII shows the vast disparity between them.

Not only the word *Fortuna* reveals their dissimilarity, but also the way in which each of them conceives of *Fatum*. To Turnus Fate is the same as Fortune, a capricious force which imposes itself upon him and for which he has no responsibility. By contrast Aeneas sees *fortuna* as chance, it is true, in our everyday sense, but he does not equate it with the word *fatum*. As a result of his descent into Hades, Aeneas has learned an essential fact of the universe, one which prevents him from ever again confusing the two terms, namely that the universe, the cosmos, is causally organized. It is perhaps not accidental that the word *fatum* has its primary meaning as "the thing uttered." The word in early Latin means an utterance of a god, an oracle, for only a divinity can

---

[5] The entire episode of the slaughter of the Latins (IX. 324ff.) by Nisus and Euryalus suggests that Euryalus is the more blood-thirsty; see 354. At 341 the full stop Mynors prints should be replaced by a colon.

perceive the connections between things. But when one reflects only a little, it is of course any utterance which is a *fatum*, for only through interpreters does one learn what a god utters. Hence every human utterance is a *fatum* in some sense. But what then does *fatum* mean in the *Aeneid*? It depends on point of view, and it is this which has given rise to much of the misunderstanding of fate in Vergil's epic. From the point of view of Jupiter, everything is fated because he perceives the causal connections between events, and between events and character; in his eyes there is no accident. But it is to him alone in the *Aeneid* that such a view is vouchsafed. All the other gods have only a limited point of view, and as a result have regard for only immediate consequences: Venus wants to protect her son, so she falls in with Juno's plan to stage that false marriage with Dido, little considering that her acquiescence will lead Aeneas to the brink of disaster. So Juno, who wants to protect Turnus, consistently employs means which only foster his anguish at his wounded pride. If the gods are limited, much more so are men. Since it is impossible for a man to foresee the consequences of any particular act or any series of acts or events until those consequences become manifest, it is only with difficulty that he can perceive their causal relationships. Indeed, it is most likely that even at his death when the pattern of his life is complete, he cannot see the figure in the carpet. So also one cannot see another's pattern. As a result, it is not uncommon to attribute to an external force consequences which were unforseen, and to call that force fate, and like Turnus to believe that it has at best only a capricious relationship with him.

Such then is speech in the *Aeneid*. Only Aeneas, never Turnus, before the final scene, gives evidence that he can understand how speech is to be used and what its limitations are. But an elucidation of the role of speech in the *Aeneid* is not enough for the understanding of the final scene of the poem. Turnus and Aeneas speak, but both also look. What, then, does it mean in the *Aeneid* "to see"?

Human sight is defined in Venus' address to her son when he contemplates destroying Helen: "I shall rip the whole cloud which, now blocking your vision, dulls mortal sight and wraps it in a dark, impenetrable mist" (II. 604–6). Clearly, normal human vision cannot wholly perceive reality. For what Venus reveals to her son's gaze is the cause for the destruction of Troy, symbolized dramatically by the gods Neptune, Juno, and Athena, supported by Jupiter (II. 624–33). No other person in the poem is granted the opportunity to learn that mortal vision is a misty cloud. The crucial word in the passage is the verb *caligat* (II. 606). It occurs only here, but the noun *caligo* recurs seven times from book III through book XII.[6] It always signifies a dark, rainy cloud through which

---

[6] As a verb: II. 606; as a noun: III. 203, VI. 267, VIII. 253, IX. 36, XI. 187, 876, XII. 466.

one cannot see, and it always appears in contexts associated with the underworld, death, and destruction. Because ordinary vision cannot fully see reality it has the potential for leading blindly to death.

In the light of these observations of the passage in book II the cloud of protection with which Venus shrouds her son and Achates as they approach Carthage and gaze upon the pictures in the temple of Juno and as they first look upon Dido takes on an ambiguous aspect (I. 411–14). If normal vision is dull, to obfuscate it further hardly seems a prudent measure, for men need all the clarity they can muster. The cloud of protection symbolizes the fact that Aeneas does not see his past nor Dido clearly, nor does Dido see him as he really is. Although Vergil alerts his readers to this possibility, it is, of course, not until book IV that this condition about each of them is realized. The failure to see reality is carefully worked out in the similes Vergil uses to describe Dido and Aeneas as they appear to each other. She appears first to Aeneas as comparable to Diana (I. 498–504), but latent in that simile is the disparity between appearance and reality. The disparity is enlarged in the pattern of the similes, and her madness and delusion reach their climax when she completely reverses the actual situation and sees herself as the hunted victim; she is identified with Pentheus and Orestes (IV. 465–73).[7] Her failure to see clearly and the consequences of that failure are brought dramatically to her consciousness in her death throes when after stabbing herself on the pyre she rises up three times, sees the light of day and falls back groaning (IV. 688–92). The description emphasizes her repugnance for and rejection of light, of life, but it also signifies that she can only die in the blaze of light which reveals to her the result of her own delusions.

The confirmation that Aeneas failed to see beyond the appearance of Dido occurs in book VI when in the underworld he sees Dido who is compared to a moon fitfully seen on a cloudy night (VI. 450–54). The simile recalls the simile of "Diana" in book I (498–504) and also puts the final bit of evidence before the reader that Aeneas in reality saw Dido at best fitfully, that he was misled by his own hopes in thinking of her as a source of safety when, as the final simile used of Dido in the epic reveals, she was in reality a harsh crag on which he could easily have been wrecked (VI. 469–71).

However, Aeneas who learned to speak truthfully, also learns to see as clearly as possible for a human being. Again, he achieves his sight by descending into the underworld. The paradoxical fact that he descends into darkness, into the obscurity of blackness in order to see, emphasizes the need for light and it also reminds one that "to see" means also "to

---

[7] For a discussion of the similes see R. A. Hornsby, *Patterns of Action in the Aeneid* (1972) pp. 89–100.

understand." The way in which Aeneas learns in the underworld is not only by seeing the organization of Hades but also by being told what he sees. The Sibyl explains the geography of Hades itself, and when he meets Anchises he learns in more detail about the organization of the cosmos and his place in it (esp. VI. 724–853). To show and to tell make it possible for one to learn. Were Anchises simply to tell Aeneas what the future will be, as everyone else does, would achieve nothing, and to show an unnamed parade of figures would be equally meaningless.

Aeneas' education is complete when he visits Evander's home, for it is here that the future Rome will be. Again in the episode, Evander like Anchises both shows and explains matters to him. Significantly the time of viewing is evening (VIII. 280), dusk, for what Aeneas sees and delights in is not the actual Rome, but the site itself in a natural and untransformed state. The future is not clearly visible, hence the appropriateness of eventide. But this point again brings to one's attention that light is needed for men to see and to act with as full awareness as possible. Throughout the poem daylight is frequently mentioned, for it is in the light of the sun that men act. Evander himself stresses the need for the clarity of light, that is why he sends Aeneas and Pallas off in the clear light of the morning (VIII. 587–91). All three of them know what they are doing and what risks each runs. Man needs light, but he also needs eyes unclouded by a physical, emotional, or intellectual impairment, hence Vergil's repeated use of *oculi* as the human organ for testing the reality of the thing seen and his use of that word as a metaphor for life.[8]

To see clearly is comparable to speaking clearly; both need a grounding in reality not in illusion. Both require testing or proving so that delusion may be excluded. In addition, though one may speak of the future through prophecy, one can see the future only in dream. Both the prophecy and the dream are untestable until the future comes to pass. Man can only accept them on trust, provisionally. To fail to do so leads to madness, to destruction. That the super achievement of seeing and speaking as Jupiter does is forever denied man does not prevent man from striving for the goal. Indeed the very condition of his existence as a person acting in a causally determined world requires that he strive if he is to accomplish what he can. The gift of the divine armor of Vulcan implies that Aeneas has learned all these lessons, for as Vergil says Aeneas rejoiced in it even though he was *ignarus rerum, ignarus* of the things which the shield portrays. As he lifted it on his shoulder he accepted his adulthood, secure in the knowledge of the past and aware of how to regard the future (VIII. 729–31).

---

[8] See, for example, I. 717, II. 68, IV. 661, 691, V. 438, VIII. 223, 254, IX. 731, X. 516, XII. 945.

Aeneas never is presented as a god nor is he ever compared with the sun (*sol*) or with light (*lux*). Instead Vergil does something more interesting. In metaphors and similes he relates Aeneas to celestial phenomena: the armor casts a reddish glow from the reflection of the sunlight and once Aeneas is compared to the star Sirius (X. 270–75) not only for his brilliant appearance but also because he is a bearer of destruction to his enemies. Vergil's refusal to compare him directly with the sun implies that Aeneas does not see or know everything as Jupiter, the sky-god, does but rather he knows as a human being.

The transformation of Aeneas' vision as much as his transformation in the use of language comes about because he knows. Turnus, on the other hand, remains captive of his own blindness (VII. 456–57). That he cannot see clearly is emphasized by the fuming torch Allecto casts upon him. His vision is clouded by preoccupations which prevent him from ever approaching a view of reality. Indeed the deception Juno practices on him indicates how cloudy a view he has, for the cloud image of Aeneas deceives him by its appearance and by its sounds (X. 680–86). Even when the cloud vanishes he never considers why he should have been so effectively deceived, and in that episode he lays blame solely on the divine world. Sight and sound deceive him because he can neither hear nor see.

The complex of ideas involving sight, light, and darkness surrounding Aeneas and Turnus reaches its climax on the final day of battle. Vergil tells that Aeneas upon his return to battle after being wounded did not deem it worthwhile to lay low in death those Rutulians who had turned their backs nor to pursue them, rather he tracked and searched for (*lustrans*) Turnus alone, Turnus *densa in caligine* (XII. 464–67). Turnus, while Aeneas has been out of action, has rampaged far and wide. In the process he has stirred up a cloud of dust and destruction. The use of the noun *caligo*, its final appearance in the poem, bears all the connotations it has acquired earlier: darkness, death, the underworld, and the obscurity of reality, man's inability to see the causes of things. The killing of others becomes Turnus' offensive and defensive protection. The imagery of the cloud has come full circle from its first appearance in book I. Turnus uses the cloud, a cloud of death, to protect himself, just as the cloud of book I was ostensibly a protection for Aeneas. Turnus, however, is not sought by a man who cannot see, but rather by one who has learned to distinguish as far as possible between appearance and reality. The use of *lustrans* with its association with the eyes, light, searching both physically and intellectually, and finally of purifying, emphasizes the attainment of Aeneas.

The imagery and the language of sight are concordant with that of speech. To see clearly and to speak accurately and so truthfully depend upon the ability to perceive reality, the understanding of the causal relationship between events and men and events. But that ability and understanding depend on the *mens* which controls the will, for it is only through the movement of the will that men act. In the *Aeneid* the will struggles to satisfy itself but it can only do so on the basis of the knowledge afforded it by the senses, especially sight and hearing, interpreted by *mens*. If the reports of the senses come through distorted, then the will acts distortedly. In the *Aeneid furor* and *ira* appear as the chief distorters. But *furor* and *ira* rise from a frustration of the will to satisfy itself.

Throughout the poem people are *amens* or *demens* in their responses and actions. Aeneas himself on awakening from his dream in which Hector warns him to flee, goes to the roof of Anchises' house where he witnesses the havoc of Troy. Madly, he says, he called for arms (II. 314). His understandable response to the situation is precisely what he is not supposed to do. The motives which prompt it are mingled, involving his anger at what is happening to his beloved city, a quite justified anger, and frustration that he is doing nothing to prevent it. A similar sense of frustration permeates Dido's responses to Aeneas' departure, and it is frustration of her will to destroy root and branch all the Trojans that drives Juno to her violence. But anger and frustration are not only connected with killing others. There is also a rage to live. Aeneas in the underworld asks his father what mad desire makes the souls of those who have died want to return to the shores of light (VI. 719–21). Anchises explains it on the basis of forgetfulness and a wish for life.

Vergil has presented a tremendous insight into the human psyche. Throughout the poem he never denies the existence of rage; it permeates every action and every scene, sometimes moderately, more often violently. *Furor* and *ira* in and of themselves have no moral content, for they have no intellectual content. Only the context in which they arise can determine whether they are justified or not. The tale of Hercules which Evander tells Aeneas is instructive on this very point. Both Cacus and Hercules are described as raging: *furis Caci mens effera* and *furens animis Tirynthius* (VIII. 205, 228). But the rage of Cacus, the embodiment of evil as his name suggests, has no legitimacy, whereas Hercules' does: he is incensed at the theft of his spoils, the cattle of Geryon. Hercules' satisfying his rage is presented as entirely fitting and as an action which issues in good for more than Hercules himself, a result which incidentally Hercules is not particularly concerned with. In addition Evander makes it quite clear that just rage does exist when he claims that all Etruria is roused *furiis iustis* for the punishment of Mezentius (VIII. 494–95). Rage is a "given," it is what we are born with, as Anchises' answer suggests. It drives us through life, as the actions of the poem show, and it dies only at death as the suicide of Dido dramatically portrays. Without rage there can be no life, for rage is the will struggling to express itself. As a result it can be either destructive or constructive for the individual and for others. It follows then that the individual's rage must be organized so that it harms neither the person nor another. Dido and Aeneas illustrate the point: the one learns that to change the will, to educate the will, is to educate the rage; the other never learns and as a result dies by her own hand.

In the last half of the poem, which presupposes the first half, rage appears in its relationship to the community of men, chiefly how the rage of one man permeates and affects the rage of others. As the Latins and the Trojans vent their rage they little consider that to satisfy it can entail death as much as life. Whether they realize it or not, they are equating life and death, as Vergil demonstrates by his repeated use of the imagery of the balance to describe the fortunes of the conflict.[9] Implicit in such an attitude is the destruction of life itself, for life is not death. Aeneas alone perceives the perniciousness of considering life and death as the same, and he rages against it when he learns that Pallas has been killed. Aeneas, furthermore, perceives that it is Turnus who has infected his allies and his enemies with the passion of this deadly equation. Aeneas' remark to Magus indicates his awareness of the infection of Turnus and its virulence among the Latin forces: "Turnus raised that despicable commerce of war when he killed Pallas" (X. 532–34). By killing Pallas, a surrogate for Aeneas, Turnus revealed that the life and death of the individual were of no moment, and Magus' attempt to bribe Aeneas with gold and silver revealed that he too equated life with an inanimate substance and so with death. The virus of the uneducated and destructive will spreads to the very flower of the Latin forces: Lausus, who rejects all counsel contrary to his desire, lamentably dies (X. 762–832). Since no other method is possible, Aeneas must use his rage against those who refuse to learn, he can do no other.

With this survey of speech, sight, and rage as they appear in the epic, one is in a better position to consider the final scene of the *Aeneid*. The fallen Turnus, humble and suppliant, extending his right hand and beseeching with his eyes, elicits the reader's sympathy as much as the sight elicited Aeneas'. Then Turnus begins to speak, and seems to admit his share of responsibility for the dreadful war waged between Latin and Trojan. But almost immediately his words reveal that he accepts no responsibility, for he says *"utere sorte tua"* (XII. 932), and his use of *sorte* reveals that for Turnus it was only chance that betrayed him. Conversely, Aeneas has won not from any superior abilities but by lot, that which is apportioned through no intervention of the individual. But as

---

[9] X. 755–57; the balance characterizes the war between the Aeneadae and the Latins without their respective leaders. The image underlies the presentation of the battle scenes in X and XI and even in IX. The justification of the balance is found in Jupiter's speech to the Council of the Gods (X. 107–10). The final appearance of the balance occurs when Jupiter is described weighing the fates of Aeneas and Turnus (XII. 725–27).

the uses of *sors* in the poem demonstrate, reality is not such a hit and miss affair, no matter what men believe.[10]

Turnus goes on to concede all to Aeneas: he has won; Lavinia is his; all the Ausonians have witnessed the defeat of their leader. Turnus' public humiliation hurts him above all else. He asks that he be returned dead or alive to his father (XII. 932–36), and the appeal of filial piety is a strong one. Yet previously Turnus has never seriously concerned himself about his father, Daunus, nor for that matter about any other father. In fact he has rejected any such plea for himself and others. But now when he thinks it may avail him to invoke such sentiments, he brings it forth. Finally, he tells Aeneas not to extend his hatred farther, *ulterius ne tende odiis* (XII. 938). In that last utterance Turnus exposes his failure to understand. Of all things that can be charged against Aeneas *odium* is not one. At no point is Aeneas shown hating individuals, as so many others do, usually those who are inspired by Juno. Only once is the verb *odi* used of Aeneas, and that is when he is described as hating delays which will end the war (XII. 431). Aeneas does not hate Turnus the man but what Turnus has wrought. Turnus pleads in reality for his life under the guise of being willing to surrender it. The language he uses is consistent with his previous practice, that is, it is magical in conception, for he hopes to persuade by coherently presenting an illusion of pious supplication to Aeneas.

Its artfulness, its rhetoric, almost persuades Aeneas. But the proof of Turnus' inability to utter the truth lies before Aeneas' eyes and betrays the duplicity of his enemy. The sight of the *balteus* and *cingula* of Pallas rouses Aeneas. With his eyes he drinks in the sight of the mementoes of his savage grief. These are not mere pictures but remnants of the dead Pallas. Once before Aeneas had gazed on reminders of his past, but on that occasion he had fed his spirit on empty pictures and the nourishment proved vain in that it only fostered his deluded sense of security (I. 464). Now confronted by reality and seeing it clearly he judges accurately what Turnus has said, and in doing so he finds Turnus a fraud. Inflamed by anger and fury at the presumption of Turnus' misuse of prayer, he denounces his fraudulence, and tells him that he must be sacrificed to Pallas. Whereupon he stabs him. Aeneas in doing so at last puts an end to the noxious pestilence which Turnus both is and fosters. The illusory world which Turnus embodied and believed in is ended on the sharp edge of reality. Vergil's use of the verb *condo* in this context *(ferrum adverso sub pectore condit* (XII. 950) recalls the opening of the

---

[10] See esp. VI. 72, VII. 254, X. 50, XI. 110, 165 where the contexts suggest more than mere chance. *Sors* does of course mean "chance" when used by men with regard to their view of their lot, but in the determined universe of the *Aeneid* in Jupiter's eyes there is no "chance."

poem where Vergil states that Aeneas is to found (*conderet*, I. 5) a city. The meanings of the verb *condo* have been explored throughout the epic: to found, to build, to bury, to hide, to conceal. Aeneas hides the knife in Turnus thereby destroying him; he buries in the darkness of death the false world of illusion and by doing so he founds his city of reality.

The departure of Turnus' soul to the underworld is characterized by the epithet *indignata*. On the one hand it bewails the failure of the scheme to persuade Aeneas to let Turnus live, and on the other it goes as an unworthy thing to the shades. Turnus had prayed to Manes that he would descend to death not unworthy of his great ancestors (XII. 646–47), but he goes forth *indignatus*, for he never has seen nor heard nor uttered the truth. His attempt to force the world to his view of reality, a palpably false view, failed as indeed it always must, for the cosmos is no capricious, haphazard chaos where black and white are the same thing, and to call one by the other is a matter of indifference.

Aeneas acts responsibly and with awareness of what he is doing. His anger and its satisfaction are justified, and his act reveals that he can willingly and freely assume responsibility for his behavior, the final proof that he is a mature man. Aeneas becomes, in one sense, an agent of the universe, but significantly this point Vergil does not proclaim. Jupiter had told the gods that the fates will find a way, that is to end the war, (X. 113) and the only way the fates can find a way is through men because it is only man who can create his own fate. The causally determined cosmos of the *Aeneid* gives rise to responsibility since men have the power to act or not to act at a given moment. But whether a man acts or not consequences follow and for them he is held accountable. Only in a universe which is chaotic can a Turnus shrug off any sense of responsibility.

In destroying Turnus Aeneas destroys also the last remnant of the golden age of innocence which was Latium, as Latinus' words to Ilioneus and the hundred orators described (VII. 202–4). But all such golden ages of innocence contain the seeds of their own destruction, for they can remain innocent only so long as they are protected both from intrusion from without and from the need to consider what it means to see, to speak and to act. Ultimately innocence means ignorance. If so, then the golden age of innocence is necessarily a world of illusion. But that does not mean that a golden age cannot be founded wherein men live in accord with both nature and each other. Evander gave the true description of the golden age, the Saturnian land, when he related how Saturnus brought together untaught tribes scattered on the high mountains and gave them laws. The age ended when the land was invaded by the Ausonians and the Sicanians, for they brought *belli rabies* and *amor habendi* (VIII. 319–27). Evander's tale points out not only the necessity of a community and of laws for a true golden age, but also that such ages can end. Nevertheless, it is this vision of the golden age which Vergil adumbrates in his epic for Augustan Rome. In demonstrating the intimate connection between sight and speech and their connection with reality and the consequences of that connection for men he shows how the individual and the society could attain their fulfillment. But Vergil is too fine an artist and too aware of human psychology to suggest that the achievement is once and forever. The struggle to become as aware as possible requires that each man struggle in each generation. This is one of the reasons for Anchises showing his son their descendants and for the history of Rome portrayed on Aeneas' shield. The battle is always within the individual and always one which affects society. That a golden age founded in reality can exist Vergil does not doubt, and such a vision is his *maior ordo*. Vergil's massive exploration of the problems attendant on such a vision, the most massive in the entire range of the imaginative literature of Greece and Rome, affords all the inheritors of the Augustan age the vision and with it the possibility of bringing it to birth.

VERGILIAN HEROES AND TOPONYMY:
PALINURUS AND MISENUS

ALEXANDER G. McKAY

Whatever its actual content and overt interest, every poem should be rooted in imaginative awe. Poetry can do a hundred and one things, delight, sadden, disturb, amuse, instruct—it may express every possible shade of emotion, and describe every conceivable kind of event, but there is only one thing that all poetry must do: it must praise all it can for being and happening. (W. H. Auden)[1]

Vergilian bimillenary celebrations during 1981 and 1982 produced a rich harvest of critical and interpretative essays on the Vergilian opera and their Nachleben. Bibliographic surveys covering both years, and extending into 1983, number something in excess of 500 titles.[2] Vergilian topography and toponymy received their due a decade or so ago, and scholars have tended to sidestep such issues since then. However, renewed study of two Campanian sites in particular during the bimillenary frenzy has inclined me to re-examine both sites and their Vergilian associations.

Vergil took pains to etch the personality of Palinurus in most sympathetic terms before his final venture into the Tyrrhenian waters.[3] As helmsman, his conduct is impeccable, alert, and responsible; his expertise with the vagaries of weather, seasonal sailings, and the stars (although Gordon Williams regards the details as incongruous)[4] is accomplished and reliable. His speedy assessment of the critical situation and his prompt manoeuvres rescued the Trojans from Scylla and Charybdis. His role as adjutant to Aeneas, after Anchises' death, even permitted him to challenge Aeneas upon their departure from Carthage—*nec nos obniti contra nec tendere tantum/sufficimus* (*Aen.* 5, 21–22). Although his role as *magister* is strangely passed over during the anniversary games at Trapani, nevertheless there is, as Putnam observed, an ironic forecast of his infinitely more

---

[1] An extract from "Making, Knowing and Judging," *The Dyer's Hand* (London 1963), Auden's inaugural address as Professor of Poetry at the University of Oxford in 1956.

[2] Consult A. G. McKay, "Vergilian Bibliography 1981–82," *Vergilius* 28 (1982) 65–80, and *Vergilius* 29 (1983), forthcoming.

[3] For Palinurus' earlier adventures see *Aen.* 3, 200–204, 269, 513–20, 561–63; *Aen.* 5, 12–25.

[4] G. Williams, *Technique and Ideas in the Aeneid* (New Haven 1983) 264–65.

tragic catastrophe in the ejection of Menoetes, *gubernator* of Gyas' ship, during the naval contest.[5] Ridicule and laughter greet Menoetes' emergence from the Sicilian sea, but enmity and death-dealing weapons await Palinurus' emergence from the Tyrrhenian sea.

Celebrations and farewells conclude the anniversary games for Anchises and the foundation of Egesta and the Trojans set sail for Italy with Palinurus in the flagship. Venus, herself a goddess with marine associations, patroness of Eryx and preserver of her Julian hopeful, negotiates with Neptune for her son's safe conduct.[6] Her request on behalf of Aeneas and the Aeneadae is granted with one exception:

> unus erit tantum amissum quem gurgite quaeres;
> unum pro multis dabitur caput. . . . (*Aen.* 5, 814–15)

Accompanied by his glamorous sea-nymphs, Neptune magnanimously calms the already serene Mediterranean and the passage to Italy begins. While others sleep, Palinurus presides gamely at his tiller during the silence of the night, resisting the inviting prospect of sleep.[7] His eyes are fixed on the stars. But Neptune's victim has been identified as Palinurus, and Sleep, in the guise of the hero Phorbas, father of Ilioneus,[8] attempts to seduce Palinurus into deserting his post. The helmsman resists the mortal blandishments but succumbs finally to unearthly means, for the god sprinkles the dew of Lethe over the pilot's temples and because the pilot still resists, heaves him overboard. Palinurus continues to cling determinedly to the tiller and wrenches away part of the stern in his fall. His cries for help are unheard by his shipmates and the fleet sails on without incident until Aeneas wakens with the sound of surf crashing on the Sirens' Isles. Aeneas realizes that his pilot is missing and assumes personal direction of the fleet through the early morning hours. His comments on Palinurus' disappearance are ironic in the extreme given the circumstances of his accident:

> o nimium caelo et pelago confise sereno,
> nudus in ignota, Palinure, iacebis harena. (*Aen.* 5, 870–71)

There has been considerable debate regarding the circumstances of Palinurus' catastrophe: was it an accident (his own account implies that turbulent seas were responsible for his being dashed from the stern); suicide,

---

[5] The naval contest: *Aen.* 5, 114–285; Gyas and Menoetes, 151–82. For discussion, Egil Kraggerud, *Aeneisstudien* (Oslo 1968) 167ff.; M. C. J. Putnam, *The Poetry of the Aeneid* (Cambridge, Mass. 1965) 75–78.

[6] Venus and Neptune: *Aen.* 5, 779–826.

[7] The final episode: *Aen.* 5, 827–71.

[8] Phorbas (*Aen.* 5, 842) equates with Homer, *Iliad* 14, 490. His heroic guise recalls the winged warrior Sleep (and Death) attending Sarpedon as depicted on the Euphronius crater in the Metropolitan Museum of Art, New York.

somnia tristia portans insonti (*Aen.* 5, 840–41) might imply despair at the interminable odyssey; or premature death from natural causes, after the pattern of Phrontis, Menelaus' pilot, who died from "the gentle arrows of Apollo" off Attic Sunium; or wilful desertion, a deliberate design to escape responsibility and add to the peril of Aeneas? The likeliest "court" verdict seems to be "accidental" death.[9]

Palinurus is the first ghost that Aeneas encounters in the underworld. The pilot's version there differs significantly from the poet's report in *Aeneid* 5; there is direct contradiction of details, and there is a firm assertion by the plaintive, apologetic ghost that the cause was by chance rather than predetermined.[10] After all, Palinurus was not aware, after Phorbas' heroic person was replaced by Somnus, that divine agency was involved in his misfortune. Drugged with Lethe's waters, bereft of his proper sense and general awareness of conditions, Palinurus reasoned afterwards that the ship had been caught in a sudden squall and that he had toppled into the sea when the ship lurched violently. Certainly he revived smartly and found the resource to swim for three nights and days against winds and current until on the fourth day he touched the Lucanian shore. Attempts to explain the contradictions by chronology of composition or as febrile lapses on the part of the poet have hardly emended or excused the situation.[11] Palinurus believed that he had fallen from the stern during a storm; Vergil informs us that he was a quasi-sacrificial victim required by Neptune, and that Sleep was the sea god's instrument. Since a change in weather is involved (Palinurus alleges a storm, Aeneas recalls a placid sea), the fault must rest with the pilot's assumptions rather than with the poet's faulty mechanics. The awesome, mysterious character of the event is underscored by its having occurred during an unnatural calm. Palinurus' protested innocence (as though to counter Aeneas' earlier assumption of Palinurus' retreat from responsibility) is altogether appropriate to the pilot's desperate longing for permission to enter the underworld and gain proper burial. Deiphobe, the Sibyl, will not permit Aeneas to respond to the entreaty. With characteristic brusqueness, she advises him that his murder will find ritual atonement and that his death place will bear his name. The sequel to

---

[9] J. William Hunt explores the range of possibilities regarding Palinurus' death in *Forms of Glory and Structure: Sense in Vergil's Aeneid* (Carbondale/Edwardsville 1973) 44–49. Cyril Connolly, *The Unquiet Grave: A Word Cycle* (New York 1945) 134–47, treats the pilot's enigmatic character and fate and suggests that Vergil strongly identified himself with the *gubernator*. See more recently David Pryce-Jones, *Cyril Connolly: Journal and Memoir* (London 1983), for Connolly's own association with Palinurus.

[10] Palinurus' appeal to Aeneas in Hades: *Aen.* 6, 346–71.

[11] On disparities and contradictions between *Aeneid* 5 and 6 see, most recently, Gordon Williams, *op. cit.* 281–82; and earlier, R. D. Williams, *P. Vergili Maronis Aeneidos Liber Quintus* (Oxford 1960) xxv–xxviii; and G. K. Galinsky, "Aeneid V and the Aeneid," *AJP* 89 (1968) 157ff.

her guarantees (Palinurus had anticipated *some* response from Aeneas) is memorable and disturbing:

> his dictis curae emotae pulsusque parumper
> corde dolor tristi; gaudet cognomine terra. (*Aen.* 6, 382–83)

The abrupt character of *emotae pulsusque* matches the sudden violence that had wrenched him from his post. The gods, and their agents, weigh heavily on the guiltless Palinurus. But the mournful hero enjoys a reprieve from his private grief "for a little while" and welcomes the toponymical compensation for a premature and violent death. The forces that ended his life's career were as final, as invincible and insurmountable, as the sea itself, as irrevocable as the Sibyl's promises.

We are left with an extraordinary portrait of a pilot, characteristically resolute but increasingly aware of insurmountable forces, and progressively countered and disoriented in his continuing service. Finally, he is physically jettisoned as a sacrificial victim to ensure the safety of the group. The manner of his death is, in many ways, comparable to the pious gestures customarily expected of travellers, and of competitors, at sea. When Cloanthus, the ultimate winner in the Sicilian regatta, sought victory, he made offerings to the sea gods:

> extaque salsos/ proiciam in fluctus et vina liquentia fundam
> (*Aen.* 5, 237–38)

Vergil's phrase, *proiecit in undas* (*Aen.* 5, 859), applied to Somnus' hurling Palinurus into the sea, has a familiar ring about it. Otherwise, Palinurus resembles the pitiable Greek hero, Protesilaus, who died first to ensure the safety and success of others; and his death on the margins of Italy is grim foretoken of resistance and death that the Trojans will encounter in Latium. Seasoned contender against the *monstrum* and *fallaces aurae* of Neptune's treacherous domain,[12] he ultimately loses his life to the terrors of Italian soil; alone and unheard as he cries for help in time of trouble, he is denied even the ultimate consolation of the man whose life he had saved so often and for whom eventually his life was forfeit.

"Water music" and "liquid tones" are terms that have often been applied to the Palinurus episode, suggesting that there is a surging, sorrowful poignancy within the verses. The reaction is subjective, but the implication of "song" is curiously embodied in the aftermath to Palinurus' fall overboard, and in the route of the Aeneadae along the Campanian shoreline. Aeneas is stirred from sleep by the sounds of breakers and, as consequence, discovers that his pilot is missing:

---

[12] *Aen.* 5, 849 (*monstro*), 850 (*fallacibus auris*). *Monstrum* here equates with a vast, supernatural creature, an agent of evil.

iamque adeo scopulos Sirenum advecta subibat,
difficilis quondam multorumque ossibus albos
(tum rauca adsiduo longe sale saxa sonabant) (*Aen.* 5, 864–68)

Quondam has exercised commentators since Servius[13] and yet it must derive, as he first argued, from the alleged suicide of the Sirens after Odysseus had navigated safely past their isles, where, as Deryck Williams comments "no enchanting voices were to be heard, only the harsh booming of the sea against the lonely rocks." The islands today are identified either with the Galli (the "Cocks"), tall rocks lying off Sorrento's southern face, or with several low-slung islands off Positano, with Capri beyond. The interval between Palinurus' mishap and death site and the Sirens' Isles suits the tranquil continuation of the fleet's voyage after the pilot's loss, and the juxtaposition of both events is hardly incidental. Palinurus' sacrificial fall suddenly becomes intelligible in the context of *quondam* efforts by enchanted sailors to reach the Sirens' Isles where things past, present, and future were available to them, and where languorous death was a consequence.[14] Aeneas has his own prophets in store, Apollo (through his Sibyl) and Anchises; the removal of the Sirens need cause him no concern. The memory of a legendary past serves only to enhance the multiple implications and associations of Palinurus' death; his last encounter coincides suggestively with the *scopulos . . . difficilis . . ossibus albos* of the Sirens' Isles and the expectation of deliverance is equally frustrated by the *gens crudelis* that aborted his landing.

Numismatics lends a measure of support for the Siren association with Palinurus' sorrowful story. Lucanian silver didrachms featuring a wild boar, running, with framing inscriptions, PAL and MOL, derive from the one-time Greek settlement at Palinurus during the sixth century B.C. PAL obviously aligns with Palinouros, the promontory site; MOL is best associated with Molpa (or Molpe), one of the Sirens who threw herself into the billowy wave after Odysseus had sailed safely past their prophetic roost.[15] Recent excavation has identified the necropolis of Palinouros and established that there was a Greek community at the site until it was abruptly terminated after a lifespan of a century or so.[16] So

---

[13] Servius, *ad loc.*, *antehac delectabili voce resonabant, tunc fluctibus solis.*

[14] For the Sirens and their final suicidal plunge, cf. Homer, *Odyssey*, 12, 39–54; Lycophron, 712f., 1463f.; Strabo 1, 2, 12 (and 5, 4, 8); Hyginus, *Fab.* 141. Consult R. Mandra, "The Sirens in the Palinurus Episode," *LEC* 7 (1938) 168–82.

[15] I have examined the coin in the Collection Duc de Lynes, Bibliothèque Nationale, Paris. For Molpe see Schol. Ap. Rhod. *Argon.* 4, 892.

[16] For Palinuran topography, consult A. G. McKay, *Vergil's Italy* (Greenwich, Conn. 1970) 241–42; Kenneth Wellesley, "Virgilian Places," *Vindex Humanitatis. Essays in Honour of J. M. Bishop*, ed. Bruce Marshall (Armidale 1980) 163–64. For excavations, see R. Naumann, B. Neutsch, *Palinuro I–II* (Heidelberg 1958–1960); E. Greco, "Velia e Palinuro," *MEFR* (1975) 81ff.

Palinurus, Aeneas' pilot, recedes from Vergil's account into even earlier associations with Greeks and a remorseful Siren and adds still more to the already exceptional dimensions of his saga.

The promontory of Capo Palinuro towers some 200 meters above sea level at the southern extremity of the territorium of Velia. Coin types and archaeological finds suggest that Sybarites were responsible for the original foundation, some time prior to the Phocaean settlement at Elea to the north. Tradition related that Palinouros was responsible for the slaughter of innocents (or an innocent) without due cause and that plague descended upon the community. In response therefore to Apollo's Delphic oracle, the Palinurans established a cult service for the murdered party and a ceno-taph as marker. Servius associates these measures with Palinurus' death, which might suggest that Vergil was drawing on a local tradition when Palinurus met with sudden death in Lucania.[17] More likely, since habita-tion at the site ceased ca. 500 B.C., Phocaean territorial expansion and aggression ended Palinouros' heyday and brought the promontory and the settlement (which may have been deliberately razed) into the neighbourly orbit of Elea. Certainly when Palinurus asked Aeneas for burial, his direc-tions are as precise as a helmsman might be expected to provide:

nunc me fluctus habet versantque in litore venti.
....
eripe me his, invicte, malis: aut tu mihi terram
inice, namque potes, portusque require Velinos.
(Aen. 6, 362, 365–66)

Aeneas is asked to return to the harbors of Velia, implying either the Velian ports at the mouths of the Palistro and Fiumarella S. Barbara rivers at Velia, or the calm waters on the northern side of the Palinurus promontory, where the river Lambro (Melpes in former days) emptied.[18] The excavators have confirmed that a modest community of fishermen survived there until the third century B.C.

The aetiology of Palinurus is adequately memorialized by Vergil but the etymology is somewhat more contentious. The physical aspect of the promontory still provides convincing reason for its having been a men-ace for ships caught in southerly gales then and now. Palinurus' mara-thon swim was harassed by southerly winds:

tris Notus hibernas immensa per aequora noctes
vexit me violentus aqua. (Aen. 6, 355–56)

[17] Servius, ad Aen. 378; respondit oraculum manes Palinuri esse placandos ob quam rem non longe a Velia ei et lucum et cenotaphium dederunt.

[18] For Velia's harbors consult Princeton Encyclopedia of Classical Sites, s.v. Elea, (later Velia) 295–96; river ports were established at the mouths of the Palistro and Fiumarella S. Barbara; and Emanuele Greco, Magna Graecia, Guide archeologiche Laterza (Bari 1981) s.v. Velia 40–50.

But his eventual "landing" evokes the harshness of natural barriers and native savagery:

> paulatim adnabam terrae; iam tuta tenebam,
> ni gens crudelis madida cum veste gravatum
> prensantemque uncis manibus capita aspera montis
> ferro invasisset praedamque ignara putasset. (*Aen.* 6, 358–61)

Vergilian autopsy becomes obvious to the visitor today, for although the southern face of the cape is entirely unapproachable, the northern side offers difficult approaches only at the base of the promontory and accessible, inviting beaches beyond. The present day marina, haven for Club Méditerrané pleasure-seekers and sailors, is located at the base of the northern face with rock-cut caves providing shelter and storage space in its lower reaches. Palinurus' "landing" crashes against rocks of the northern bay; sharp and sheer, they offer him no opportunity for a firm grasp and so, distracted and vulnerable, he is easy prey for hostile weapons. Once slain and stripped, his body is left in the surf that moves restlessly along the length of the beach reaching towards Velia some 20 kilometers distant.

Before tackling the etymology of the cape we should recall that Vergil's *animae dimidium*, Horace, suffered shipwreck at Palinurus in 41 B.C., while returning from Philippi; he cites the event in a Roman ode (*Odes* 3, 4. 28: *Sicula Palinurus unda*), and it may even affect the Pyrrha Ode (*Odes* 1, 5) where the marine imagery and the language offer intriguing parallels with the distress of the Vergilian pilot consigned as victim to Neptune by Venus' compromise. Octavian's last, desperate measures against Sextus Pompey almost came to a catastrophic end in the same gale-driven waters at Cape Palinurus in the summer of 36 B.C. Lashed by frenzied south winds, a match for those that beset the storm-tossed Palinurus, Octavian's armada was left in disarray and ruins.[19] The hope of the Julian cause was almost eclipsed in the waters where Aeneas' savior-figure floundered. Vergil's memory of the conflict with Sextus Pompey was deeply ingrained: it included the military conversions at Cumae and at the Portus Julius; maybe it also included the tradition, part scandal, part fact, of Octavian's deep sleep just before the final engagement with Sextus Pompey between Sicilian Mylae and Naulochus. According to Suetonius, Octavian had to be roused from sleep to give the signal for the start of the decisive engagement. Although Octavian may have been heard to defy the countermeasures of Neptune, the repeated storms and shipwrecks, and may have undertaken to win his naval battle without Neptune's support,[20] Vergil supplied drastic means to win the sea deity's support through the sacrifice of Palinurus, Neptune's appointed victim.

---

[19] For Octavian's mishaps during hostilities with Sextus Pompey, see Appian, *B. C.* 5, 88–90, 98–99; Dio Cass. 49, 1; Vell. Pat. 2, 80.

[20] Suetonius, *Augustus* 16.

Of Palinurus' wind-swept locale and destructive intrusions into Vergil's historical era, there is adequate testimony. The likeliest etymology for the cape also seems obvious in the poet's "playful" association of waves and winds in his account of Palinurus' final condition:

> nunc me fluctus habet versantque in litore venti. (*Aen.* 6, 362)

Versant and *venti* together provide a summary reflection of the pilot's career, plying the tiller through the ocean's waves and sensing and reacting expertly to the winds that are associated with maritime travel. Neptune's realm, although properly the measureless seas, in Vergil's narrative seems more often that of the winds. Aeolus is his subject, but Neptune's intrusions into the epic are commonly in association with gales and storm blasts. (Dwellers by the Mediterranean are generally more alive to winds scudding across sheets of water than with the waves that rise thereafter. Pilots are particularly attuned to the sound and impress of winds and guide their vessels according to its inclination.) Palinurus' name comprises *palin*, suggesting "reversal" and *ouros* "wind," implying that the cape's etymology contained notice of its windswept, calamitous character, the cape where winds run counter to the desired direction, where wrecks may occur and adverse gales are common. The "etymologizing" verse (362) serves other designs as well; not only Homeric but Euripidean reverberations can be detected.[21] Heyne was first to suggest that the corpse's plight may derive from Euripides' Trojan plays, *Hecuba*, *Helen*, and *Heracleidae*. The last refers to shipwrecked sailors who reach land successfully after being rejected by winds; Palinurus' rejection is final however. He comes to Italy as a returning Dardanid (as son of Iasius, Dardanus' half-brother)[22] but meets rejection and death; the Heracleidae share the "homecoming" pattern but are ultimately successful in their quest. The Euripidean tie further intensifies the pathos of the Palinurus episode.

But Palinurus' adventure actually surmounts a palimpsest of models: Odysseus' prodigious swim after leaving Calypso's isle (*Odys.* 5, 313ff.); Patroclus' ghostly apparition to Achilles (*Iliad* 23, 65–101) where the request for burial to enable his ghost to cross the infernal river is intensified by a farewell handshake (*Iliad* 23, 75); the death of Phrontis, Menelaus' "mindful" pilot off Cape Sunium for whom a sorrowing Menelaus built a tomb and offered the requisite burial services (*Odys.* 3, 278–85); maybe

---

[21] Homer's Elpenor (*Odys.* 10, 551–60; 11, 51–83); Euripides, *Hecuba* 28–30 (Heyne's association), *Helen* 405–7, *Heracleidae* 427–32. For detailed discussion of etymology and paradigms, consult Z. Philip Ambrose, "The Etymology and Genealogy of Palinurus," *AJP* 101 (1980) 449–57.

[22] Cf. M. Owen Lee, "The sons of Iasius and the end of the Aeneid," *Augustan Age* 1 (1981–82) 13–16. Palinurus, the helmsman, and Iapyx, the *longaevus* physician (*Aen.* 12, 420–29) are identified as brothers, sons of Iasius. But Iapyx also suggests Antonius Musa, Augustus' personal physician.

even the Polygnotan mural in the Cnidian Lesche at Delphi, where Phrontis, the only bearded hero in sight, was depicted as steersman with two boat-hooks, standing amidships, according to Pausanias.[23] Homer's Elpenor is demonstrably influential (Pausanias saw his likeness too, in the Polygnotan painting, alongside Odysseus, and wearing, instead of clothes, a mat, "such as sailors customarily wear") but similarities are outnumbered by differences.[24] Both are unburied, and sleep is involved in both deaths. But Elpenor's character differs markedly from that of Palinurus: inexperienced, stupid, lacking in martial vigor (Raymond Clark calls him "an incompetent and exasperating bungler")[25] his sleep, which is his undoing, stems from an excess of wine, but Palinurus' death is product of a "lethal" attack; Elpenor was incapable of finding the ladder at the edge of Circe's palace roof and plummeted to his death below, whereas Palinurus, startled awake by the chill of the sea, swam for three days and nights to reach land. If Palinurus be accepted as an embodiment of heroic virtues, Elpenor's faults are certainly uncommonly human, and his desertion by his hard-pressed companions may be a token of their disregard or contempt. And yet there is irony in the eventuality, for, like Palinurus, who finds burial and a "memorial service" from his murderers, Elpenor is the sole companion of Odysseus who wins decent burial.

Palinurus' fall, and the sea tragedy associated with him, finds precedent too in the tragic fall of Icarus, Daedalus' son, the event which the despondent father could not include in the door reliefs which he fashioned for the Apollo Temple at Cumae.[26] Icarus' death, of course, occurs in blazing sunlight; Vergil's pilot, and Leucaspis is another,[27] encounters his doom in darkness. Icarus died in the seas which later bore his name; Palinurus contributed his name to the promontory where he died. And the grief which Daedalus found so overwhelming is matched by that of Aeneas, not only for Palinurus, but for all the loved and lost whose destinies were cut short and whose promise was curtailed.

Vergil's instances of death by drowning, and of "the unburied corpse on the deserted shore" are frequent enough in the first six books of the epic to excite reflection about their symbolic value. Just as Palinurus is depicted finally, in Aeneas' vision, as an anonymous cadaver, stripped and mutilated by savage foes, carried to and fro by the surf along the

---

[23] Pausanias 10, 25, 2.

[24] Pausanias 1, 29, 8.

[25] For treatment of Misenus and Palinurus, consult R. J. Clark, *Catabasis: Vergil and the Wisdom Tradition* (Amsterdam 1979) 152–54, 157–58; the quotation appears on p. 161; and T. A. Dorey, "Homer and Vergil: The World of the Dead," *Orpheus* 3 (1956) 119–22 (especially 119–20, on Elpenor).

[26] *Aen.* 6, 30–33.

[27] Cf. G. Thaniel, "Ecce . . . Palinurus," *Acta Classica* 15 (1972) 149–52 for Leucaspis as Orontes' pilot.

beach, so too Priam's corpse is left on Sigeum's strand, headless and unburied,[28] and Dido prays for a comparable ending for Aeneas:

> *sed cadat ante diem mediaque inhumatus harena.* (*Aen.* 4, 620)

Servius, however erratic in judgment sometimes, realized that this repeated "quadretto" in larger, varied contexts must derive from the death of Pompey the Great in Egypt.[29] The glory that leads but to the grave, as Icarus, Priam, Palinurus (and Misenus) would suggest by their careers, is a characteristic Vergilian theme; their deaths are reminders of the inescapable presence of evil, of the distressful human condition which condemns mortals to wander through life (and death, sometimes) without joy, to encounter death and oblivion at the end.

Misenus' career is no less sympathetically rendered by the poet than that of Palinurus. He appears first rousing the Aeneadae to action against the loathsome Harpies (*Aen.* 3, 1239–44). As trumpeter he knows no equal:

> Misenum Aeoliden, quo non praestantior alter
> aere ciere viros Martemque accendere cantu. (*Aen.* 6, 164–65)

His patronymic, son of Aeolus, befits his profession; as incomparable master of a wind-instrument, he shares a mastery with his father, the ruler of the winds and Neptune's warden of fractious creatures. Vergil's retrospective on Misenus' career and experience heightens respect for his military heroism:

> Hectoris hic magni fuerat comes, Hectora circum
> et lituo pugnas insignis obibat et hasta.
> postquam illum vita victor spoliavit Achilles,
> Dardanio Aeneae sese fortissimus heros
> addiderat socium, non inferiora secutus. (*Aen.* 6, 166–70)

His final engagement, an event which Vergil decisively undercuts by his qualifying interjection, is yet another challenge to unearthly powers, the anguiform deity Triton, child of Neptune and Amphitrite:

> sed tum, forte cava dum personat aequora concha,
> demens, et cantu vocat in certamina divos,
> aemulus exceptum Triton, si credere dignum est,
> inter saxa virum spumosa immerserat unda. (*Aen.* 6, 171–74)

Emboldened by his artistry and distracted by ebullient but frustrated heroic instincts in a pacific setting, Misenus challenged the divinities to a

---

[28] *Aen.* 2, 557–58.

[29] Servius, *ad Aen.* 2, 557: *Pompei tangit historiam.* See also John L. Moles, "Virgil, Pompey, and the *Histories* of Asinius Pollio," *CW* 76 (1983) 174–82 for the argument that *Aen.* 2, 557–58 was influenced by Pollio's account of and reflections on the death of Pompey the Great.

contest. Triton responded as champion and defeated Misenus in the conch-blowing competition. The loser (although Vergil questions the severity of the retribution in light of the circumstances) is drowned in the foaming rocks beneath the promontory where Misenus had played out his arrogant action.

Warned by the Sibyl that his entry into Hades required the burial of a lost companion and the procural of the Golden Bough, Aeneas and Anchises, unaware of any loss until then, sought grimly for the missing person. Eventually Misenus' corpse was discovered lying unburied on the Baiae-Misenum shoreline. Immediately, adhering faithfully to the Sibyl's instructions, a funeral pyre was commissioned for the much-lamented trumpeter. During the search for firewood, Venus' doves led Aeneas to the Golden Bough. The pyre was completed and, after appropriate services for the deceased, it was set alight. The ashes of the dead man were gathered in a bronze urn, and an impressive tumulus was heaped over his remains "beneath the windy hill" and the hero's oar and trumpet served as markers.[30] Once again, topography provided a platform for Misenus' final act and an outline for the tumulus, repeated in reduced scale, which housed the trumpeter's remains. Cape Misenum is a massive, flat-top hill, some 167 meters high; it dominates the seascape in the Cumaean environs and on the Bay of Puteoli.[31] Although some prefer to locate the Misenus episode nearer to the acropolis of Cumae, at Torregaveta perhaps, beyond the Acherusian Swamp (Lago del Fusaro), or at Monte di Procida, Vergil's tendency to telescope space and time makes the likelihood of the tragic encounter more reasonable at Cape Misenum itself. Distances may be formidable (Cumae and Misenum are 11 kilometers distant) but heroic legs are stouter and distances enlarge and diminish with the ease of an accordion.[32]

Sources for the Misenus episode are, as with Palinurus, diverse. Elpenor's drop from Circe's roof is distinctly comparable; the erection of the funeral pyre and the enactments around its charred remnant hark back to the rites for Patroclus in *Iliad* 23, 110ff. The account of the tree-felling, which derives from Ennius' version of the Homeric original, underlines that factor decisively.[33] Achilles' final *munera* to his deceased beloved match Aeneas' pious concern and thwarted love for his lost companions.

[30] *Aen.* 3, 239–44 (the Harpies); *Aen.* 6, 160–82, 212–235.

[31] For topography of Misenum, consult M. Borriello, A. d'Ambrosio, *Baiae-Misenum, Forma Italiae* 1, Vol. 14 (Firenze 1979); Stefano De Caro, Argella Greco, *Campania, Guide archeologiche Laterza* (Bari 1981) 65–73; and A. G. McKay, *Ancient Campania II: Naples and Coastal Campania*, s.v. *Misenum*, 1–39 (Plate 1, p. 6).

[32] For the disputed locale cf. R. J. Clark, *op. cit.*, 152–53; id., "Misenus and the Cumaean Landfall: Originality in Vergil's Use of Topography and Tradition," *TAPA* 107 (1977) 63–71.

[33] For the tree-felling, cf. Homer, *Iliad* 23, 114ff.; Ennius, *Ann.* 187–91; *Aen.* 6, 179–82.

For Misenus' earlier activities there is a remarkable pictorial rendering. The Tabula Iliaca, from Bovillae, now in the Musei Capitolini, Rome, depicts episodes from several components of the epic cycle: *Iliad, Aethiopis, Little Iliad* and *Iliupersis*, all in close conjunction. One episode, called Stesichorean in the relief but now generally discarded as a Stesichorean "original," portrays Aeneas, with Ascanius and Anchises, in company with Misenus, so named, carrying his trumpet and embarking with the family group for Hesperia. The inclusion of Misenus with the "pilgrim" family is intriguing. Lycophron included him in Odysseus' company but gave no notice of his prospects or achievements in Italy. His association with Aeneas in Hesperia probably initiated with Varro. Dionysius of Halicarnassus certainly consigned Misenus' death to the harbour of the Opicans which was named after him. The inclusion of Misenus in the Tabula Iliaca probably stems from the popularity of Vergil's epic. Galinsky has argued, persuasively, that the relief is probably Augustan and so likely to have been influenced by "something greater than the *Iliad*." But Galinsky's assumption that the hero is standing on a promontory, although heights are consistent with his performances in the *Aeneid*, seems strained. The platform is better identified with the embarkation platform at the Sigean jetty and may even be a reflection of the naval facility at Portus Misenensis which was developed by Octavian-Augustus.[34]

Misenus' funeral rites, and the preparation of the pyre, are extremely detailed, so detailed that it has been called the *locus classicus* for elaborate Roman funerary ceremonial. The ritual, as Bailey and others have observed, contains both Greek and Roman features.[35] The Greek, or heroic elements seem to derive largely from Homeric models, from the last rites for Patroclus and Hector. But there are indications too that Vergil competed not only with Homeric paradigms but with Ennius too in the details regarding the tree-felling for the funeral pyre. Quinn has suggested that the Vergilian "version" was meant to recall the famous passage "to set himself alongside Ennius, and against Homer."[36] Most striking is Vergil's obvious attempt to gain an atmosphere of austere, large-scale primitivism. The Ennian lines, quoted by Macrobius (*Sat.* 6, 2, 27), impart a grim, antique note to the funeral which is singularly important and suitable for the funeral of a one-time companion of Hector. By recalling that earlier association, Vergil induces his reader to reflect on the past strengths and heroic accomplishments of the Trojans. But Misenus' death ("premature" is Vergil's usual implication in *indigna*,

34 For the Tabula Iliaca relief consult A. Sadurska, *Les Tables Iliaques* (Warsaw 1964); and G. K. Galinsky, *Aeneas, Sicily, and Rome* (Princeton 1969) 107–9 (with plates and drawing).
35 Cf. R. G. Austin, *P. Vergili Maronis Aeneidos Liber Sextus* (Oxford 1977) 102. Cyril Bailey, *Religion in Virgil* (Oxford 1935) 287ff.
36 Kenneth Quinn, *Virgil's Aeneid: a critical Description* (Ann Arbor 1968) 367–68.

but "resentful" is implied elsewhere, particularly in Turnus' case) is something less than heroic when set beside Hector's; the struggle, the agony, are no longer public and impressive but isolated and evidently unseen. Misenus' death results from his insane challenge, and his defeat is marked only by Triton's blast ringing over the waters between Misenum and Ischia.

Roman aspects of the burial ceremony for Misenus are easily identified. Some of them may derive from Etruscan or Italic practices; some may even derive from "heroic" Macedonian funerals, or the obsequies of Hellenistic royalty which Romans sought to emulate.[37] Vergil alters some of the normal sequence in the service, perhaps to lessen the immediacy of the funeral for his readers. The washing and anointing of the corpse normally came after the *conclamatio* by family and intimate friends. When the corpse had been washed and anointed, it was normally dressed in a toga; Misenus' body is draped in purple, a color which Servius advises was meant to recall the blood of a sacrificial victim.[38] If so, the symbolism is peculiarly apt for Misenus whose death seems a material offering to ensure Aeneas' immunity in his underworld adventure that lies ahead. The tremendous bier, with the couch atop, is designed to give heroic measure to the deceased and to the ceremony. With heads averted, to miss the soul's departure from the body, the Trojans ignite the pyre with torches, and after the corpse is consumed, the ashes are drenched with wine, and the burnt bones and ashes collected by relatives (Corynaeus?) and placed in an urn for lodging in the tomb. The offerings for the deceased, incense, a costly meal (cakes?), and bowls of oil, are consumed in the blaze. The lustration, designed to purify the Trojans from the pollution of death, is performed three times with Corynaeus encircling the assembly, using a branch of fruitful olive as sprinkler. Augustus, according to Servius, banned the use of laurel, customary before his time, because it was associated with his own birth and was used to crown triumphant generals.[39] The processional movement implied in the lustration closed with the *novissima verba*, the last farewell to the deceased. Vergil's ritual, however antique the origins, has implications of present forms. The Trojans have, as elsewhere, been identified with contemporary Romans, and Vergil signals as much in his use of *more parentum* to impart a sense of contemporaneity in connection with the turning aside from the deceased when the pyre is ignited (*Aen.* 6, 223–24).

Palinurus' sorrow was alleviated "for a little while" by the promise of expiatory rites, a tomb, and sacrifices at the site:

---

[37] On Roman funerals, consult Jocelyn M. C. Toynbee, *Death and Burial in the Roman World* (London 1971) 39ff., 43ff.

[38] Servius, *ad Aen.* 3, 67 (derived from Varro).

[39] Servius, *ad Aen.* 6, 230: *noluit laurum dicere ad officium lugubre pertinere.*

et statuent tumulum et tumulo sollemnia mittent,
aeternumque locus Palinuri nomen habebit. (*Aen.* 6, 380f.)

Misenus is provided with a tumulus and a memorializing promontory:

at pius Aeneas ingenti mole sepulcrum
imponit suaque arma viro remumque tubamque
monte sub aërio, qui nunc Misenus ab illo
dicitur aeternumque tenet per saecula nomen. (*Aen.* 6, 232–35)

In both instances, as Austin remarked, Vergil "could link past with present in living history."[40] Two heroes, whose names survive in well-known heights, both with Julian associations, are part of the experience of travellers along Italy's shores, impressive monitors of Italy's Tyrrhenian shores. But these are only outward signs and immediate associations. By associating them with the personal grief of Aeneas and his company, Vergil hints at larger ramifications than antiquarian concern with legendary associations and local pride in the configurations of Italy. Charles Segal sensed larger implications: "Aeneas can bury Misenus, to be sure, but he is not consoled, any more than he is for the other losses to come. The 'eternal name' of Misenus in 234–35 is not described as a consolation; it is given in an impersonal and matter-of-fact way, as a bit of aetiological lore."[41] The same inconsolable character surrounds the Palinurus episode. The tragedy of the human condition is an essential part of both episodes, heightened by the conjunction of Aeneas' symbolic "death and return" within which both heroes find themselves. Misenus and Palinurus have no such privileged status; their memorials testify to the inability to transcend mortality. Their lineage, Misenus, son of the wind god, and Palinurus, son of Iasius, half-brother of Dardanus, is insufficient to provide them with more than visible and durable memorials, with historical markers of their mortality.

If the Portus Misenensis had been activated before 31 B.C. (and there is some reason for suggesting that it had been designed and completed between 31 and 23 B.C.), Vergil had a splendid, even momentous historical association for the hero and his promontory.[42] Portus Julius, the Lucrine harbor which included Lake Avernus and the Bay of Puteoli in its make-up, Vergil hailed enthusiastically as a man-made wonder in

---

[40] R. G. Austin, *op. cit.*, 108.

[41] C. P. Segal, "Aeternum per saecula nomen: The Golden Bough and the Tragedy of History," *Arion* 4 (1965) 617–57; quotation appears on p. 637.

[42] For the early years of the Misene naval base, consult John H. D'Arms, *Romans on the Bay of Naples* (Cambridge, Mass. 1970) 136–37; A. G. McKay, *op. cit.*; C. I. L. X, 3357 (pre 27 B.C.); Strabo 5, 4, 6 (Lucrinus useless as a marina, hence closed); Propertius, *Elegies* 3, 18 (Avernus excluded from Baian waters and Herculean causeway a busy thoroughfare again). Chester G. Starr, *Roman Imperial Navy* 14, dates the Misene installations between 27 and 15 B.C.

Georgics 2, 161–64.[43] The successor naval base, easier of access and more commodious with its landlocked harbor (today's Mare Morto), was a worthy successor to Portus Julius. The outer harbor, *monte sub aërio* (*Aen.* 6, 234), with impressive breakwaters, was designed to accommodate the active fleet and training exercises.

The confrontation with Palinurus' corpse and the request for burial recalls a situation and monologue peculiar to sepulchral epigrams. So too, with Misenus, the summary of past achievements at the outset of the Misenus episode echoes epigrams where the deceased is addressed in his grave. Horace's Ode to Archytas (*Odes* 1, 28), the drowned man on the Calabrian shore, coincides remarkably with Palinurus' condition when the dead man asks the passer-by for a handful of sand as burial. Three handfuls of dust will suffice to enable the merchant sailor to proceed with the corpse's good will.[44] The Misenus episode, particularly at the close, has the pathos of an epitaph and, in combination with the contemporaneity of the burial rites, has a disturbing immediacy for the reader. Vergil leaves one with a sense that the Misenus episode had some exceptional relevance for the poet's era.

Actually, there is remarkable independent testimony about the poet's involvement with the Misenus passage. The Donatus *Life* relates that Eros, Vergil's freedman and *amanuensis*, during his advanced years, used to relate that Vergil, in the midst of a recitation completed two 'half lines' impromptu. *Misenum Aeoliden* (*Aen.* 6, 164) was already in the text when Vergil added *quo non praestantior alter*; and again, after *aere ciere viros* . . . (165) he was inspired to append *Martemque accendere cantu*, and both verses were immediately inserted into the text. The specific reference to the Misenus episode leads one to suppose that these lines, and so the entire episode, claimed some particular interest and favor after the poet's death, and that Vergil personally had devoted particular care to its perfection, perhaps on the eve of the recitation of *Aeneid* 6 to Augustus at Atella in 23 B.C. At any rate, the anecdote permits us to peer into the processes of poetic creativity and into the artist's techniques of composition. One is reminded of the incomplete masterpiece of Daedalus who was unable to render Icarus' fall; Vergil evidently found it difficult to complete the Misenus counterpart until inspiration struck. But the question inevitably arises: why should these particular lines be singled out for comment by Eros, and why should they be retained in the tradition? Were they perhaps among the best known and

---

[43] For Portus Julius, ancient testimony and physical details, consult A. G. McKay, s.v. *Avernus & Lucrinus*, 7–30, 214–25 (with plates and map).

[44] On Horace *Odes* 1, 28, consult R. G. M. Nisbet, Margaret Hubbard, *A Commentary on Horace's Odes Book 1* (Oxford 1970) 317–37; and R. J. Clark, *op. cit.* 158. Horace's model may be either Vergil (23 B.C.) or Varro's *Sesquiulixes*, a Menippean satire.

respected of Vergil's verses, so well known that Eros could refer to them with the assurance of familiarity on the part of his audience?

The passage has already been cited as the *locus classicus* for Roman burial practices. Its stark, archaic aspects marry gracefully with Hellenistic epitaphic elements. But there is another aspect, the fruitless character of obsequies (*cineri ingrato*, 213) that recurs later in Anchises' last words regarding Marcellus:

> his saltem accumulem donis, et fungar inani
> munere . . . . (*Aen.* 6, 885–86)

Like Palinurus, Marcellus is hard to discern in the underworld's penumbra, but once identified, Anchises offers a heartbreaking recital of his virtues and promise denied. His death brings *ingentem luctum* (868); he is the supreme embodiment of Trojan-Roman youth, whose resting place will be the Augustan Mausoleum, Tiber-side, and whose premature death will give rise to universal lamentation.

Vergil was not alone in composing a tribute to the deceased son of Octavia, Augustus' sister, and Julia's husband since 25 B.C. Death came to him at Baiae in 23 B.C. after unsuccessful therapy there with the ministrations of Antonius Musa, the court physician. Propertius III, 18, an *epicedium*, or lament, for M. Claudius Marcellus, was probably composed immediately after the youth's death since it alludes to the funeral procession moving towards Rome and his final interment.[45] In his catalogue of sites in the Baian environs Propertius includes the seemingly inactive Portus Julius (*clausus ab umbroso qua ludit pontus Averno*, 1), the steaming pools of Baiae's sulphur springs, and nearby Misenum (*qua iacet et Troiae tubicen Misenus harena*, 3). The Herculean causeway, pierced by Agrippa's engineers in designing the Portus Julius, now resounds to traffic noise with Lucrinus once again relegated to oyster beds and maritime villas. The entire area, Propertius remarks, has been saddened by a recent death, a death which he portrays as drowning: *his pressus Stygias vultum demisit in undas* (9). The waters off Baiae, with their pleasurable and underworld associations, are perceived as another route to Hades, a passage on a par with Avernus itself. And the ghost still haunts the place of death, hovering between the world of the living and the dead, awaiting burial: *errat et in vestro spiritus ille lacu* (10).

Propertius evidently conceived his epicede for Marcellus after the pattern of Misenus' death in the same environs. The description of Marcellus' death, *his pressus Stygias vultum demisit in undas* is entirely à propos to Misenus' unhappy death on the same shores. And the

---

[45] On Propertius III, 18, consult W. A. Camps, *Propertius Elegies Book III* (Oxford 1966) 137–43; L. Richardson, Jr., *Propertius Elegies I–IV* (Norman, Oklahoma 1977) 391–95.

pathetic reflections on the disparity between his fortunate status and his sudden death meld intriguingly with the honorable succession Misenus enjoyed, from being Hector's companion to becoming Aeneas' aide, and again, an abrupt death. The bravura of both young men is remarkable; the denial of promise is as dolorous for the Julian house as for Vergil's Aeneas.

Palinurus and Misenus, together, constitute not so much doublets as complementary figures in Vergil's epic narrative. Their careers are not dissimilar; they are both embodiments of Trojan heroism and endurance with accomplishments to their credit beyond the ordinary. And they have earned the respect and affection of their leader. Their patronymics, *Aeolides* and *Iasides*, confer distinction among Trojan heroes. But their fame is ultimately posthumous. Their lives are forfeit to the destiny which embraces Aeneas and Ascanius. Quasi-sacrificial victims to ensure the security of the Trojans and of Aeneas, they give their lives in the divine plan as innocent and forlorn individuals. Aeneas, Augustus, and Vergil had all experienced personal grief and sorrow; they knew that the continuity of life must involve crude and sorrowful ruptures with the past. Monuments, like promontories, stand eternally; but memorials are small solace for the dearly departed. Wendell Clausen has caught the sense of Vergil's grasp of tragic mortality better than most and his remarks are entirely applicable to the heroes under review: "Aeneas weeps for the dead or for those he thinks dead, for Orontes, for Amycus, for Gyas, for Cloanthus. *Fortemque Gyan fortemque Cloanthum* (brave Gyas and brave Cloanthus): the cadence is strangely affecting; the repetition somehow and the regretfulness of the tone suggest the futility of what has happened and of what will, in all probability, happen again."[46]

---

[46] Wendell Clausen, "An Interpretation of the Aeneid," in *Virgil: A Collection of Critical Essays*, ed. Steele Commager (Englewood Cliffs, 1966) 75–88 (quotation on p. 81, referring to *Aen.* 1, 220–22).

STRUCTURE AND SOURCES OF HORACE, *ODE* 1,12*

PETER LEBRECHT SCHMIDT

According to the historian Cassius Dio (56,34) the *pompa funebris* of Augustus (September 14 A.D.) consisted not only of the *imagines* of the emperor's family, but also of the images of those Romans, starting with Romulus and ending with Pompey, who had distinguished themselves in war or politics. This orientation of early and republican history towards *one family* and *one Iulius* no doubt surpassed the accepted framework of gentiliciar representation, and was to become a traditional element of the ideology of the principate.

It seems certain that this selection of exemplary personalities was based on Augustus' own will.[1] He had pursued the same intention when he filled the niches of the *exedrae* and the intercolumniations of the porticoes in his *forum* (dedicated 2 B.C.): To the left and right of the temple of Mars Ultor there stood statues larger than life not only of the *Iulii*, but, once more, of the *viri summi*, starting as before with Romulus, *qui imperium populi Romani ex minimo maximum reddidisent: Hinc videt Aenean oneratum pondere caro/ et tot Iuleae nobilitatis avos;/ hinc videt Iliaden umeris ducis arma ferentem, claraque dispositis acta subesse viris.*[2]

Such *imagines*—waxmasks, busts or statues as the Roman art of gentiliciar representation developed—were traditionally on view in the *atrium* of the Roman nobles' townhomes. There a young nobleman might well look up to his ancestors, to those who had attained at least the aedileship, the first curule office, and especially to those who had crowned their *cursus honorum* with the offices of *praetor, consul* or *censor*, or their military career with a triumph.

---

*Nicholas Horsfall has saved my English from graver anomalies; for the remaining mistakes in language and matter (as, of course, for the distinctively German flavor) I am solely responsible.

[1] Cf. Suet. *Aug.* 101,4 and H. T. Rowell, "The Forum and Funeral *Imagines* of Augustus," *MAAR* 17 (1940) 131ff.; D. Kienast, *Augustus: Prinzeps und Monarch* (Darmstadt 1982) 123ff.

[2] Suet. loc. cit. 31,5; Ovid, *Fast.* 5,563ff. and cf. P. Zanker, *Forum Augustum: Das Bildprogramm* (Tübingen 1968) 14ff.; P. L. Schmidt, *RE Suppl.* 15, 1978, 1637f. (possible author: Hyginus); P. Frisch, *ZPE* 39 (1980) 91ff. (in ignorance of my suggestion; possible author: Augustus himself); Kienast, op. cit. 173f.

Public opinion in the age of Augustus quite spontaneously compared Augustus as *pater patriae* to a *pater familias*.[3] In his forum he is standing surrounded by his ancestors and the *summi viri*. Therefore it has often been suggested that the Hall of Fame in the *exedrae* and porticoes was inspired by the *imagines maiorum*. In this way Roman art of representation—originally an expression of the *dignitas* of the ruling class as a whole, but in each instance an articulation of variety and competition—is channelled into the claim to power and the need for legitimacy of a regime concerned for its dynastic continuity.

Its republicanizing ideology expressed itself above all in a building program. Rarely did architecture serve as so direct a medium of political propaganda as under the influence of Augustus. He and his advisers succeeded—to a hitherto unprecedented degree—in turning public buildings into the vehicles of a political program. On the one hand the republican tradition is glorified and at the same time the mighty record of past achievements brought to its conclusion. On the other dynastic claims, combined with but a remembrance of the republic, imbued notably the series of great monuments of the principate when finally established through both figurative implications and explicit texts: the *Arcus Augusti* (next to Caesar's Temple) together with the *fasti consulares et triumphales* (19 B.C.), the monumental inscription commemorating the *ludi saeculares* (17 B.C.), the *ara Pacis* (9 B.C.), the arch for the princes L. and Caesar corresponding to the *Arcus Augusti* (3 B.C.), and finally the *forum Augustum* with its statues and *elogia*, whose attempt to influence public opinion manifested itself in the copies of the pictorial and textual programs spread throughout the provinces.[4]

After the publication of the newly found *elogia* (1933) and the synthesis of the old and new material by Degrassi (1937)[5] two comparable texts inevitably attracted corresponding scholarly attention, Horace, *Ode* 1,12 (v. 33ff.), and of course the Parade of Heroes in Virgil's Nekyia, *Aeneid* 6 (v. 756ff.). Both lists of names were thought to be directly inspired by the *summi viri* of the *forum Augustum*[6]: *excudent alii spirantia molius aera . . .* and *vivos ducent de marmore vultus* (v. 847f.)

---

[3] Cf. Zanker, op. cit. 26, n. 18 and, for the wider propagandistic context, p. 5; *Forum Romanum: Die Neugestaltung durch Augustus* (Tübingen 1972) 14ff., 23f. See also L. Braccesi, *Epigrafia e storiografia* (Napoli 1981) 39ff.

[4] Zanker, *Forum Augustum* 27; T. Hölscher, *Staatsdenkmal und Publikum* (Konstanz 1984) 26ff.

[5] *Inscriptiones Italiae* 13,3 (Roma 1937).

[6] Cf. D. L. Drew, "Horace, *Odes* I.XII and the *Forum Augustum*," *CQ* 19 (1925) 159ff.; T. Frank, "Augustus, Vergil, and the Augustan *Elogia*," *AJPh* 59 (1938) 91ff.; H. T. Rowell, "Vergil and the Forum of Augustus," *AJPh* 62 (1941) 261ff. For Drew's hypothesis see already K. Hiemer, "Zwei politische Gedichte des Horaz," *RhM* N.F. 62 (1907) 229ff.

were supposed to refer to the series of bronze and marble statues created by Greek artists. Virgil was also assumed to have had in mind this architectural ensemble, when he envisaged the temple palace of Latinus, the *regia Pici* (*Aen.* 7, 170ff.). In the vestibule of this palace the poet imagined not only Latinus' forbears, Picus and Saturnus, but also the tradition of ancient Italy in a wider sense (. . . *Italusque paterque Sabinus/ . . . Ianique bifrontis imago/vestibulo astabant, aliique ab origine reges*), and also warriors of exceptional courage.

The Greek gods and heroes selected by Horace (*Ode* 1,12, 19ff.) were also seen to allude to works of art exposed in the *forum*. The chronological difficulty presented by the fact that the temple of Mars Ultor though already vowed in 42 was dedicated only in 2 B.C. was met by the hypothesis that at least the *forum* itself together with its niches must have been open to the public as early as the twenties.

In 1945 Degrassi's[7] sceptical arguments silenced such vague assumptions: for among the heroes there stood also Tiberius' brother, the elder Drusus, who died in 9 B.C. According to Degrassi *forum* and temple, encircling wall, porticoes and statues were built continuously from about 12 B.C. on. That, however, leaves open the question of whether the lists in Virgil and Horace relate only the the rhetorical tradition of historical *exempla* in general, or to a specific impulse, perhaps not architectural but literary.

This paper tries to answer that question concentrating on Horace *Ode* 1,12 and especially on v. 25ff. A German will base the introductory résumé of the poem quite naturally on Kiessling-Heinze[8]:

> Of whom will you sing, heavenly Muse, man, *heros*, or god, in the province of poetry? (stanzas 1–3). Among the gods it is Jupiter, who reigns over the world without equal. Nearest to him is Minerva, valiant in battle, and you, too, Liber, Diana and Apollo my song shall praise (4–6). I shall commemorate Hercules and the Dioscuri, saviours at sea; who will follow next, Romulus, Numa, Tarquinius Superbus, or the heroic death of Cato? (7–9). I shall exalt those who by the sacrifice of their own or of their offspring's life bought Rome's victories, or laid the foundation for success by their traditionally simple way of life. Marcellus' star is still rising, but all others are outshined by the *sidus Iulium* (10–12). You, Jupiter, chosen by fate

---

[7] *Scritti vari di antichità* (Roma 1962) 283ff.

[8] *Oden und Epoden* (Berlin 1930), new edition with bibliographical additions by E. Burck from [8]1955 to [10]1960; the following overall interpretations are also helpful: Th. Birt, *Horaz' Lieder* 1 (Leipzig 1926) 64ff.; E. Fraenkel, *Horace* (Oxford 1957) 291ff.; R. G. M. Nisbet/M. Hubbard, *A Commentary on Horace: Odes Book* 1 (Oxford 1970) 142ff.; H. P. Syndikus, *Die Lyrik des Horaz. Eine Interpretation der Oden* 1 (Darmstadt 1972) 135ff.; V. Bejarano, "Poesia y politica en Horacio," *EClás* 20 (1976) 241ff. Contributions to details will be cited in the following notes; cf. also W. Kissel, *Horaz 1936–1975: Eine Gesamtbibliographie.* ANRW II, 31,3, (Berlin/New York 1981) 1491.

as Augustus' guardian: Let him triumph over his foes on earth, as you smite with your thunderbolt the sacrilegious from Olympus (13–15).

Our ability to paraphrase the poem triads of solemnly moving stanzas provides a first hint towards the corresponding basic structure of the poem, which in its turn must be seen as an imitation of a poetic model: Many scholars attach great importance to the quotation in v. 1 from the beginning of Pindar's second Olympian. Notably Fraenkel[9] examines here as usual the adaptation of Pindar in detail and emphasizes the fact that the ode, which consists of five triads, thereby transposes the sequence "Strophe-Antistrophe-Epode," five times repeated by Pindar, into the medium of the Sapphic ode. This must, however, also mean that Horace tries to transpose the Pindaric poem as a whole—in respect both of structure and of intention—into the Augustan environment. In that case it is not enough to interpret the introductory quotation, as is often done, purely as a motto; rather it is to be taken as a first indication which evokes the literary background and acquaints the informed audience with the intended function of the text.

Let us follow the initial sequence of questions (*Quem virum aut heroa . . . sumis celebrare, Clio, quem deum*) one by one: Pindar immediately gives a swift and direct answer; he names, each in his category, Zeus, Hercules and Theron. In Horace's ode, however, the triple question functions first of all as *dispositio*; typically for him the answer is given in a more roundabout, subtle and complex way. He does not, as Fraenkel understands, replace each individual object of praise with a group (gods, heroes and men, triads 2, 3 and 4). Among the gods Jupiter is clearly preferred both in sequence and consequently in rank (v. 13 *quid prius dicam . . .*). Athena is next (v. 19f. *proximos illi tamen occupavit / Pallas honores*), but after a considerable distance.

Sequence as rank, that is to say, as a functional principle of arrangement, is also what is at issue in v. 33ff.: which Roman comes closest to the Greek heroes? Here we find again the *prius* of v. 13, and at the end of the passage the *sidus Iulium* outshining all the lesser stars, v. 46ff. Where Pindar's answer is absolute, Horace's is relative: Jupiter, as in Pindar, surpasses all other Olympians; the man—*quem virum*—Augustus, the actual addressee of the poem, is shown on the one hand in the final triad as reigning below the shadow of Jupiter's wings, on the other in line with the Roman, especially the republican tradition. Triads

---

[9] Loc. cit.; cf. also G. Pasquali, *Orazio lirico* (Firenze ²1964, (ed. A. La Penna) 739ff., 838f. Horace develops the Pindaric theme from question (vv. 1–12 = Pindar, v. 1f.) to answer (v. 13ff. = vv. 3–11) to final prayer (v. 41ff. = v. 12ff.), that is, he integrates the matter pertaining to his own historico-panegyrical situation into the Pindaric framework. For the rest (v. 15ff.) the second Olympian goes its own way. See also n. 17 for the problem of the triadic structure.

two and five, dedicated to the relationship between Jupiter and Augustus, surround the actual center of the poem where one has to look for the answer to the still open question *quem heroa*.

This center with its string of names has evoked the most varied associations and has thus forced interpreters into divergent explanation and even sometimes into conjecture, the last resort of philological desperation.[10] If we take the Pindaric sequence of questions in the prooemium (triad 1) seriously, we have to emphasize the fact that Horace in distinction to Pindar does not set off Hercules. In contrast to *quid prius dicam solitis parentis/laudibus* (v. 13f.) *dicam et Alciden* is conventional. On the other hand the dividing line between the heroes (as former men to be worshipped) and the eminent actors of history that has to be drawn traditionally between Romulus and Numa (v. 33) is in no way marked; on the contrary: the fact that Romulus is afflicted by Horace's doubt (*dubito*) who is to be granted second place after the Greek heroes (*post hos*), raises the other competitors to quasi-heroic importance. That the nimbus of the younger Cato competes with the aura of the distant past is as such less surprising than that his heroic suicide is juxtaposed against all chronology with the last Roman king Tarquinius Superbus; we must keep this difficulty in mind.

By confusing the chronological order in the next two stanzas Horace avoids the impression of just giving a simple sequence of important historical events, thus again keeping alive the awareness of the near-equality of all Roman heroes selected for praise. By his careful choice he can appeal implicitly to the collective memory of his public that may associate the historical occasion with the individual achievement. Implied are six outstanding moments of crisis and final success in wars from the early fourth to late second centuries, decisive for the imperial history of Rome: (1) Camillus against Veii and the Gauls (v. 42); (2) Curius Dentatus and the war against the Samnites (v. 41f.); (3) Fabricius Luscinus in conflict with Pyrrhus (v. 40f.); (4) Regulus and the 1st Punic war (v. 37); (5) Aemilius Paullus, one of the consuls at Cannae, in the 2nd Punic war (v. 38); and finally (6) Aemilius Scaurus[11] as the embodiment of the last external threat to Rome, the invasions of the Cimbri and the Teutones (v. 37). The catalogue is carefully divided into two basic categories of *contemptus mortis et doloris* (Regulus, Paullus who died on the battlefield, Scaurus who took his son for a coward and drove him to suicide) on the one hand, and modesty, *frugalitas, continentia, moderatio* (the rigid incorruptibility of Fabricius and Curius, the moderate reaction of Camillus

---

[10] E.g. Peerlkamp's *Marcellis*, see n. 12.

[11] The plural denoting Scaurus and his son, cf. *De vir. ill.* (= Hygin?, cf. *RE* loc. cit. 1644ff.) 72,10; Val. Max 5,8,4; Frontin, *Strat.* 4,1,13; Ampel. 19,10. It is unnecessary to look for another Scaurus outside the *exempla*-tradition, as do Nisbet–Hubbard, op. cit. 157f. and Bejarano, loc. cit. 268f.

called back from exile to help against the Gauls) on the other hand.

In this order of historical merit, beginning with v. 25ff., the catalogue parallels in third place the invocation of the gods after (1) Jupiter and (2) Pallas, v. 21ff.; *neque te silebo* corresponds with *referam*, v. 39. As Hercules, however, is neither absolutely nor relatively put on the same level with Jupiter and a clear second cannot be made out (v. 33ff.), the whole group of heroes in distinction to the gods is brought closer together.

This line of thought is interrupted by one Marcellus (v. 45f.) who is quite naturally identified by the scholar too well read in history as the elder, while the contemporary audience was supposed to think just as spontaneously of the younger who as nephew of the *princeps* and husband (25 B.C.) of his daughter Julia was his destined successor: *Claudium Marcellum significat Octaviae Augusti sororis filium—Neben den großen Helden der alten Zeit kann Marcellus nur den berühmtesten dieses Namens, den Eroberer von Syrakus und Sieger von Clastidium meinen.*[12] The ancient commentator's view is also supported by the consideration that it was hardly possible to say of the undisputedly famous figure of the elder Marcellus that his glory still permitted growth.[13] Moreover, his appearance after the preceding well-balanced series of events and motifs would have been pointless, that is, inconsistent with Horace's usual poetic procedure. Pindar (*Nem.* 8,40ff.) had compared the growth of ἀρετὰ to the growth of a tree to which Homer (*Il.* 18,56f.) had also compared the young Achilles. Horace combines both allusions applying them to the seventeen- to eighteen-year-old prince whose *fama* is still rising, but may one day outshine all other heroes, as now does the *sidus Iulium* (v. 46ff.).

Horace is thinking of Augustus himself . . . . A direct reference to Julius Caesar is unlikely—Gai Caesaris stellam dicit: the plain statement of Porphyrio convinces again in contrast to the complicated interpretation of modern commentators[14] who are forced to take *sidus* metaphorically

---

[12] *Porphyrio*, ed. D. Holder (Innsbruck 1894) 20, followed e.g. by A. Magariños, *Emerita* 20 (1952) 83ff.; Syndikus, op. cit. 147f.; Kiessling–Heinze, op. cit., followed by Nisbet–Hubbard, 145, 161f., who see Horace "no doubt also hinting at the Princeps's nephew and son-in-law"; but whoever wants two *Marcelli* or even the whole family to be meant should be attracted by *Marcellis* (Peerlkamp); cf. Birt, op. cit. 73f., and G. Williams, *TORP* (Oxford 1968) 271 and "Horace *Odes* I.12 and the succession to Augustus," *Hermathena* 118 (1974) 147ff., esp., 148, n. 10 (on 154). For the political situation of 24 see Williams, *Hermathena*, loc. cit., and Kienast, op. cit. 85f.

[13] Contra Nisbet–Hubbard 162, but *longum semper fama gliscente per aevum* (v. 63 in the Regulus-digression, Sil. Ital. 6,62ff.) reckons from the historical context of the excursus, that is, from the first Punic war. For Jerome the matter is clear (In *Ephes.* 619 [PL 26, 535] = Rufin. Apol. contra Hieron. 44 [CC 20,80]): *Parvulus crescit et occulto aevo in perfectam adolescit aetatem* = Horace v. 45f.: *Crescit occulto . . . aevo fama Marcelli.*

[14] *Porphyrio*, loc. cit. (and e.g. Birt, op. cit. 73; "Daβ unter letzterem [sc. dem Julischen Gestirn] nur der vergöttlichte Julius Cäsar gemeint sein konnte, steht fest") against

and to cope with the repeated mention of Augustus here and again in the otherwise clearly set off final triad.

Those who sufficiently take into account the cult of the emperor, its development and its symbolism as background for such flickering lights, will grasp the importance of Caesar's star within Augustan ideology, and consequently in Augustan poetry too.[15] The contemporary addressee therefore would again quite naturally have taken the *sidus Iulium* as alluding to the consecrated adoptive father of the *princeps*. It is well known that already in 44 a celestial phenomenon appeared which could be taken as a sign that the dictator in Roman terms was raised among the gods, *Caesaris animam inter deorum immortalium numina receptam*, as Augustus noted later in his autobiography.[16] Octavian in any case knew how to nourish popular belief by connecting the natural phenomenon with Caesar's consecration. In addition he put up a number of statues crowned with Caesar's star. In Virgil's ninth *eclogue* (v. 46ff.) Caesar's *astrum* guarantees the ripening of crops and grapes; in Propertius 4,6,59f. Caesar looks down from the stars into the battlefield at Actium.

No doubt Augustus' adoptive father heroized according to Greek notions is also meant in Horace; *micat* looks back to *refulsit* of verse 28. Caesar outshines as *heros* not only all mortals, but also Hercules and the Dioscuri, as the moon is brighter than all lesser stars. Horace is complimenting the princeps by ending the poem in a kind of dynastic climax— Marcellus (v. 45f.), Caesar (v. 46ff.) and Augustus himself (the final triad). The genealogical aspect in the praise of Iuppiter as *parens* (v. 13, *generatur* v. 17) of the Muse, of the selected Greek gods and heroes corresponds with the synthesis of Roman history culminating (as later in the *forum Augustum*) in the *gens Iulia* and in Augustus between the

---

Nisbet–Hubbard 162 (and Magariños, op. cit. 85f.; Fraenkel, op. cit. 296) who omit to mention that a few years earlier the temple of the Divus Iulius, showing the star in the tympanon, was inaugurated by Octavian in the Forum Romanum, cf. Zanker, *Forum Romanum* 12f. Those who accept *Marcellis* understand consequently the *gens Iulia*, cf. Pasquali, op. cit. 744f.; Williams, *Hermathena* loc. cit. 148ff., also Kiessling–Heinze, ad loc. For the official position (implied or outspoken criticism of civil war and dictatorship, emphasis on the apotheosis) see R. Syme, *The Roman Revolution* (Oxford 1939) 317f.; L. R. Taylor, *Party Politics in the Age of Caesar* (Berkeley/Los Angeles 1949) 179f.

[15] Cf. in general S. Weinstock, *Divus Julius* (Oxford 1971) 370ff. (who unfortunately for the Horace passage ceded to the philological *communis opinio*, p. 378f., 383); H. Gesche, *Caesar* (Darmstadt 1976) 169f.; Kienast, op. cit. 24f., 180f.; for artistic and literary representations, K. Scott, *CPh* 36 (1941) 257ff.; D. Pietrusiński, *Eos* 68 (1980) 273ff. The young Caesar turned the presumably ill-boding prodigium (of a comet?) into a lucky star, cf. I. Hahn, *AAntHung* 16 (1968) 239ff.; the *thronos Caesaris*, however, was to be seen only in the southern sky, cf. Plin. *nat. hist.* 2,178.

[16] Plin. *nat. hist.* 2,93f., (H. Malcovati, *Imp. Caes. Aug. Operum fragmenta* [Torino ³1948] 86ff.), cf. also *Iul. Obs.* 68 (= Livy); Sen. *nat. quaest.* 7,17,2; Suet. *Caes.* 88; Cass. Dio 45,7,1 and F. Bömer, *BJ* 152 (1952) 27ff.; Serv. *auct. buc.* 9,46; *Aen.* 8,681.

generations of Caesar and Marcellus.

Thus the central triads 3 and 4 are more closely connected and distinctly separated from the surrounding Jupiter/Augustus triads 2 and 5. The "heroical" centre of our poem is unified by a kind of "Ringkomposition" which contrasts the Greek heroes (st. 7/8) with the future and the already consecrated Roman heroes (st. 12) by simile (Marcellus) and visualization of their celestial power. Moreover the central stanzas 9 and 10 are bound together by the catalogue of Roman *exampla*, especially by the clausula *Catonis nobile letum* which anticipates the following fates; the underlying structural plan is handled in a flexible way.[17]

And yet the two central triads are again independent from one another when seen in the light of a subtle allusion to another, this time Latin literary source. The stanzas 7–9 are talking about *seven* heroes (Hercules and the Dioscuri, three kings, and Cato), stanzas 10–12 about *seven* celebrities (Regulus, Scaurus and Paullus, Fabricius and Curius, Camillus and Marcellus) plus *one* (Caesar). This play with numbers—7 + 7 + 1—addressed to well-informed ancient readers so far has escaped all modern commentators. It is the reversed disposition of Varro's *Imagines sive Hebdomades*. This prosopographic summary of Varro's historic works since the late fifties appeared from about 45 B.C. on. In fifteen books (1+7+7) it presented 700 *viri illustres*. The introductory book which anticipated the double sequence of the following books contained fourteen outstanding personalities, seven Greeks and seven Romans representing seven human activities which were then dealt with in a Greek and Roman book each, *reges* in 2/3, *duces* (generals and politicians) in 4/5, poets in 6/7, prose writers in 8/9, *opifices* (doctors, architects etc.) in 10/11, *artifices* (artists) in 12/13 and finally in 14/15 the authors of the seven liberal arts.[18]

The number 7 determined the structure of the work as a whole and in detail. It comprised 7 x 100 names, the number of books was 1 + 2 x 7, the first book consisted of 2 x 7, and each following book of

---

[17] Our results (*quem deum = Iovem*, triad 2; *quem heroa = Caesarem*, triads 3 and 4; *quem virum = Augustum*, triad 5) obviate, I believe, most of the objections levelled against a too rigid (and conceptually problematical, cf. especially Fraenkel, op. cit. 292f., 295f.) understanding of the triadic structure; cf. C. Becker, *Das Spätwerk des Horaz*, (Göttingen 1963) 114,3; Williams, *TORP* 270ff.; Syndikus, op. cit. 136ff. The discussion between A. Treloar (*Antichthon* 3 [1969] 48ff.; 6 [1972] 60ff.; 7 [1973] 60f.), A. J. Dunston (ibid. 54ff.) and H. D. Jocelyn (5 [1971] 68ff.; 7 [1973] 72ff.) peters out; undecided also N. E. Collinge, *The Structure of Horace's Odes* (London 1961) 104f.

[18] Cf. the discussion ap. F. Ritschl, *Opusc. philol.* 3 (Leipzig 1877) 508–92; also H. Dahlmann, *RE Suppl.* 6 (1935) 1227ff. The modern neglect of this important work is mirrored by B. Cardauns, "Stand und Aufgaben der Varroforschung (mit einer Bibliographie der Jahre 1935–1980)," *AAWM* (1982) 4,11, who, however, omits here to collect the minor contributions of the unfortunately alphabetical bibliography. My reconstruction is partially new, the arguments for which will be found in a book which I'm preparing together with N. Horsfall.

7 x 7 heroes. But it was not this typically Varronian pedantic disposition, but an abundance and vividness of pictures hitherto unseen which must have struck the ancient reader, who till then was unspoiled in this respect, as sensational. Even as late as the elder Pliny the *Imagines* were appreciated as *benignissimum inventum*, as a gift worthy of the envy of the gods, because it did not just bestow immortality, but distributed it all over the world, so that the persons portrayed might be omnipresent (*nat. hist.* 35,11). For the pictorial representation of the celebrities, which were identified only by an (often traditional) epigram, was the real innovation of the work. Varro's achievement is impressive even if Pliny should be right in some cases: *quin immo etiam, quae non sunt, finguntur, pariuntque desideria non traditos vultus.*

The common knowledge of the *Imagines* is taken for granted in the Varronian center of our poem. The original sequence "outstanding personalities" (B. 1)-"normal celebrities" (B. 2–15) is turned into a striking climax by putting Caesar at the end. Moreover the number 7 as underlying theme, which contrasts with the structural weight of the triads, can only be explained by Varro's influence: all in all the poem names twenty-one praiseworthy persons: five gods (Jupiter, Pallas, Liber, Diana, Phoebus), the fifteen heroes and Augustus. The twenty-one names are distributed in a latent parallelism featuring again the number 7; Jupiter is followed by seven Greeks (Pallas to the Dioscuri, altogether 5 stanzas), the three Roman kings by seven Republican heroes and these in turn by three members of the Julian dynasty (4 stanzas).

The structure of the Horatian ode, evoking that of the Pindaric poem as well as that of the Varronian prosopography, shows precise poetic calculation. This, however, results in more far-reaching questions to be asked of the function of these transtextual relations. Our poem, as other Pindarizing odes (3,4. 4,4.14), at first gives the impression of an official statement—thus Gordon Williams,[19] who takes its historicity sufficiently into account: "The ode is evidence of the way in which Horace received concrete political information and processed it for incorporation in his lyric poetry." Written in 25/24, it builds on Augustus' military success and Marcellus' achievement in Spain. As an *epinikion* in the full sense of the word, it integrates the allusions to Augustan ideology (the *princeps* as the second founder of Rome equivalent to Romulus, a religious reformer like Numa, v. 33f.) into an overall picture painted with colors of war and victory: Pallas is defined as *proeliis audax* (v. 21); Apollo as a terrifying archer; the *viri summi* symbolize the decisive wars of Republican history; and the final triad models the reign of Augustus according to the ideal of Alexander (v. 53ff.) and disparages the enemies of the empire as rebels (*iusto triumpho*, v. 54).

---

[19] *Hermathena* 153.

Thus Horace on the one hand participates here and elsewhere in what Syme calls "The organization of opinion"[20] even without acceding to the request that he write a panegyrical epic. This is not to be misunderstood as a one-way street: compared with Pindar the volume of praise which the polyphony of the text indicates is clearly lowered. At the same time Horace by answering the question *quem virum* (=Augustus) takes an unambiguous position which—probably in accordance with the *princeps'* wishes—stays within the framework of a strictly republican tradition and systematically precludes a crossing of the borderline towards the cult of the ruler.[21] Deserving men may have been heroized after their deaths or may be in the future, but that is history's decision.

Varro's pictorial system had comprised Greeks as well as Romans, politicians and writers, men of theory and practice. Horace selects only *reges* and *duces*: this reduction of the Varronian program embedded in the Pindaric context is geared to evoke Roman history as essentially republican tradition. The reference to the *princeps*, once more, remains discreetly indirect; Romulus, not Aeneas, the family hero of the *gens Iulia*, appears as the symbol of Augustan rule. Roman republican history culminates in Augustus. Only after the publication of our poem did he in 23 B.C. procure for himself a legal basis for his monarchical power by the permanent *tribunicia potestas* and the *imperium proconsulare maius*. But in 24 B.C. it was still possible to believe in *rem publicam . . . in libertatem vindicavi* (*Mon. Anc.* 1) or *rem publicam ex mea potestate in senatus populique Romani arbitrium transtuli* (34) or else to try to commit the *princeps* to these maxims.

The conjuring up of republican heroes might explain, too, why the younger Cato instead of Iunius Brutus,[22] tyrannicide and founder of the republic, contrasts almost provocatively with the last king, Tarquinium Superbus. Augustus' idea of history had no place for the vanquished of revolution and civil war—e.g., the Gracchi—as we know from the repertory of his *forum* and the biographies of Hyginus.[23] So far the canonization of Roman history as an exemplary prosopography, beginning with Varro's and Atticus' *Imagines* and approaching its final form in Livy and Hyginus, had not yet been completed. Its meaning and components were still in a state of flux. The *nobile letum* of Cato in Horace heads a sequence of exempla who by their sacrifice contributed to the salvation of the *res publica*. His suicide is thus interpreted as a renunciation of self-destruction of

---

[20] Op. cit. 459ff.; cf. also for the more personal aspects, N. Horsfall, *Poets and Patron. Maecenas, Horace and the Georgics*, Publications of the Macquarie Ancient History Association, No. 3 (North Ryde, Australia 1981).

[21] Fraenkel 296f.

[22] Cf. Williams *TORP* 272 and *Figures of Thought in Roman Poetry* (New Haven 1980) 13ff. E. Fantham very kindly made me aware of the last title.

[23] Cf. *RE*. loc. cit. 1657.

the old republic and thereby as a salutary action for the new one. Now, Horace implies, Augustus' main ambition should be to take its restoration really to heart, and that includes the reconciliation with the republican resistance. Augustan rule is accepted within the boundaries of its own ideology and taken at the word of its proclamations.[24]

[24] Cf. R. Merkelbach, *Philologus* 104 (1960) 149ff. and, for the "Catonism" of this "new-style republic," Syme, op. cit. 506f. and Taylor, op. cit. 178ff.

LITERATURE, PATRONAGE, AND POLITICS:
NERO TO NERVA

J. P. SULLIVAN

Literature, particularly ancient literature, has to be understood in its historical context before we can judge it. It has been the fashion recently to focus our critical gaze on just the work of art itself, not the personality of the artist, not the moulding pressures of the time or the genre or the tradition. Some critics therefore have tended to examine the extant literary works in isolation, leaving the impression that most Greek and Roman writers, although writing for fame and willing enough to use contemporary material, simply did their best in their chosen literary form and that was that. But it is arguable that all superior art, art that is not purely derivative, is a triumph over almost intractable *données*: the poverty of subject or language, the lack or excess of models, the deadening weight of a tradition or the uncharted path that faces the *avant-gardiste*. Art is the product of a human being subject to the pressures of his personal, literary, political, and indeed economic environment. The artist may transcend the crippling effect of such influences, but we cannot assume that such influences did not actively affect the nature of his art. Art is not produced in a vacuum, but in a matrix. The age of Nero and the Flavian Emperors is a particularly fruitful period for the study of the interrelation of these forces, both because of its extensive literature and because of the documentary evidence of the pressures exerted on individual writers.

Tacitus and Pliny are in agreement that literature does not flourish under tyranny; we, with our greater experience of man's endurance and ingenuity, may feel more sympathy with Jorge Luis Borges's remark: "A dictatorship is good for writers. Censorship challenges them to make their points with ever greater care and subtlety." From an economic point of view, it has been observed that a system of private literary patronage is usually found alongside a despotic or at least highly aristocratic and oligarchical form of society, where the bounty of individual benefactors becomes a necessity. The connection between literature and politics, and between art, economics and political advancement, as well as the rivalries that stem from this, is nowhere more evident than in the Augustan, Neronian and Flavian periods.

Many works of art with a message, poems and novels with partisan content, fail, tempting us to think that art and contemporary propaganda cannot mix. What is too time-bound, we feel, is sure to end in artistic failure. But perhaps the opposite is the case. The work of art that is *not* rooted in its historical reality is more likely to be a failure, because it will feed on nothing but the imitation of past literature without understanding the pressures and the intellectual immediacy which generated its models. The fusion of the writer and his age produces the artistic tension that ensures both comprehension by contemporaries and continued appreciation, perhaps of a different sort, by later generations. The *Aeneid* survives as a revered classic because Vergil grappled with contemporary issues, not just with Homer. The same may be said of Swift's *Gulliver's Travels* and Orwell's *Animal Farm*.

The Neronian age, without denying due honour to Flavian or Antonine literature, is surpassed only by the Augustan age for the number and fertility of the poets and prose writers it produced. Seneca, Lucan, Persius, Petronius, Silius Italicus, Calpurnius, Siculus, Columella, the Elder Pliny, the Greek epigrammatists, Lucillius, Cerealius and Nicharchus, and the Stoic Philosophers Annaeus Cornutus and Musonius Rufus are represented by extant works, but even more writers are lost. Much of the credit for this literary Renaissance must be given to the Emperor himself. It may even be said that his devotion to the arts cost him his throne and his life. "*Qualis artifex pereo!*" A pacific emperor who added little territory to the Empire and who managed to close the temple of Janus twice, unlike Domitian he did not count among his many enthusiasms a taste for military leadership or for inspection tours of his legions in the provinces. In another display of poor judgment, despite the urgings of his freedman Helios, he lingered in Greece from September 66 till January 68, while massive discontents among various elements of the state festered unchecked. Greece, he said, was the only nation that truly appreciated his artistic gifts.

Nero's aesthetic bent contributed in another way to his downfall. His philhellenism in both its political and histrionic manifestations added to the outrage of the senatorial class. Yet the young Nero had begun his reign auspiciously enough. In his first speech on attaining the purple, a speech ghost-written for him by his tutor Seneca, he had promised to rule *ex praescripto Augusti* (Tac. *Ann.* 13.4; Suet. *Nero* 10). Few had been deceived about the realities of power in Augustan times. The political state created by Augustus was always and inevitably on the side of the reigning monarch, just as the earlier Republican constitution was tipped on the side of hereditary families and wealth. But Augustus had tried to conceal those realities under constitutional veils. Yet the natural tendency of the principate to absolute monarchy, aided by the supineness (or realism) of many members of the senate, was openly hastened by Nero, particularly after 62, once he felt the basic lack of sympathy among them for his style of life and the ways he used his power. Nero was moving towards what appeared to some as a monarchy of the Hellenistic type and to others something worse, the capricious rule of a Caligula. The image of the great Ptolemaic patrons of arts and letters with their libraries, court poets, and divine status proved too much of a temptation. Nero hankered for the glory that was Greece: the senators looked back to the Grandeur that was Rome—particularly as embodied in the senate.

The dramatist Ernst Toller wrote that "History is the propaganda of the victors" and since Nero was a loser, it is small wonder that the senatorially-biased histories that have survived make Nero out to be a monster, although we know from Josephus and Martial that there were also histories that put Nero in a far more favorable light; for many years after his death parts of the Empire awaited his miraculous return with hope and credulity. Indeed nothing proves the power of literature more than the fact that the usual picture of Nero himself is the hostile depiction conveyed to later generations by Tacitus, Suetonius and Dio Cassius.

The evidence for Nero's own artistic activity and his encouragement of the activity of other writers and artists is found in all of our chief sources. Tacitus notes his early and lively interest in carving, painting and singing (not to mention his passion for horses). The historian even grudgingly recognises in him an educated talent for versifying (*Ann.* 13.3). And it is not surprising that Nero should be so interested in literature, particularly poetry, since he was tutored not only by the learned Alexandrian pedagogue Chaeremon, who would have drawn attention to his native city's greatest poetic luminary, Callimachus, but also by one of the most brilliant writers of the age, Seneca, who produced four books of poetry as well as some tragedies (Prisc. *lib.* 7.759).

That Nero really wrote poetry himself is guaranteed by Suetonius (*Nero* 52), who was able to inspect some rough drafts which came into his hands, presumably when he had access to the imperial archives. These may have been drafts presented to the literary circle which Nero established in 59 and which went into session after dinner. Tacitus' remarks are worth quoting in full for their sneering innuendo and their uncharacteristic disdain of literary artifice:

> ne tamen ludicrae tantum imperatoris artes notescerent, carminum quoque studium adfectavit, contractis quibus aliqua pangendi facultas necdum insignis erat. Hi cenati considere simul et adlatos vel ibidem repertos versus conectere atque ipsius verba quoquo modo prolata supplere, quod species ipsa carminum docet, non impetu et instinctu nec ore uno fluens.   (*Ann.* 14.16)

But the emperor did not wish his stage talents to be his only avenue to fame. He affected also an enthusiasm for poetry. He brought together round him associates with some ability in versification, whose talents had not yet attracted public attention. After dinner they all sat down and strung together verses they had brought along to the meeting or improvised on the spot, and they aided Nero in his own efforts, whether they were drafts or extemporizations. This is obvious from the very impression given by his poems: no vitality, no inspiration, and an inconsistent tone.

There were not only poetry workshops, but also lyre-recitals at Nero's house. His instrumental skills were honed by one of the most famous musicians of the day, Terpnus, who used to give him lessons, also after dinner. This was his preparation for entering the contests which he himself established, the *Ludi Iuvenales* of 59 and the *Neronia* of 60 and 65. These were official occasions, which were to culminate in the many contests Nero entered during his triumphal tour of Greece in 66 and 67 when he won no less than 1808 prizes and dedicated the wreaths on the Capitol.

Nero was twenty-one by this date when he started the circle, fretting under his mother's domination and the restraining influences of Seneca and Burrus. Perhaps the latter felt that this interest in poetry was a harmless enough occupation. At any rate, Seneca's nephew Lucan seems to have been recalled from Athens to join it. The very existence of such a circle is surely proof of Nero's genuine, if jealous, literary interests. Moreover philosophical debates varied the poetic diet, even if inconclusive dialectic and sectarian squabbles rather than the pursuit of truth provided the interest and amusement. What Tacitus may have overlooked, however, is that membership of this circle often led to admission to Nero's *consilium principis* and, where appropriate, to high office or other tangible prizes. The list of its possible members therefore deserves close scrutiny.

There is the consul of 65, M. Julius Vestinus Atticus, whose barbed jokes, based on close intimacy with Nero, eventually led to his downfall during the Pisonian purges. There is M. Cocceius Nerva, the future emperor (96–98), whom Nero hailed as the Tibullus of his day (Ma. 8.70; cf. 9.26 and Plin. *Ep.* 5.3.5). Nerva held the offices of *sevir* and *quaestor urbanus*, but the significant aspect of his career is his vigorous part in the suppression of the Pisonian conspiracy. He and Tigellinus were honoured not only with triumphal insignia but also with statues in the Forum and the imperial palace. He became praetor in 66. In view of the sensitivity of the Pisonian conspiracy, we may conclude that Nerva was high in Nero's councils. Presumably his interest in poetry, which declined with time, if it was ever serious at all, was a large factor in cementing the reciprocal friendship.

Another future emperor who was part of the circle and who also seems really to have admired Nero's compositions was Aulus Vitellius.

His earlier successful career suffered no setback under Nero and evidence of his participation in Nero's literary activities is to be seen in his presidency at the *Neronia* and his loyal demand for a recital from the *liber dominicus* after he became emperor himself (Suet. *Vitell.* 4–11).

Yet a third ruler of Rome may have been a member of the circle. This was the future emperor Titus, who would have been seventeen years old in 59. Although a close friend and fellow schoolmate of Britannicus, Nero must have been assured of his loyalty or captivated by his artistic talents: a ready orator in Latin and Greek, an equally accomplished poet in both those languages, he was notable also for his skill at the highly esteemed art of extemporization. He was in addition a good singer and a trained and agreeable musician (Suet. *Tit.* 3). His martial abilities helped, but after holding military tribunates, he received a quaestorship and in 67 the command of a legion in Judaea. Would we know of his peacetime poetic talents unless they were displayed at court in his youth? After 64 or thereabouts he was immersed in military matters or civil administration.

T. Silius Italicus, author of the *Punica*, was also probably a member of this circle. He appears to have been a gratuitously active or overly loyal prosecutor at this period (Plin. *Ep.* 3.7). His consulate in 68 would seem to confirm this. Significantly he supported Vitellius, who retained his affection for Nero, in the succession struggles of that year. He probably wrote the *Ilias Latina*, as the acrostics at the beginning and end of the poem *ITALICUS . . . SCRIPSIT* indicate; certainly the work belongs to the period before 69, since there is a flattering reference to the Julio-Claudian house (*Augustum genus claris submitteret astris*) between verses 899 and 902 (cf. vv. 236, 483), and the author shows Alexandrian tastes, the dominant influence in Neronian poetic circles. In any case, since Silius was a devoted and loyal friend of Nero's, who blossomed later as an epic poet, it is unlikely that he did not participate, however prentice his hand, in the court's literary activities.

A. Fabricius Veiento, another minor writer, also rose to high honours and influence under Nero. He was a friend of Nerva's and as praetor he was involved in another of Nero's enthusiasms, chariot racing. His only known publication was the *Codicilli*, an exercise in a long-lived genre which seems based on a practice going back to Augustan times and earlier, the parody of wills and testaments for malicious purposes. Fabricius however attacked the senate and the priestly colleges; despite Nero's known fondness for satire and indeed tolerance of lampoons against himself, he may have gone too far and provoked serious hostility. His enemies accused him of abuse of his position at court, the selling of offices and state privileges. It was for this that Nero exiled him.

Another literary man was the consular Cluvius Rufus. He is known best for his later, well-informed, but doubtless revisionist history of

Nero's reign and beyond. He must have had a place in the circle, since he was Nero's impresario for his stage appearances even in Greece, and had presumably demonstrated the appropriate artistic leanings. He also wrote a treatise on the theatre, a sure way to Nero's heart.

Another member of the circle was surely C. Calpurnius Piso, who, until enemies began their insinuations against both Seneca and himself, had been an apparently close supporter and friend of the emperor. His intimacy with Nero was such that it was proposed by the conspirators in 65 that Nero be struck down in Piso's lovely villa at Baiae, since Nero enjoyed his visits there and took few precautions (Tac. *Ann.* 15.52). Calpurnius Siculus, who is the best candidate for the authorship of the *Laus Pisonis*, which was written by a young poet on the make if ever there was one, represents him as eulogizing the emperor and thanking him before the senate for his consulate. Although Piso's *forte* was oratory, he also wrote light verse and lyrics and shared with Nero a fondness for the lyre, an accomplishment of which few senators would be proud (Tac. *Ann.* 15.48). The future conspirator must have been then an eager and active participant in the literary activity of the court.

The most significant member of Nero's circle in the eyes of later critics was, of course, Lucan. With his precocious poetic gifts and, more importantly, his uncle Seneca's influence at court, he was introduced early to the circle, and it was in this ambience that there developed the friendly competition with Nero described in the Voss Life. One of Lucan's rewards for his talents and initial friendship with Nero was a premature quaestorship and an augurate. Lucan's poetic output, considering that he died in his twenty-sixth year, is staggering, even when we allow for his talent in extempore composition. He treated the perennial theme of Troy in his *Iliacon*; he churned out epigrams and ten books of miscellaneous poems (the *Silvae*). For our purposes it is enough to point to the *Laudes Neronianae* of 60 as evidence of the friendship that was to sour into treason by 64. The cause alleged was Nero's jealousy of Lucan's poetic genius which prompted a deliberate affront; Nero walked out on Lucan during one of his recitations. More probably Lucan's connection with the Stoic circles in which Annaeus Cornutus and Persius moved and the strong Republican sympathies visible in even the first books of his poem on the Civil War would have alarmed the political sensitivities of the princeps. Nor would there have been lacking new members of the circle, hostile to even the waning influence of Seneca and his family, to point this out. A prime candidate would be Petronius.

T. Petronius Niger, Nero's arbiter of elegance, joined the circle later, after his consulship in 62 and after his successful governorship of Bithynia. Indeed he achieved such influence with Nero that he aroused the jealousy of Tigellinus, who engineered his downfall. If *entrée* into this circle was a proven road to fast political and material advancement as well as more formal influence on Nero's decisions, then we have a plausible explanation for the rapid growth in the number of poetasters and other amateur writers that we hear of in Persius' first satire:

scribimus inclusi, numeros ille, hic pede liber (1.13)

Nero's genuine devotion to literature, to dramatic performance, to declamation, and to the other arts, did not blind him to their political usefulness. Nero was particularly assiduous about conciliating the populace; he was jealous of everyone who could touch the heart of the masses (Suet. *Nero* 53; Tac. *Ann.* 13.31). One obvious way he enhanced his popularity and his safety was through his own enthusiasm for the stage and the circus and the provision of spectacular entertainments. Of course Nero's artistic talents, however welcome to the Roman people, were greeted even more tumultuously in Greece and the Greek-speaking areas of Italy such as Naples, where drama and music were then as now the objects of lively passion.

There were of course other literary circles and also a more mischievous side to such gatherings, which may account for Domitian's hostility to them (Tac. *Agr.* 2.3). It was at a particularly crowded dinner, given by P. Ostorius Scapula, that Antistius Sosianus, now praetor, recited his slanderous poems against Nero. Cossutianus Capito, Tigellinus' son-in-law, promptly accused him of treason. Nero, who was normally tolerant of such abuse and not above writing scurrilous verse himself, allowed the infamous *lex maiestatis* to be revived for the first time in his reign (in 62) and Antistius was banished.

This is an illustration of the sometimes dangerous connection between literature and power, but Seneca had seen the connection long ago. There can be little doubt that, until 62 and his forced, or voluntary, retirement from court, Seneca took a great interest in the literary activities of Nero's court. His incessant production of erotic verses and epigrams, or serious tragedies and scientific and philosophical treatises, sometimes with an overtly political cast (the *De Ira* and *De Clementia*) can be largely explained by extrinsic motives. Seneca could not have afforded to neglect the power to be gained by those who were admitted to these gatherings. One charge made by his enemies later was that Seneca had started writing verse more frequently now that Nero had developed an affection for it (Tac. *Ann.* 14.52). In view of Nero's predilection for the stage and dramatic recitals, it is not unreasonable to date some of Seneca's tragedies to the period after 59 rather than earlier. This could be part of the poetry his enemies are referring to.

The death of Burrus and the philosopher's semi-retirement meant that Nero fell under the influence of very different advisers from those he formerly had (Tac. *Ann.* 14.52). Among the imperial advisers would be those who espoused very different political, philosophical, and literary principles from those of the Annaean family. Ofonius Tigellinus at this period replaced Burrus as a co-commander of the Praetorian Guard and the philosophy that, in its Roman form, differed in so many ways from Stoicism would gain influence after 62. Epicureanism was to have its representatives not only in Calpurnius Piso, but also in Petronius. It is most unlikely that the refined tastes of the *arbiter elegantiae* would not be felt in the literary and critical activity of the court.

With such imperial encouragement the proliferation of other literary and political circles outside the palace is easy to understand. An identifiable group is that of the Calpurnii, whose most prominent member was C. Calpurnius Piso, the arch conspirator in 65. Its philosophical bias was probably Epicurean; its literary views conservatively classical, and its politics initially cooperation with the imperial regime. Stoic circles existed also, such as that of Thrasea Paetus in which Persius and Cornutus moved. It was in these circles that the aspiring poet would find his rich patron; that new literary enterprises could be tried out; that subversive or libellous writings could get their first hearing. They offered opportunities for poetic, philosophic and political writing; and their potentialities for propaganda, the moulding of opinion, personal attacks, and even the fashioning of plots must not be underrated. Apart from the *Apocolocyntosis* of Seneca, we know little enough of the form these malicious and personal literary attacks took. Nero himself had insulted the flabby Afranius Quintianus in a more direct way, driving him into the arms of the Pisonian conspirators (Tac. *Ann.* 15.49). Lucan in turn had written a similar *probrosum carmen* about the emperor and his associates, so joining the praetor Antistius Sosianus and Fabricius Veiento.

The complimentary effusions of Calpurnius Siculus deserve attention. In the pastoral eclogues he claims that his real desire is literary fame rather than money (or position), a protestation we may take with a grain of salt. He had presumably gained entry to Calpurnius Piso's salon and repaid his patron with effusive praises: Piso's ancestry, his eloquence; his amiability; his courtesy to the emperor during his consulship; his culture; his poetic and musical accomplishments; even his skill at Roman chess. Piso is to be his Maecenas, and he has even higher hopes. Piso is to bring his verse to the attention of Nero and crown the favours he has already done him. Here the otherwise insipid court poetry catches our attention by sounding certain political notes.

Before these themes can be appreciated a glance is needed at the first and prime example of literary polemic and propaganda in the Neronian age, Seneca's *Apocolocyntosis*, a scathing attack on the recently dead emperor Claudius combined with a fulsome eulogy of young Nero. The work reflects the prejudices and objections held by the senatorial class against the late emperor: Claudius' penchant for enfranchising provincials; his subjection to his freedmen; his excessive preoccupation with legal work and his private kangaroo courts. Essentially it is criticism of imperial attacks on the privileges and security of the upper class. Nero had promised to govern in the manner of Augustus, so Augustus delivers the vicious foray on Claudius' blatant departure from the Augustan model of government. This is one of the most significant elements in the satire. The compliments to the young Nero on his beauty and promise are handsome enough, though brief, being intended to solicit grateful acceptance of the passing over of Britannicus, Claudius' legitimate son, in favor of his adoptive son. Equally important are the propaganda motifs that Seneca introduces: Augustan principles; the new Golden age; peace; justice; beauty; and culture. These are the notes echoed by Calpurnius Siculus in the *Eclogues*.

The interesting aspect of the *Apocolocyntosis*, then, is that a Neronian ideology has been established from the start: an image had been created by Seneca, which aspirants, such as Calpurnius Siculus, to fame, fortune and power had to incorporate into their more personal flattery of Nero's good looks, godlike presence or poetic skills. Calpurnius Siculus may stand as one in place of many examples of the typical "court" poetry of the period, that is to say, poetry one of whose prime aims is flattery of the emperor and whose motivation, besides fame, is social advancement and pecuniary reward. This was to be carried to far greater heights by Martial and Statius. Theocritus' *Idylls* and Vergil's *Eclogues* are the models, indications of the type of poetry favoured in Nero's literary circle and despised by Persius. The propaganda notes in the flattery would by now be familiar: the return of *aurea aetas* of Saturn; the rebirth of the rule of Numa; the restoration of justice by kindly Themis; the end of civil war; bright peace; clemency; the freedom of the senate; the abolition of bribery for public office; and the comparison of the emperor with a superior deity. All this in *Eclogue* I (cf. especially vv. 42–88), repeating not only the motifs of the *Apocolocyntosis*, but also of the *De clementia*, written about 55–56.

The so-called Einsiedeln Eclogues, which are by different hands, may give us a further insight into the literary and political warfare of the period. The second, deliberately recalling the opening of Calpurnius' Eclogue 4, presents a critical variation on the praises of the new Golden Age inaugurated by Nero, to the effect that there was a serpent in the Neronian Garden of Eden. Too established a peace, too widespread a prosperity, would have its dangers also and could lead to moral decadence. The speaker Mystes even says *satietas mea gaudia vexat* (v. 9). But there is no evidence for our assuming a political hostility in the writer, which is not the case with the first Einsiedeln Eclogue, dateable to late 64 or 65, after the fire of Rome, and possibly from the circle of Calpurnius Piso, where pastoral had been used for political purposes earlier. A suitable irony would be to couch adverse comment on Nero in

the same form, particularly now that Piso himself was becoming
estranged from Nero. Again, the central poem of Calpurnius' collection
is the model. The structure is conventional, a contest between Thamyras
and Ladas. Thamyras desires to sing Nero's praises; Ladas sings of
Apollo, a theme Thamyras promptly incorporates by identifying Nero
with the god: *hic vester Apollo est*! Then comes the satiric exaggeration
of Nero's poetic talents and vanity with unmistakable allusions to Nero's
alleged burning of Rome, a topic constantly associated with Nero's Trojan epic and particularly with its probable conclusion in the burning of
Troy.

> tu quoque, Troia, sacros cineres ad sidera tolle
> atque Agamemnoniis opus hoc ostende Mycenis:
> iam tanti cecidisse fuit! gaudete ruinae
> et laudate rogos: vester vos tollit alumnus! (1. 38–41)
>
> You also Troy, must raise your sacred ashes to the stars and display
> this work to Agamemnon's Mycenae! Now your destruction was
> worth such a price! Rejoice in your collapse and praise your funeral
> pyres: your nursling raises you up!

The sarcastic note of this veiled allusion to Nero's youthful speech secur-
ing exemption from all public taxes for the inhabitants of Troy is confirmed when Homer puts his golden wreath on Nero's head and Vergil
tears up his own works in frustration (1.45–49).

This is just one literary genre practised in Neronian circles and we
can see that not even in the idealized countryside are politics divorced
from poetry and song, if they ever were. The significance of the pastoral
on the development of propaganda and as a convenient vehicle for
appeals to patrons could hardly be overlooked after Vergil's example.
The distancing effect of the artificial milieu and the convenient use of
humble *personae* served to conceal blatant flattery and damaging criticism alike. Not so distanced is Persius' attack in his satires on the whole
literary and moral ambience of the Neronian Age, since political and
personal themes were not the only ammunition which could be used in
Neronian literary battles. Critical principles and writing styles were also
at issue.

There seems little doubt that some form of Callimacheanism was the
prevalent poetic mode at this period, harking back to the fashions of the
Neoterics and the Augustan elegists. Callimacheanism pervaded such
poetic forms as didactic poetry, pastoral, epigram, hymn, elegy, and the
so-called epyllia. The style is fundamentally learned, indeed *recherché*,
and oftentimes obscure. For subject matter its practitioners preferred
recondite myths, ingenious catalogues, scientific information, aetiology,
love and death, scenes of town or country life, and general discussion of
the art and appropriate themes of poetry, in particular the *recusatio*, the

poet's refusal to write on certain subjects. The critical terms were λεπτός ("smooth") and τόρος ("delicate"), which came over into Latin critical vocabulary as *tenuis* (or *gracilis*), *levis*, and *teres*; ἀγρυπνίη and μαρτυρήσις led to the Roman concepts of *doctrina* and *doctus*.

The renaissance of the Neronian Age saw a rise in the critical fortunes of Callimachus in Rome and also the beginning of his imminent decline as critic and poetic model. The nadir of his reputation was to be later represented by Martial's 10.4, in which the epigrammatist rejects all mythological themes to write about mankind. The reader who does not wish to know himself should read the *Aetia* of Callimachus (vv. 9–12). But the attacks on Callimacheanism can already be seen in the epigrams of the period. The first criticism we have is of one notable Callimachean verse practice— ingenious periphrases for time. It occurs in the *Apocolocyntosis* (ca. 2), where Seneca offers us nine parodic lines of poetry to describe the time of Claudius' death: between twelve noon and one o'clock, October 13th, as he then tells us in prose. Seneca criticizes the practice elsewhere (*Ep.* 122.11–14) and cites some examples from Julius Montanus, an inferior poet writing in the age of Tiberius. The prevalence of such poetic periphrases can be confirmed from the verse practice of Columella in Book 10 of *De Re Rustica* (published about 62–64). His inspiration is Vergil's *Georgics*, and an acceptance of didactic poetry, a favoured Callimachean genre, needed no defence from him and Callimachean touches abound: periphrases for time and the seasons; obscure mythological descriptions of constellations; a digression on the origins of man; a geographical list of places where cabbages grow; and, finally, he introduces myth or αἴτια associated with such various plants as myrrh and hyacinth. He offers therefore good evidence for the standard poetic mode of the Neronian period, as does Calpurnius Siculus.

Seneca's parody in the *Apocolocyntosis* then is well founded. This sort of thing had become a tired, and tiring, mannerism which was flourishing unchecked among pre-Neronian and Neronian versifiers, a hypothesis for which the prize witness is Persius. The products of Nero's own literary tastes and those of his cronies such as Nerva and the author of the *Ilias Latina* merely provide further evidence.

That Nero's own poetry was predominantly neoteric, that is to say, ultimately Callimachean in inspiration, is easy to prove, since Martial describes his poems as *carmina docta*, *doctus* being a key word in neoteric circles that had kept its critical implications. And one of the few sure lines of Nero's that survives

colla Cytheriacae splendent agitata columbae,

with its variant (AbaB) of "the golden line" is obviously neoteric. Among his poems we find a composition on Poppaea's amber hair; Callimachus chose a similar subject for his *Lock of Berenice*, translated into Latin by

Catullus; and later Statius, another admirer of Callimachus, was to write poetry on Earinus' hair (*Silv.* 3.4). His father who had once soldiered with Nero, was a devoted Callimachean (*Silv.* 5.3.156f.). The neoteric quality of Nero's verse can even be detected in one aspect of his *Troica*, where, according to Servius (*ad Aen.* 5.370), Nero makes Paris the strongest champion of the Trojans. This unexpected story is very much in the spirit of Callimachus. This and the introduction of a little-known king of Troy, Cynthius, into the poem, are other signs of his neoteric tastes. The most decisive evidence, however, for the Callimachean affiliation is the poem he recited in 59 at the *Iuvenalia*, entitled *Attis*, or *The Bacchantes* (Dio 62.20).

The most devastating rejection of Callimacheanism in the poetry of the Neronian age is to be found in Perius' choliambic prologue to his Satires. It is couched, not surprisingly, in *recusatio* form, the refusal to write "what the age demanded." In a few lines Persius bluntly states that modern poets are in business because it is a way to social and material advancement, to patronage by the Emperor or by the rich. The first satire makes it clear that Persius prefers the poetic isolation of the satirist to outmoded and lifeless Callimacheanism as a way of writing poetry, even in its falsely modest and self-deprecatory forms. Despite their elaborate art, which produces a false impression of seriousness disguised as levity, contemporary productions of this sort are ultimately *trifling*, which is of course to turn back on the neoterics their own mock-modesty as a weapon.

The whole of Persius' *Satire* 1 is to be interpreted as an attack on contemporary poetry, which Persius sees as reflecting contemporary morality, and both are bad. Persius' whole *oeuvre* exemplifies the art form Persius proposes to practise in the place of the hated and decadent genres then current: he will write satire. Satire could now stand on its own feet as an art form. Its apologies for its lowly language, like the apologies of the neoterics and the elegists, serve the same function: to disguise thinly and formally its serious claims, which are of course supported by its scathing attacks on both traditional epic and tragedy and also the favoured Callimachean genres of elegy, epyllia, and pastoral. The general target of Persius' criticism is obvious, but a much debated question is whether Persius is more specific about the victims of these satiric darts.

The *Vita Persi* clearly states that Persius *did* attack Nero:

> vehementer saturas componere instituit. . . . sibi primo, mox omnibus detrectaturus cum tanta recentium poetarum et oratorum insectatione, ut etiam Neronem illius temporis principem inculpaverit.

Similarly the *scholia antiqua* (ed. Jahn) allege that there are quotations from Nero's verses between verses 93 and 102 of Persius' first satire. Nor does the scholiast tell us merely once of Persius' quoting Nero. He informs us that the poet inserts bombastic endings used by Nero and he then attributes the four quoted lines to the emperor. Juxtapose now Dio's evidence (62.20) that Nero gave a performance with his own lyre accompaniment at the *Ludi Iuvenales* of a composition which had some such title as *Attis* or *Bacchantes* ("Ἀττιν τινά ἢ Βάκχας) with the relevant lines of Persius:

> summa delumbe saliva
> hoc natat in labris, et in udo est, Maenas et Attis.
> (1.104-5)

This enervated thing, this *Maenad* and *Attis*, swims on the lips, on top of the spittle and stays in the wet.

Persius is insisting that compositions such as *Attis* (or *The Maenads*) are effeminate and superficial. He has earlier quoted (or composed) seven whole or part lines, most of which would appropriately belong to a poem of the subject of Attis. Not unexpectedly, Maenads and Bassarids figure: *Berecyntius Attis, Bassaris et lyncem Maenas flexura corymbis*. The probability is that they are really by Nero. As for the danger of such open quotations or allusions, are they any more dangerous than the contemptuous condemnation of a poem with a title curiously similar to that of a composition which the emperor had put on at a thronged public performance less than three years before, and perhaps even more recently than that? A similar thrust at Nero may be detected in verse 128 (*et lusco qui possit dicere 'lusce'*), since Nero had written a satire entitled *Luscio* against the ex-praetor Clodius Pollio (Suet. *Dom.* 5). The theme of Attis had been handled by Catullus (Cat. 63) and it would therefore seem to be a typically neoteric subject, since with Attis is associated Cybele, hailed by Catullus as *dea domina Dindymi*, and *Magna Mater*, who in turn was the subject of a poem by Catullus' associate Caecilius (Cat. 35.13–18).

It has to be remembered, of course, before we make Persius into a moral hero that Persius' satires were written for a small circle of friends and not published before his death in 62 and perhaps much later. The theory that Persius is just imitating the modernist style for parodic purposes is somewhat weak. *Parodier tout le monde, c'est parodier personne*. Indeed, Persius' critical and satirical ends were best served if he attacked the most prominent exponent of the type of poetry he denounces, the man mainly responsible for the inordinate scribbling and reciting in upper class circles.

Persius of course was a Stoic and a passive resister of the literary and moral decadence of Nero's reign as he perceived it. Gaston Boissier, however, long ago proposed the theory that the opposition to the emperors was predominantly led by Stoics, who were morally and politically opposed to the principate. In fact, the opposition to any emperor consisted predominantly of senators who were vulnerable to imperial authority and mistrust and who deplored the erosion of senatorial power and privilege. Only a few, among whom perhaps should be included Lucan, dreamed of restoring Republican *libertas* of the old oligarchic sort. The best the senatorial order, in its more realistic mood, could hope for was a better ruler than the current emperor, preferably one of their own such as Nerva. The rallying cry of *libertas* still had some value for the more discontented senators; the concept was symbolized in literature and philosophy by the figure of the younger Cato, fortuitously a notable Stoic. Cato was therefore venerated as the last hero of the Roman Republic, the champion of Republican *libertas* both against Caesar, and, had there been real need, Pompey also.

The symbolism of Cato the Younger becomes extremely important in the ideological and literary debates that seem to have thrived in Neronian salons and contemporary publications. Lucan's imposing portrait in the *Pharsalia* is paralleled in Seneca, although Seneca carefully uses him as the ideal Roman Stoic, not as the great champion of Republican liberty. It is a pity that we have lost the various near-contemporary pamphlets which alternatively built up and destroyed Cato's reputation: the laudatory pamphlets by Cicero, Brutus, Fadius Gallus, and Munatius Rufus which confronted the hostile productions of Julius Caesar, Aulus Hirtius, and, eventually, the aging Augustus. But the generally favourable verdict of the Augustan period is enshrined in Vergil's *Aeneid*, Horace's *Odes* and later writers who depended on them.

Even for those like Seneca, who entertained no serious hope of restoring the Republic, Cato and other Republican champions could function as symbols for a more powerful and independent senate, more active magistracies, and greater freedom of speech. Both Seneca and Lucan are predominantly political writers. Seneca pragmatically hoped for a better emperor, perhaps better institutions. Seneca's nephew, Lucan, enshrines the youthful and idealistic view that the Republic could, and should, be restored, identifying himself more and more with the senatorial class and smarting from the insults of Nero. Disillusion with Nero was swift among some senatorial groups; by 62, a pivotal year, the emperor's excesses, whether artistic or domestic, had alienated all but his closest cronies. Lucan, a dupe of the myth of Catonism, expressed their ideals in increasingly perfervid language as the *Pharsalia* progressed.

The works written in Seneca's exile prove the highly political nature of his writings. Even the *Consolatio ad Helviam* contains overt political elements in attempting to clear his own name of the charge for which he had been exiled to Corsica: adultery with Germanicus' daughter, Julia Livilla. The *Consolatio ad Polybium*, written about 43 to the powerful freedman of Claudius, which Seneca later tried to suppress, is even less palatable. The only purpose of the pamphlet was to secure his return from exile. Polybius had just lost a brother and Seneca seized his opportunity; the philosophical sentiments are conventional enough, but the gross flattery of Polybius himself and of the emperor Claudius go beyond even the generous conventions of Roman eulogy (cf. 2.1, 2.4, 2.6, 3.2, 3.4, 6.2 and 6.4). Seneca's references to the emperor's clemency pointedly allude to his own plight (6.5; 18.9). Claudius is praised for his manly bearing of the burdens of Empire. He is compared to Atlas holding the sky on his shoulders (7.1). His vigilance, his industry, his tirelessness, his self-sacrifice (7.2–3) are praised in turn by the future author of the *Apocolocyntosis*. On his return from exile, however, Seneca almost immediately added a third book to his *De Ira*. Here again the occasional nature of much of Seneca's writing is clear. Protected by the power of Agrippina, he indulges in more or less covert criticisms of the emperor who had exiled him. The motivations behind the pamphlet are further underlined by Seneca's referring to exile, his own fate, as an example of imperial cruelty combined with cowardice. A similar attack can be detected in the *De Brevitate Vitae*, probably written in 49 (or 55). This time the darts are directed against Claudius' antiquarianism and his pedantically argued extension of the *pomerium*.

The *De Clementia* was written in late 55 or early 56 and was addressed to Nero. It makes clear that Seneca accepted the realities of the principate. He accepted its absolute power and its immunity to legal sanctions. The supposed question Seneca sets himself is how this supreme power is to be guided. Seneca puts into Nero's mouth a protestation that, with all this power, he exercises it with an even temper, unprovoked by human obstinacy and devoid of vainglory. He exercises it above all with mercy (*clementia*) and so can, at any time, look the gods in the face. This sort of pamphlet, *Advice to a Ruler*, is of course familiar from many national literatures, Machiavelli's *Il principe* being perhaps the most distinguished and notorious. It is literature as an instrument of indirect government, although there are few indications of the success of such writing. Seneca's pamphlet certainly provides no exception to the rule.

The basic message of the treatise is that Nero has inherited a trust, the state, and he must be able to boast that his principles have faithfully guarded this trust. He is credited with bringing Rome security, justice, and, above all, *libertas* (1.1.8–9), again that grace note of imperial propaganda, equally prominent in Pliny the Younger when he praises Trajan, but, Seneca insists, Nero is most admired for his clemency, which he must extend even to the behaviour of dogged champions of Republican (or senatorial) liberty such as Thrasea Paetus. Seneca then is appealing also to the senatorial order. Without the emperor there would ensue the destruction of Roman peace and the ruination of Rome. Seneca's anticipation of civil war consequent on the forcible removal of the emperor was to be amply fulfilled in 69, the year of the Four Emperors. Noticeable is Seneca's constant use of the symbolic figure of Julius Caesar and Augustus to drive his point home (e.g. 1.9–10). Clearly Augustus was still a potent propaganda symbol because he had tried hard to cover up his absolute power and had taken more care than most emperors to conciliate the senate. It was no accident that, despite several plots, he enjoyed the longest reign of all the Julio-Claudian rulers.

Seneca's pen, however, was not simply at the service of the state. He had to think also of himself. When the aging philosopher felt that his own power was slipping from him in 62, he attempted retirement from the court. It was now that Seneca wrote the *De Otio*, a self-justificatory dissertation on the appropriateness of Seneca's decision, whether forced upon him or not, to withdraw from public affairs. In it he covertly expresses his disappointment with the present political situation in Rome and perhaps his own loss of influence.

But Seneca's pen had been deployed in his own interest far more vigorously when he had come under attack. In 58 P. Suillius Rufus, an old enemy of Seneca's, was brought to trial and condemned (Tac. *Ann.* 13.42–43; Dio 61.10). In his defence Suillius voiced criticism which many of Seneca's opponents, perhaps even his friends, must have shared. What branch of learning, asked Suillius, brought Seneca three hundred million sesterces in his four years of friendship with the emperor? Suillius further accused Seneca of shameless legacy hunting and exorbitant interest rates on his loans to Italy and the provinces, of being a hypocrite who preached Stoic doctrine and indifference to wealth, while displaying a rapacious and worldly temperament. Seneca's answer to these charges was his treatise *De Vita Beata.* ". . . those creatures who applaud my eloquence, run after my money, court my favour, and praise my power. They are all my enemies or, much the same thing, can become so" (2.4). He propounds the eclectic Stoic doctrine that virtue is the foundation of happiness, pleasure or worldly goods. He defends his acceptance of legacies (23.2), and, very obliquely, his sex life (27.5). Seneca's defence is that he is *not yet* the Stoic sage, but, in any case, wealth for a Stoic is a matter of "indifference." He prefers to be rich because of the opportunities that wealth provides for the exercise of virtues such as generosity. Even Cato the Younger, the persistent symbol of Stoic and Republican propaganda, is cited as an immensely wealthy man.

The adversaries in this dialogue take on a life of their own. Only in the later *Moral Epistles* does Seneca display such venom. He calls them spiteful excrescences, the enemies of all the best men (*malignissima capita et optimo cuique inimicissima*, 18.1). He compares them to little dogs (19.2). It is they his detractors who are envious; it is they who are the real slaves of money, not Seneca (22.5).

Seneca's important treatise, *De Tranquillitate Animi*, apparently belongs to the same historical context and should therefore be dated between 60 and 62. This too is an *apologia* for Seneca's political activity and worldly power and seems to reflect his growing unease about his position at court, perhaps even his worries about Nero's growing hostility towards him.

After the later *De Otio*, however, Seneca, in semi-retirement, began to write predominantly philosophical or scientific books, but between 63 and 64 he wrote, intermittently, the *Epistulae Morales ad Lucilium*, which are by far the most interesting of Seneca's surviving works, since they offered a more flexible form in which to express his preoccupations. Ostensibly an exposition of various aspects of Stoic philosophy, interlaced with anecdotes, they could take account obliquely of court politics and a radical change of tone in the later letters toward Epicureanism and Epicureans in society shows the increasing bitterness that Seneca was feeling about some of his supplanters, a feeling which may have driven him ultimately to involvement in the Pisonian conspiracy of 65, and thus a rejection of his earlier moderating role in Neronian governance.

Seneca's nephew Lucan took a harder line earlier in his subversive epic, the *Pharsalia*, in which he reveals himself as an emotional Republican from the beginning. The core of Republican ideology was that, from Julius Caesar on, the *de facto* heads of the Roman state held their power illegally, whatever their pretensions, and that power must be restored to the *senatus populusque Romanus*, which in effect meant the Senate, of which Lucan, following his quaestorship, was naturally a member. *Libertas senatoria* is the heart of the matter and Cato was part of the baggage of the senatorial "liberal imagination," and it was Nero's most prominent critic, Thrasea Paetus, consul in 56, who wrote a life of Cato. Seneca too had found in Cato the nearest possible embodiment of the Stoic *sapiens* with his indomitable courage, indifference to worldly possessions and personal misfortunes, and his championship of the cause of freedom against both Caesar and Pompey. But it was left to Lucan to paint the most ideological picture of that flawed Stoic saint and express through him the aspirations and nostalgic longings of a minority of the senatorial class for a Republic that could never be brought back. For a balanced evaluation of Lucan's epic one must turn elsewhere; our interest here is in its political implications and its place in Neronian literary warfare. Confusion about this has been caused by the deliberately grotesque and fulsome flatter of Nero in Book 1 (33–66). This very detachable passage, actually, has only a conventional purpose: it is there to hide something, even to protect the poet. Had Lucan lived to finish and publish his epic, or had the Pisonian conspiracy succeeded, the modern reader would have known nothing of this eulogy except through some gossip-writer. In these few lines Lucan claims that if civil war was the only way fate and the gods could bring forth Nero to rule Rome, then the city had no regrets. Nero of course is not mentioned again after 1.33–66, and the whole of the epic embodies the opposite conclusion. Nothing could justify the civil war and its results, least of all the house of the Julio-Claudians (*Caesareae domus series*), of which Nero was but the latest horrible example.

The epic reflects Lucan's profound pessimism about destiny and the nature of most men. He even disregards the Stoic doctrine of the ultimate benevolence of providence. Whether the praise of Nero found in Book 1 is conventional or ambiguous flattery, a political insurance policy, or a stroke of disguised impudence, it is of little weight against the evidence of the whole poem from Book 1 onwards. Naturally Lucan's anti-Caesarism, which may have been at least partly responsible for the ban on Lucan's publication of the books after I–III, grew progressively stronger, as the poet's own circumstances worsened.

From the start Lucan's *Pharsalia* had an ideological basis, as had Vergil's *Aeneid*. The primary aim no doubt was to write a great poem, but literature and politics have often been close bed-fellows. Lucan's epigrammatic and rhetorical style, his epic innovations, are at the service of a mission which became more and more urgent, as discontent with Nero grew. The *Pharsalia* is a lament for the losses of the great Civil War. The last, most important casualty, had been Republican liberty; the next most tragic loss was Cato, the embodiment of all Republican and Stoic virtues. Correspondingly, the epic is an attack first on Caesar the destroyer and then on Caesarism.

Other symbolic figures than Cato are deployed. There are heroic figures such as Regulus and Brutus; hated representatives of unconstitutional government such as Marius, Cinna, and Sulla; or terrifying external enemies such as the Gauls, the Parthians, Hannibal, and Jugurtha. More difficult for Lucan's use would be the politicized symbols derived from Roman religion and mythology. In the propaganda battles that raged during, and long after, the Civil War it was important to enlist on one's side as many of these religious symbols as possible: in battle cries, inscriptions, regimental names; on coins or monuments, and naturally, in the partisan literature of the time. The Julian clan claimed direct descent from Venus through Aeneas and his son Iulus, and he, the ancestor of the Julian house, is also the founder of Rome, and Vergil's *Aeneid* solemnly celebrates the claim. But neither Julius Caesar nor Augustus were content with such a distinguished heavenly connection. Augustus in particular tried to organize his religious champions systematically: Jupiter, Apollo, Venus, Mercury, Vesta, Juno, and Mars are prominent among his Olympian backers. *Pax*, *Fortuna*, *Honos* and *Virtus* are among his more abstract supporters.

Lucan however is as adept here as any writer and the crucial word he chose was *Libertas*, which then became the key symbol of his poem. Politically, the battle of Pharsalia is the spatial and temporal pivot of the work since it was after this battle that *libertas Romana*, and the Republic itself, came to an end. Julius Caesar destroyed it because of his ambition and self-aggrandisement and thanks to his awesome energy and preternatural abilities. Only Cato, with whose death at Utica the *Pharsalia* would probably have ended, was to emerge from the catastrophe of the civil war with a lustre undimmed in death, even though it would be inappropriate to describe him as the *hero* of the poem in a formal way. This approach to historical epic therefore allowed the epic to dispense with the commonest source of its symbolism for expressing the author's values, mythology. *Fortuna* and *Fatum* are as close as he comes to the traditional invocation of the divine working in mortal affairs. Divine machinery, moreover, is useless for eliciting sympathy for the vanquished, since they must have been defeated because the gods or the fates desired this result for their larger purposes. Lucan therefore chooses morality or immorality; ambition or altruism; dedication to freedom or the acceptance of slavery, as the determinants of his characters' action rather than messengers from Olympus or heaven-sent dreams. How events fall out remains the decision of Fortune or destiny; but the responsibility for how men behave is their own.

Nero's newer friends and advisers of the Epicurean stamp were not to let such Stoic subversion remain unchallenged. Again literature was used to pay off private and political scores in the way Seneca had revenged himself on Claudius in the *Apocolocyntosis* and on Suillius and other critics in the *De Vita Beata*. Discretion and subtlety without the naming of names still played a part in the opaque denigration of intimates and contemporaries, which now dominated court literature and obviously titillated Nero and his intimates.

After being governor of Bithynia and consul in 62, T. Petronius Niger had entered the small circle of Nero's literary cronies, where he had ingratiated himself by his wit and cultural interests (Tac. *Ann.* 16.18–20). What could be more natural for him than the exercise of his literary and political skills in amusing Nero and his friends with serial readings of his picaresque Menippean satire? The *Satyricon* is a strange and baffling work unless it is firmly set in the ambience of Nero's court. The allusions and parodies woven into it make no sense otherwise. Petronius was at home in Nero's court until the very end, and the combination in his humorous saga of funny, obscene and vulgar elements with elevated literary criticism and parody would obviously appeal to an emperor who had himself combined disreputable sexual tastes, a passion for wrestling and chariot-racing, a fondness for rowdy night-wanderings in the lower quarters of the town, with an unprecedented enthusiasm for lyre-playing, dramatic acting, and poetic composition. In consolidating his position and pleasing his master, Petronius had two obvious targets for his critical and parodic talents: Lucan and Seneca, who were both by this time (63–64) out of favour; their presence on the cultural and intellectual scene alone can explain certain features of the *Satyricon*.

To begin with Lucan had published Books 1 to 3 of the *Pharsalia* and then been forbidden by Nero to disseminate his work through public recitations or overt publication. Lucan's deviation from the traditions of epic, not to mention his anti-Caesarism, had left him open to hostile critics. It is easy therefore to appreciate the thrust of the attack on the *Pharsalia* by Nero's *arbiter elegantiae* in chapters 118–124 of the *Satyricon*, the so-called *Bellum Civile*, and the critical preface that introduces it. The allusions and imitations of Lucan, which are meant to be recognized by the knowledgeable audience, rely mainly on Books 1–3. In the criticism that prefaces Eumolpus' reworking of the material of the *Pharsalia* (*Sat.* 118) Petronius does not say anything original: epic poetry is not easy; it is certainly no easier than producing a scintillating and epigrammatic speech for the law court—a hit here at Lucan's youth and an allusion to Nero's ban on Lucan from legal practice. Further shafts may be detected in allusions to inadequate *doctrina* and epigrammatic lines that stand out from the texture of the narrative—always a temptation for Lucan. Lucan had intended to write an accurate, if ideologically biased, account of the Civil War, and this whole aim becomes the basis of Eumolpus' most fundamental criticism: poets should not deal in historical fact like the historian. Inspiration operating along the traditional epic lines, an aura of mystery, divine interventions and superhuman wonders, these are the requirements for a successful historical epic. The criticism, whether critically sound or unsound, fits nothing so aptly as Lucan's *Pharsalia*. The verbal parallels with Lucan and the coincidence of themes make the relationship undeniable. There seems also a political aim over and above the implicit denigration of Lucan's talents as a poet. This was, again in deference to Nero, the defence of Julius Caesar against Lucan's Republican bias.

Caesar is made the hero of the poem and is likened to Jupiter and also to Hercules (*BC* 206), a demigod traditionally associated with Stoicism and so with the Republican side. Lucan, for his part, had subtly attempted to link Cato with that hero. Most significant, in terms of Augustan propaganda and Neronian court politics, is the partisan division among the Olympians. On balance Caesar is given better divine help for warfare than the Republican side as represented by Pompey. Analysis makes it clear that the *Bellum Civile* is simultaneously a literary and political attack on Lucan's *Pharsalia* and that it would be appreciated as such by Nero. This attack, however, is a digression in the *Satyricon*. Far more pervasive is the allusion to, and frequently parody of, Seneca's writings. The uses to which Petronius puts his Senecan material may be classified in two ways: the first consists of a pastiche of Senecan prose and Seneca's Stoic meditations on such matters as the decadence of the age; the vanity of human wishes and man's subjugation to fortune; and the uneasy conscience of the evil-doer. They are revealed as parody by the ridiculous contexts in which they appear or by the disreputability of the characters voicing the sentiments. The second is the dramatic use of Senecan material to throw scorn on its philosophical implications. This is generally found in the *Cena Trimalchionis* and one example should suffice. Seneca's famous *Epistle* 47 on the proper treatment of slaves protests that slaves are fellow-human beings, subject to the same Fortune, and therefore dining with one's slaves, selectively, is commendable. In the *Cena*, Trimalchio's drunken invitation to his household to join the company at table (*Sat.* 70.10), his maudlin remarks about their common humanity despite their ill fortune, all make good sense as straight satire on a vulgar and pretentious freedman, but how much more point do they gain if the listener has Seneca's letter in mind?

The literary feud between the rising, or now established, arbiter of elegance and the two most brilliant ex-members of Nero's court circle, Lucan and Seneca, is susceptible of many explanations. A dominant motive would have been to cater to Nero's artistic jealousy, but there was also an obvious antipathy between the styles of life and thought favoured by the two sides. The feud was not one-sided. In Lucan's libelous poem of 65 against the emperor and the most powerful of his friends it is unlikely that Petronius was overlooked. Seneca's more oblique response is to be found in the sustained tirade on the *turba lucifugarum*, the crowd of night-owls, who turn darkness into day with their lengthy potations (*Ep.* 122.5–8). Seneca attacks their material luxury, their desire for notoriety, their eagerness to appear different, the elaborate elegance of their table and their way of life. The description squares very closely with Tacitus' account of Petronius' elegance, luxury, and his custom of turning night into day. Significantly in these later letters Seneca suddenly adopts a hostile tone towards Epicureanism in general, in sharp contrast to his earlier sympathetic references to Epicurean doctrine.

The last piece of evidence to be adduced is tenuous and may be passed over lightly. Certain epigrams from the *Anthologia Latina* (396ff.) are attributed to Seneca, some attacking personal enemies; 412 and 416 seem to belong to a time when Seneca is being undermined by enemies at court rather than from exile. The two poems in question are complaints of the malicious, if witty, backbiting of enemies. In 412 the enemy invoked is not only verbally malignant, but he writes satirical poems as well:

> carmina mortifero tua sunt suffusa veneno,
> at sunt carminibus pectora *nigra* magis.

> Your poems are full of deadly venom, but your heart is more *black* than your poems.

Was this enemy's *name* also as black as his heart? Was Seneca covertly alluding to T. Petronius Niger? Certainly the description might suit the courtier:

bellus homo es? valide capitalia crimina ludis.

You're a fine fellow, aren't you? You really play deadly games.

The epigrams, if they are authentic, would confirm further that literary feuds, or political quarrels conducted in verse, were a constant feature of court life and that Seneca suffered from them. His own poems and certainly his *Letters to Lucilius* indicate that he could and did hit back.

The *Apocolocyntosis* and the *Eclogues* are two fairly notable works which mix adulation of the present Emperor with denigration of his predecessor in different proportions and using different techniques. Another important work, the pseudo-Senecan *Octavia*, written only slightly after Nero's death, does much the same thing through the medium of tragedy. The action of the play is set in the year 62, when Nero's first wife, Claudia Octavia, is being divorced by Nero to enable him to marry Poppaea Sabina, whose wedding night is, for dramatic purposes, juxtaposed with Octavia's departure to exile and eventual death. The plot of the play is whether Nero can be swayed by popular opinion, by Seneca, or by the significantly unnamed Prefect of the Praetorian Guard to change his decision. He is inexorable. To add more portentous dimensions to the unfolding of the simple action the ghost of Agrippina is introduced to predict in convincing detail the actual manner of Nero's death (vv. 629–32). The main purpose of the play is not to present the sad fate of Octavia by a sympathetic observer; it is rather, as Marti argues, a fierce denunciation of the character and crimes of the late emperor, and, what is more, through vindictive criticism of the folly and cruelty of his mother and his adoptive father, Claudius, it turns into an indictment of the whole Julio-Claudian line including Augustus, who is attacked by Nero himself (vv. 504ff.). Nero is constantly described as a ferocious *tyrannus* and the list of his crimes lengthens as the play progresses: the execution of his mother, adoptive brother and numerous members of the upper classes who were obstacles to his desires or threats to his security. His incest with his wife and sister, his hatred of the aristocracy and senate, his cruel treatment of his wife in favour of a vengeful and lascivious mistress are also added to the indictment. At one point he threatens to fire Rome to get revenge on the ungrateful populace, who supposedly support Octavia.

Seneca's part in the play is to stress the duties of a good prince, the *concordia ordinum*, the importance of popular feelings. The anonymous praetorian prefect, in real life the bloody Ofonius Tigellinus, is presented, for the author's purposes, as pleading for mercy for Octavia. (This dates the play to the reign of Galba before Tigellinus' execution by Otho). It has been suggested that the emphasis on the good will and power of the people points to Galba, a populist according to his coinage, as the beneficiary of the anti-Julian propaganda in the work. But the author is too cautious to predict the outcome of that troubled year. He expresses distrust of popular power and favour, as reflected in the fates of previous reformers (vv. 877ff.), and this undercuts his earlier regrets for the vanished power of the Populus Romanus.

The author, probably Annaeus Cornutus or possibly Seneca's friend Lucilius Iunior, sees clearly that the murderous and incestuous behaviour of the Julio-Claudian line was due to the fact that the legitimacy of their power and succession depended on a relationship with the revered Augustus. To marry or even commit adultery with one of his female descendants was a deadly danger for any prominent Roman, as was being a descendant oneself. Incest was used to preempt external marital connections and judicial murder to eliminate Julio-Claudian competitors. That is why Nero's brutally realistic description of Augustus' bloody behaviour before he was safely established on the throne is important. The very foundation of the Julio-Claudian pretentions to legitimated autocracy by a sort of divine right is thereby destroyed. Image making and breaking was a characteristic of the year of the Four Emperors. The negative propaganda against the Julio-Claudians, particularly Nero, most visible in the *Octavia*, was offset by the attempts of Otho and Vitellius to capitalize on their connections with Nero and gain the popular support that still attached to the memory of the great *artifex*. The propaganda battles were often waged on coins with promises of *victoria, concordia, libertas, securitas* or *pax* for the Roman people. Only Vitellius made use of literary means to bolster his position when he called for a performance of some of Nero's *cantica* and loudly applauded them in order to identify himself with that Emperor's imperial policies (Suet. *Vitell.* 11).

Although the Flavian Emperors (69–96) did not go to the extravagant lengths of Nero, they were all interested in fostering literature, especially Domitian. Their support had several motives and, despite Martial, imperial patronage and favour still offered substantial rewards. Vespasian appointed the first professor to be paid from public funds in Quintilian, and the young, epic poet Saleius Bassus was given half a million sesterces (Tac. *Dial.* 5.2; 9.8), although this was only a tenth of the reward given to Eprius Marcellus for his prosecution of Thrasea Paetus in Nero's time. Titus, who had belonged to Nero's literary circle, was presumably pleased by Martial's sometimes tiresome *Liber de Spectaculis to* celebrate his official inauguration in 80 of the great Flavian amphitheatre begun by Vespasian. Commissioned or not, official favour for this no doubt helped to propel Martial to the international fame he boasts of in his first book of epigrams.

Domitian, like Nero, was a poet himself. His institution of the Capitoline games is proof enough of that, since they incorporated literary and musical contests as did the revived *Ludi Saeculares*. He may well have recognised his affinity to Nero, but he did not have Augustus' tolerance

of, or pleasure in, *Spottgedichte*; he punished impolitic historical writing
and theatrical satire alike (Suet. *Dom.* 8.10), although anonymous satire
circulated as in Nero's reign (Ma. 10.5; Suet. *Dom.* 14). The Flavians, as
a new dynasty, not unnaturally encouraged favorable notices of themselves as well as anti-Neronian progaganda. The spate of histories unfa-
vorable to Nero dates from this period, along with the new excesses in
imperial eulogy. Domitian needed more help from his panegyrists than
did his predecessors, particularly as he grew more and more unpopular
after the revolt of Saturninus (88–89). His personal campaigns against
the Chatti, against the Dacians, and the Sarmatians may seem to the
modern historian victories for prudence and common sense, including
the settlement with the Dacian king Decebalus, who was bought off with
subsidies and practical aid in the shape of a corps of engineers. But to
Tacitus and Suetonius, they were all pathetic shams and failures, whatever the triumphs and honours demanded for them. Martial and Statius
both were aware of this and they stress the Emperor's achievements in
war and generosity in peace wherever possible.° Martial tries to present
Domitian as being sorely missed by the city whenever he is away cam-
paigning or highly popular with the mob on his frequent appearances at
the games (6.34.5–6).

Naturally as the poets fed the vanity and alleviated the insecurity of
the Flavian emperors, the blazing self-righteousness of the members of
the senatorial order increased as they saw their shaky position and privileges further eroded by Vespasian's dilution of their elite number with
provincials, and Domitian's increasing reliance on equestrians for important posts, even in a senatorial province. Domitian's assumption of the
censorship *in perpetuo* alarmed them further. The war of the pamphlets
did not cease altogether then and it proved equally dangerous to Helvidius Priscus, author of a *Life of Cato*, and later to Senecio, who worked
on a Life of Helvidius himself.

Even Domitian's social and moral reforms did not cut much ice with
senatorial writers. The younger Pliny goes to great length to disparage
even reforms of which he approved (cf. Plin. *Pan.* 46). So it was left to
the poets to provide the vigorous approbation they offer Domitian for his
attempts to improve morality, efforts of which he seems to have been
very proud (Ma. 6.4). This sometimes leads them into curious areas.
Somewhat strange, for example, are the verses written on Domitian's
ordinance against castration (Suet. *Dom.* 7; Dio. 67.2, 3). Statius, rather
indelicately, introduces the theme into the poem commissioned in 94 by
Domitian on the occasion of Earinus' dedication of his shorn hair to the

---

°e.g. *Theb.* 1.16ff.; *Silv.* 1.25ff., 79ff.; f.1.11ff., 39ff; 4.2.14, 66.7; and Ma. 2.2; 4.1, 3; 5.19;
6.4, 10; 7.1, 2, 5–8. 80; 8 praef., 1–2, 4, 8, 11, 15, 21, 26, 36, 39, 50, 54, 65, 78, 80, 82; 9.1,
3, 6, 24, 31, 34, 35, 64–65, 79, 91, 101.

temple of Aesculapius in his native city of Pergamum (*Silv.* 3.4.73–77). Earinus of course was himself a eunuch. The subject occurs also in his poem on the construction of the Via Domitiana (*Silv.* 14.3.13–15). Earinus was a favorite subject of Martial's also, as we might expect (9.11–13, 16, 17), and he too scarcely keeps all his references to castration (9.6, 8) separate from his encomia of the emperor's favorite, which may indicate that it was an open subject for discussion and that the ban, though enacted earlier (cf. Ma. 2.60; 6.2), was somehow connected with Earinus.

The *exordia* of epics on whatever subject, since this was the most elevated literary genre, were tempting places to locate deferential or fulsome compliments to the current emperor and further the claims of the Flavians to be the proper rulers of Rome. And it is interesting to compare the different imperial compliments introduced into the four epics which have survived from the Flavian era. C. Valerius Flaccus (d. 93), at the opening of the *Argonautica* and addressing Apollo, links the Flavian house with the god by his invocation of the deified Vespasian, whose vicarious victories in Wales, Northern Britain and Scotland won by Cerealis, Frontinus, and Agricola, he suggests, would be splendid material for an historical epic. Valerius then suggests that the poetic genius of Domitian should recount the overthrow of Judaea and Titus' destruction of Jerusalem (1.7–14); and it is he who will raise temples and institute divine cults in his father's honour.

Silius (ca. 25–101) probably thought of himself as continuing the *Aeneid*, his devotion to Vergil being notorious. He was to narrate in the *Punica* the consequences of Dido's curse upon Aeneas' descendants and describe its fulfillment in the Punic War. Only the first six books perhaps appeared in Domitian's time, since there appears to be a modest compliment to Nerva at the end of Book 14. If the Julian house was good enough for Vergil it was certainly so for Silius, who, it has been suggested already, had belonged to Nero's poetic circle and ended up as consul in the year of his demise. How was he to deal with Nero's Flavian successors? The former Neronian consul, with all the confidence of a man with nothing to lose, simply invokes the Muse on opening his poem and closes it (17.650–55) with a salutation to Scipio Africanus, true scion of Capitoline Jupiter.

How different are the introductory flourishes of Papinius Statius (ca. 45–96)! At the beginning of the *Thebaid*, the poet protests that he would not as yet dare tackle subjects such as Domitian's defence of the Capitol in 69 or his Northern triumphs from the Rhine, the Danube, and Dacia. He prays that Domitian will refuse to join the other gods for all their urgings and that the time will then come when he can with greater strength and expertise do justice to his great achievements (1.16–33). The *Achilleid* also is made out to be just a prelude to some long, though still unconfident, poem on an emperor who has won laurels in the arts of poetry and war both (*Ach.* 1.14–19).

But it is to Statius' *Silvae* and to seven books of Martial's epigrams that the fastidiously curious turn to discover the sort of praise that the latest and last scion of the Flavian house, though not the modern reader, would find congenial. The longest piece of this kind is Statius' ecphrastic poem on the great equestrian statue of Domitian erected in the Forum Romanum. It was a commissioned piece like the statue itself and was dashed off in less than forty-eight hours. The themes emphasized in the poem are external war and internal peace (vv. 37, 51). Domitian's puissance in both are symbolized by the statue of Pallas Minerva, his favorite goddess, who is perched on his left hand. The groaning of the mighty plinth beneath the weight of Domitian's genius might remind the uncharitable of Lucan's description of Nero's weight as a threat to the heavens (*sentiet axis onus, Phars.* 1.57). His German conquests are represented by the trodden locks of the captive River Rhine, a theme further emphasized in his address by the tutelary deity of the area, Romulus, who adds for good measure a reference to the Civil Wars ended by the Flavian dynasty. This poem and the *Eucharisticon* (*Silv.* 4.2) on the great splendour of Domitian's lavish feast to which the poet was invited are adequate illustrations of how far poets were prepared to go in their presumably acceptable adulation. G. W. E. Russell once remarked to Matthew Arnold "Everyone likes flattery; and when it comes to Royalty you should lay it on with a trowel."

From Martial we get the same idea of what conventions and subjects were agreeable to the reigning autocrat. Book 8 of the epigrams is in fact dedicted *Imperatori Domitiano Caesari Augusto Germanico Dacico.* This book, in keeping with Domitian's pretensions to be the great reformer of Roman morality, is free of the more licentious epigrams on which Martial's reputation is unfortunately (and wrongly) based. The book presents, however, an adequate selection of imperial motifs, and it needs little supplement from elsewhere. Martial has no objection to Domitian's assumption of such addresses as *Dominus Deus* and does what he can to weave the concept into his verses (e.g. 8.4). In both poets exaggeration is preferred to Augustan subtleties.

Martial and Statius had several other patrons in common. Among the most prominent of these were the poet Arruntius Stella, the freedman Claudius Etruscus, Atedius Melior, and Lucan's widow, Argentaria Polla. It is a worthwhile exercise to compare the different ways the quest for patronage and benefits took in the case of each poet. Especially significant are the poems addressed by both to Argentaria Polla, Lucan's widow, on the occasion of the birthday of the poet (Ma. 7.21–23; *Silv.* 2.7). They are interesting because they appropriately combine the anti-Neronian motifs of Flavian propaganda with genuine regret for a great genius and more conventional and subdued praise of an important woman patron. One of Martial's three is worth quoting as an illustration:

Haec est illa dies, quae magni conscia partus
    Lucanum populis et tibi, Polla, dedit.
Heu! Nero crudelis nullaque invisior umbra,
    Debuit hoc saltem non licuisse tibi.   (7.21)

This is that day which, aware of its great nativity, gave Lucan to the
world and to you, Polla. Ah! cruel Nero and for no death more
hated, this at least should not have been in your power.

This is brief and to the point. Statius' poem (*Silv.* 2.7) by contrast is
much more ambitious. Addressing Lucan, he exclaims:

sic et tu (rabidi nefas tyranni!)
iussus praecipitem subire Lethen,
dum pugnas canis arduaque voce
das solacia grandibus sepulchris
(o dirum scelus! o scelus!) tacebis   (*Silv.* 2.7.100–4)

And so (*like other short-lived heroes*) you were ordered—the wick-
edness of the mad tyrant!—to go down in precipitous haste to Lethe,
and while you are singing of battles and in your lofty tones bring
comfort to imposing sepulchres, you will fall silent.

Statius' attack is more sustained since he also attributes the burning of
Rome to the Emperor and pictures him pursued in hell by the avenging
torch of his murdered mother Agrippina (vv. 60–61; 118–19). He is also
more fulsome about Polla's own merits (vv. 83–88). In short, a bravura
piece of great literary interest.

There is a dimension lacking in the Flavian literary picture, since we
do not find as before the use of poetry as a weapon in a fight for real power
at court and in the *consilium principis* as we do in the reigns of, say, Nero
and Claudius. Despite Tacitus' discussion of this in the *Dialogus*, only
Maternus in his *fabulae togatae* seems to have been a practitioner and then
for principle rather than actual power. None of the Flavians encouraged
senatorial literary activity centering around the court and none of them
was so star-struck by literary gifts as to attribute to such writers political
talents. Moreover, even Domitian, who welcomed delation, did not like the
venting of venom under artistic guises at all—unlike Nero at least in this.
But that there were literary and critical rivalries is obvious enough from
the pages of Martial. In fact Martial himself was clearly involved in a literary feud with Statius. Not surprisingly, for here were two great poets who
were very close contemporaries, neither rich (cf. Stat. *Silv.* 5.3.117–18 and
Martial *passim*) nor Roman by birth, and both in need of imperial and
other patronage. Genius and talent unfortunately do not always go hand in
hand with magnanimity or even tolerance. Striking is the ominous silence
about each other, despite their many common patrons. Statius pointedly
omits Martial from the list of Spanish literary lights at *Silv.* 2.7.24–35. Such
silence implies dislike or indifference and a determination to give no posthumous fame or contemporary notoriety to another. Having such elevated

and dignified patrons, the contending poets found themselves "Willing to wound and yet afraid to strike." So Statius, in the dedicatory letter to Atedius Melior prefacing Book 2, refers to his lighter poems, on Melior's tree and his parrot (*Silv.* 2.3, 4) as *leves libellos quasi epigrammatis loco scriptos*, a deliberate slighting of the art and potential seriousness of the epigrammatist's mode. Martial's apparent reply was written about 95, near the date of Statius' death. It is the famous *apologia pro opere suo*, of which the significant lines are:

> Qui legis *Oedipoden* caligantemque Thyesten,
>   Colchidas et Scyllas, quid nisi monstra legis?
> Quid tibi raptus Hylas, quid *Parthenopaeus* et Attis . . . ?
> Quid te vana iuvant miserae ludibria chartae?
>   Hoc lege, quod possit dicere vita "Meum est."

> Read of Thyestes, Oedipus, dark suns,
>   of Scyllas, Medeas—you read of freaks.
> Hylas' rape . . . ? Attis . . . ? Parthenopaeus . . .?
> Why waste time on fantasy annals? Rather
>   read my books, where Life cries: "This is me!"
>   (trans. by Peter Whigham)

The reference to Parthenopaeus, son of Atalanta, one of the seven champions sent against Thebes (*Theb.* 4.246ff.) can hardly be accidental; and it should be noted that Parthenopaeus is brought on stage last in Statius' parade of the Seven, where the poet devotes more attention to him than to the rest. The cheaper jibe (9.19) at a certain "Sabellus" who praises the baths of "Ponticus" in three hundred verses in order to get invitations to dinner cuts close to the bone in the light of Statius' 65 line poem on the Baths of the freedman Claudius Etruscus (*Silv.* 1.5), which would have appeared not many years before the epigram.

They may even have had entrée to Domitian through different court personages. Flavius Abascantus, the imperial *libertus ab epistulis*, was the particular patron there of Statius, whose *epicedium* on the former's dead wife Priscilla is prefaced by a letter mentioning the closeness of their wives' friendship and also the poet's own loyalty to the court. Martial's main contact was the palace chamberlain, and *libertus a libellis*, Parthenius (4.45; 5.6; 8.28; 9.49; 11.1; 12.11); he was regarded as the proper intermediary to get Martial's poetry into the Emperor's hands. Abascantus is not mentioned by Martial and Statius is silent about Parthenius.

What was the Spanish poet to do with the sudden departure of his imperial patron, whose memory was now damned by the senate? Cocceius Nerva (96–98), the new emperor, had been the Tibullus of his day according to Nero (Ma. 8.70.7), but he had abandoned his learned Alexandrian elegies as soon as they ceased to be valuable in politics; he turned his attention to the law and became a respected jurist and a sound member of the senatorial body. There can be little doubt that

Martial's close literary associations with Domitian and the Flavian house in general was detrimental to him in his search for imperial patronage. (The neglect of Statius' epic after 96 is also noteworthy.) And, besides, Nerva had taken over from Domitian a very tight fiscal situation and financial exigencies may have made him less generous than might be expected in a ruler. Small wonder then that Martial reluctantly decided to return to his native Bilbilis in 98. The poet's discontent may be seen in the preface to Book 12. His attempts to get into the good graces of Nerva and Trajan (98–117) were presumably futile, although he did his best. Book 11 contains eulogies of the new Emperor for his general acceptability to all, particularly the senate who had so quickly made him their own, and his lack of censoriousness (11.4, 5, 2). Published only in 101, his epigram to Nerva (12.6) acclaims him as the gentlest man ever to occupy the imperial *aula*; a poet who has brought back *Fides, Clementia, cauta Potestas*, banished fear, and importantly for Martial, restored to senators the once dangerous right to be financially generous to others. He compliments him on his steadfast honesty in the black days of Domitian's rule (vv. 11–12):

> Sed tu sub principe duro
> Temporibusque malis ausus es esse bonus.

He had of course already joined the senatorial order in damning Domitian's memory as a misplaced fragment of his verse preserved by a scholiast on Juvenal indicates:

> . . . Flavia gens, quantum tibi tertius abstulit heres!
> Paene fuit tanti, non habuisse duos.   (*Lib. de Spect.* 33)
>
> . . . How damned was the Flavian Line by that third heir!
> Was it worth the benefits of the earlier pair?   (trans. J. P. S.)

Other minor attacks, which had to be somewhat muted to make the unavoidable hypocrisy less blatant, may be found in the revised edition of Book 10, published in 98. Prayers for Trajan's speedy return from Germany (10.6; 7) are to be found in company with a plea for greater liberties for patrons and greater support for clients (10.34). But compliments on his military reputation (12.8) and his donation of Domitian's treasures to the Capitoline (12.15) are perfunctory by comparison with the poems on Domitian and his inner circle. Martial may have felt by now that it was hardly worth the effort, so tainted was he by his former imperial associations. And Nerva had presumably preferred the more subdued praise of a friend of Martial's, the conscientious Sextus Julius Frontinus, who just casually mentions *Nerva Augusto, nescio quo diligentiore an amantiore rei publicae imperatore* (*Aq.* 1), very much in the way Silius had briefly thanked him for his honest administration.

Some points from Tacitus' *Dialogus de oratoribus*, which is set in the mid-seventies A.D., are worth noting in conclusion. This interesting discussion is between Curiatius Maternus, two lawyers and an expert on oratory. Maternus has just written and recited the day before a much-discussed tragedy on Cato, presumably another subversive *fabula togata* on the theme of *libertas*. The play supposedly caused offense in high and powerful quarters and his friends argue for the elimination of the offending matter. It is perhaps odd that in the contrast of the advantages of oratory, security, power, reputation and personal satisfaction (*Dial.* 5.4–8) with those of poetry, Maternus should speak of poetry's charm and its seclusion from the unpleasantness of politics and public life and claim that poetry harms no one. Yet Neronian politics in general indicate that the statement is deliberately naive, as Aper points out (*Dial.* 10.6–8), forcing Maternus to admit that he himself had broken the power of the odious Vatinius in Nero's time (*Dial.* 11.2). More significantly he claims that even if he did eliminate offensive views from his *Cato* they would only crop up again in his *Thyestes*, a hint to us that the tragedies of Seneca and even the epics of Statius are worth examining for the contemporary political issues raised in mythological guise. But that would take us too far afield from our survey of the more directly personal use of literature to win friends and influence and injure rivals and enemies, a feature of the literature of the early principate which is often forgotten in the contemplation of those seemingly serene and aloof classics.

HULLEY LECTURERS

1. John N. Hough, University of Colorado at Boulder: "The Greeks Face Their Space Age: The Challenge of the Hellenistic World." (December 8, 1965)
2. David Daube, Regius Professor of Law at Oxford University: "Evasions of Laws at Rome." (January 17, 1966)
3. Karl K. Hulley, University of Colorado at Boulder: "Aristophanes, The Verbal Cartoonist of Athens." (February 16, 1966)
4. W. K. C. Guthrie, Laurence Professor of Ancient Philosophy at Cambridge University: "Man as Microcosm—The Idea in Greek Thought and Its Legacy to Later Europe." (April 28, 1966)
5. Ernst Fredricksmeyer, University of Colorado at Boulder: "Alexander the Great and the Genesis of the Ruler Cult." (December 1, 1966)
6. Hugh Lloyd-Jones, Regius Professor of Greek at Oxford University: "The Theology of Sophocles." (February 9, 1967)
7. Hara Tzavella-Evjen, Visiting Assistant Professor at the University of Colorado at Boulder: "The Aesthetic Approach to Cretan and Mycenaean Art." (March 1, 1967)
8. David Daube, Regius Professor of Law at Oxford University: "Philosophical Aspects of Roman Law." (April 27, 1967)
9. Alan Watson, Douglas Professor of Civil Law at the University of Glasgow: "Roman Republican Jurists' moral Views about Slavery." (November 28, 1967)
10. John E. Coleman, University of Colorado at Boulder: "Explorations in the Island of Keos." (January 11, 1968)
11. Roger A. Hornsby, the University of Iowa: "The Classics Reviewed: Ancient Literature and Modern Criticism." (February 27, 1968)
12. David F. Heimann, University of Colorado at Boulder: "Did St. Jerome *Really* Hate Women?" (April 25, 1968)
13. Hugh Lloyd-Jones, Regius Professor of Greek at Oxford University: "New Portions of Menander's *Samian Women*." (March 11, 1969)
14. Cedric H. Whitman, Francis Jones Professor of Classical Greek at Harvard University: "Existentialism and the Classic Hero." (April 30, 1969)
15. John B. McDiarmid, University of Washington: "The Changing World of the *Oresteia* Trilogy." (November 17, 1969)
16. Ernst Badian, State University of New York at Buffalo: "Alexander the Great and the Greeks." (March 11, 1970)
17. Harold D. Evjen, University of Colorado at Boulder: "Aeschylus—Legal Philosopher or Merely an Excellent Dramatic Poet?" (April 14, 1970)
18. Hazel E. Barnes, University of Colorado at Boulder: "Homer and the Meddling Gods." (January 27, 1971)
19. Alexander Gordon McKay, McMaster University: "The Vergilian Underworld." (February 25, 1971)
20. Donald Sutherland, formerly Professor of Classics at the University of Colorado at Boulder: "The *Odyssey*, Or Epic on the Loose." (October 25, 1971)

21. Bernard Knox, Director of the Center for Hellenic Studies: "Medea—Hero, Goddess, Woman." (May 3, 1972)
22. Stephen J. Becroft, University of Colorado at Boulder: "Euripides' *Heracles*: The Weakness of the Strong." (November 16, 1972)
23. Michael C. J. Putnam, Brown University: "The Achievement of Virgil." (March 8, 1973)
24. Joy K. King, University of Colorado at Boulder: "Propertius' Programmatic Poetry." (April 23, 1973)
25. Charles P. Segal, Brown University: "The Raw and the Cooked in Greek Literature: Structure, Values, Metaphor." (November 13, 1972)
26. Hunter R. Rawlings, III, University of Colorado at Boulder: "The Historian as Exile." (April 23, 1974)
27. William M. Calder, III, Columbia University: "Misinterpretation of Greek Tragedy." (October 30, 1974)
28. John N. Hough, Professor Emeritus, University of Colorado at Boulder: "A Funny Thing Happened to Plautus' Jokes." (March 18, 1975)
29. John P. Sullivan, Provost of Arts and Letters, State University of New York at Buffalo: "Horace and Propertius: A Literary Feud?" (April 3, 1975)
30. Zvi Yavetz, Tel-Aviv University: "*Forte an dolo principis*—The Great Fire in Rome, 64 A.D." (April 24, 1975)
31. Hazel E. Barnes, University of Colorado at Boulder: "Three Philosophical Myths: Plato, Nietzsche, and Huxley." (September 23, 1975)
32. Clifford J. Dull, Visiting Assistant Professor at the University of Colorado at Boulder: "The Ancestry of Mary: Its Political Importance on Jesus' Life." (March 1, 1976)
33. Benjamin D. Meritt, Institute for Advanced Study and the University of Texas at Austin: "Epigraphy: The Handmaid of History." (March 11, 1976)
34. Charles Rowan Beye, Boston University: "The Epic of Gilgamesh: An Anticipation of Themes in European Literature." (November 27, 1976)
35. Hara Tzavella-Evjen, University of Colorado at Boulder: "Works and Days at Lithares in the Third Millennium B.C." (March 7, 1977)
36. Charles Edson, University of Wisconsin at Madison, "The Other Alexander: Alexander the Molossian and Alexander the Great." (April 25, 1977)
37. Peter L. Schmidt, University of Konstanz: "Roman Philosophy, Society, and Literature in the Time of Cicero." (December 1, 1977)
38. E. Christian Kopff, University of Colorado at Boulder: "The Simile Language of Achilles in Homer's *Iliad*." (February 14, 1978)
39. Peter M. Green, University of Texas at Austin: "*Carmen et Error: Prophasis* and *Aitia* in the matter of Ovid's Exile." (January 30, 1979)
40. Ernst Fredericksmeyer, University of Colorado at Boulder: "Alexander: King of Asia and God." (April 11, 1979)
41. Michael W. Haslam, University of California, Los Angeles: "Homer Makes History." (November 28, 1979)
42. William M. Calder, III, University of Colorado at Boulder: "Ulrich von Wilamowitz-Moellendorff and Friedrich Nietzsche: The Struggle over *The Birth of Tragedy*." (May 8, 1980)
43. Ulrich K. Goldsmith, Professor Emeritus of Germanic Languages at the University of Colorado at Boulder: "Ulrich von Wilamowitz-Moellendorff

and the *George Circle*: New Documents." (October 28, 1980)

44. Sander M. Goldberg, University of Colorado at Boulder: "Terence and the Death of Comedy." (February 18, 1982)

45. William M. Calder, III, University of Colorado at Boulder: "Seneca's *Thyestes*: A Paradigm for Survival." (November 18, 1982)

46. Hara Tzavella-Evjen, University of Colorado at Boulder: "Homeric Medicine." (March 2, 1983)

47. Albert Henrichs, Harvard University: "The Modern View of Dionysus from Nietzsche to Girard." (April 28, 1983)

48. Harold D. Evjen, University of Colorado at Boulder: "The Olympic Games: Theories of Origin." (March 15, 1984)

49. Michael Gargarin, University of Texas at Austin: "The Beginnings of Greek Law." (April 4, 1984)